The A
DICTIONARY
OF
HEALTH
CARE
ADMINISTRATION

P9-DUM-806

Arnold S. Goldstein, M.B.A., J.D., LL.M.

Professor

Health Care Administration and Law
Northeastern University
Boston, Massachusetts

Senior Partner

Meyers, Goldstein, and Kosberg
Specializing in Health Care Law
Chestnut Hill, Massachusetts

AN ASPEN PUBLICATION®

Aspen Publishers, Inc.
Rockville, Maryland
1989

Editorial Services: Jane Coyle Garwood

ISBN: 0-8342-0077-5

Printed in the United States of America

1 2 3 4 5

To my wife Marlene

for her dedication
in seeing this project through

PREFACE

As the field of health care undergoes radical and fast-paced change, so does its language. *The Aspen Dictionary of Health Care Administration* is a reference book of current health care terminology. It is designed to help health care professionals communicate more effectively.

This dictionary is written primarily for health care practitioners and administrators, but I envision its use in far wider circles. Students in health care administration, nursing, health education, and other allied health programs will find it a helpful adjunct text. Government officials, regulators, and policymakers may gain new insights into emerging trends in health care. Lawyers, business people, and even patients, who are the ultimate consumers of health care services, will find the dictionary convenient in understanding specific terms. *The Aspen Dictionary of Health Care Administration* is also a treasury of health care words and phrases. It can be a pleasurable journey for those who simply enjoy browsing through its pages to discover how today's health care system works.

A few comments about the preparation of this book are offered. Terminology is limited to the major or commonly used terms comprising the broad foundation of a modern health care vocabulary. Therefore, the dictionary is not completely exhaustive, but it is reasonably complete. The terms have been carefully selected from numerous sources, including professional journals and texts and government publications. In addition, I have drawn from my own considerable library and lexicon of terms accumulated during two decades of active involvement in health care administration. Hopefully, the completeness, accuracy, and usefulness of the definitions contained in the dictionary will compensate for any oversights.

The dictionary contains several features to make it a helpful reference tool. In a definition using a term which is itself defined within the dictionary, that term has been printed in italics (except for very common terms) the first time it appears. This indicates that the reader will find the definition of that particular term in its proper alphabetical location. Many of the definitions include a list of closely related terms that also should be reviewed to understand a given concept. Using related terms, it is possible to pull together words focusing on the topic and obtain the broadest possible comprehension of the subject.

Commonly used abbreviations and acronyms are listed in Appendix A. These abbreviations and acronyms are listed under their complete wording in the dictionary. A reader confronted with an acronym should start with the appendix and then turn to the text for the full definition. In addition to a simple definition, many of the entries include one or more examples, a brief discussion or historical perspective of the term in question, and references to, or questions from, formal legal and official definitions of the term.

A book is seldom the work of only the author. I am indebted to Professors Carl Nelson and David Rochefort at Northeastern University, who have immeasurably enriched my health care vocabulary. I am also grateful to my editor at Aspen Publishers, Inc., Stephen Mautner. His infectious enthusiasm encouraged me to undertake and complete this project. It is my wife Marlene, however, who is the book's true architect. Her tireless secretarial efforts and editorial instincts made this book a reality.

Aa

AA: See *Alcoholics Anonymous.*

AAAHC: See *Accreditation Association for Ambulatory Health Care.*

AACHP: See *American Association for Comprehensive Health Planning.*

AAHCF: See *American Association of Health Care Facilities.*

AAHE: See *Association for the Advancement of Health Education.*

abortion: Termination of a pregnancy before the fetus has attained viability, i.e., become capable of independent extrauterine life. Viability is usually defined in terms of the duration of pregnancy, weight of the fetus, and, occasionally, the length of the fetus. It has been traditionally assumed that viability is attained at 28 weeks of gestation, corresponding to a fetal weight of approximately 1000 g. This definition is based on the observation that infants below this weight have little chance of survival, while the mortality rate of infants above 1000 g declines rapidly. Different types of abortions are distinguished: early, less than 12 completed weeks of gestation; late, more than 12 weeks; induced, caused by deliberate action undertaken with the intention of terminating pregnancy; spontaneous, any abortion other than induced, even if externally caused, for instance, by trauma or treatment of an independent condition; therapeutic, performed as treatment for the pregnant woman. See also *stillbirth.*

abstinence: Deliberate restraint from using harmful substances, such as drugs, alcohol, and tobacco; may also include restraint from other items, such as certain foods.

abuse: Improper or excessive use of program benefits, resources, or services by either providers or consumers. Abuse can occur intentionally when services that are excessive or unnecessary are used; when the appropriate treatment for the patient's condition is not used; when less costly treatment would be as effective; or when billing or charging does not conform to requirements. Abuse should be distinguished from *fraud,* in which deliberate deceit is used by providers or consumers to obtain payment for services that were not actually delivered or received, or to claim program eligibility. Abuse is not necessarily either intentional or illegal. The term can also extend to child abuse or drug abuse. See also *drug dependence.*

acceptability: An individual's (or group's) overall assessment of medical care available to the individual (or group). The cost, quality, results, and convenience of care, as well as provider attitudes, may be appraised to determine the acceptability of available health services. See also *access* and *availability.*

access: An individual's (or group's) ability to obtain medical care. Access has geographic, financial, social, ethnic, and psychic components and is thus very difficult to define and measure operationally. The goal of many government health programs is to improve access to care for specific groups or equity of access in the whole population. Access is also a function of the *availability* of health services and their *acceptability.*

accession number: The number sequentially assigned each order as it is entered into medical records.

accident: An unexpected, unplanned event that typically involves *injury.*

accident and health insurance: *Insurance* under which benefits are payable in case of *disease*, accidental *injury*, or accidental death.

accidental bodily harm: An injury to the body of an individual as a result of accident.

accountable: Responsible or liable. To account means to furnish a justification or detailed explanation of financial activities or responsibilities, or to furnish substantial reasons or convincing explanations for the activities. Accountability entails an obligation to disclose periodically to all directly and indirectly responsible or properly interested parties, in adequate detail and consistent form, the purposes, principles, procedures, relationships, results, incomes, and expenditures involved in any activity, enterprise, or assignment so that they can be evaluated by the interested parties. The concept is important in health *planning* and *regulation* programs (such as *health systems agencies*) that should be accountable to the public and those individuals and groups affected by their actions. There is no specific or detailed agreement on what accountability is or how to assure it. Health planning policies, for example, contain a variety of provisions designed to make the planning activities accountable: for example, agency governing boards often must have a *consumer* majority; the affected parties must be represented on agency governing boards; all data, files, and meetings must be open to the public; and decisions must be made according to established public procedures and criteria.

accreditation: The process by which an agency or organization evaluates and recognizes a program of study or an institution as meeting certain predetermined *standards*. The recognition is called accreditation. Similar assessment of individuals is called *certification*. Standards are usually defined in terms of physical plant, governing body, administration, medical and other staff, and scope and organization of services. Accreditation is usually given by a private organization created for the purpose of assuring the public of the quality of the accredited programs or institutions (such as the *Joint Commission on Accreditation of Healthcare Organizations*). Accreditation standards and individual performance with respect to such standards are not always available to the public. In some situations, state governments recognize accreditation in lieu of *licensure* or accept it as the basis for licensure; in others, accreditation may be a requirement for licensure. Public or private payment programs often require accreditation as a condition of payment for covered services. Accreditation may be either permanent or effective for a specified period of time. Unlike a license, accreditation is not a condition of lawful practice but is intended as an indication of high-quality practice. Where payment is effectively conditioned on accreditation, however, it may have the same effect.

Accreditation Association for Ambulatory Health Care (AAAHC): A nonprofit association chartered to improve the quality of care provided by ambulatory health care organizations. It sets uniform standards for ambulatory health care and conducts voluntary reviews of ambulatory health care facilities.

Accreditation Council for Facilities for the Mentally Retarded (ACFMR): A national accrediting body for institutions providing medical care and housing for the mentally retarded.

accredited record technician (ART): An individual who graduated from an accredited program on medical records systems and passed a national examination. ARTs supervise daily activities of medical records units in assembling and analyzing records and indexing and classifying diagnoses and operations performed during the patients' hospitalization.

ACHA: American College of Hospital Administrators. See also *American College of Healthcare Executives*.

ACHE: See *American College of Healthcare Executives*.

ACNHA: See *American College of Nursing Home Administrators*.

acquisition cost: The immediate cost of selling, underwriting, and issuing a new *insurance policy*, including clerical costs, agents' commissions, advertising, and medical inspection fees. Also refers to the actual cost paid by a pharmacist or other retailer to a manufacturer or wholesaler for a supply of *drugs*. Also the cost of obtaining physical plant or equipment.

activity director: An organizer of recreational and social activities in a long-term care institution. See also *recreational therapist*.

actual charge: The amount a *physician*, other *practitioner*, or health care *provider* actually bills a patient for a particular medical service or procedure. The actual *charge* may differ from the *customary*, *prevailing*, and *reasonable charges* under *Medicare* and other insurance programs. See also *fractionation*.

actuary: In *insurance*, a person trained in statistics, accounting, and mathematics who determines policy rates, *reserves*, and dividends by deciding what assumptions should be made with respect to each of the risk factors involved (such as the frequency of occurrence of the *peril*; the average benefit that will be payable; the rate of investment earnings, if any; *expenses*; and *persistency* rates) and who secures valid statistics on which to base these assumptions.

acute care: Short-term health care, typically within a hospital, with an *average length of stay* of less than 30 days.

acute disease: A *disease* characterized by a single episode of a fairly short duration from which the *patient* returns to normal or previous state and level of activity. While acute diseases are frequently distinguished from *chronic diseases*, there is no standard definition or distinction. It is worth noting that an acute episode of a chronic disease (for example, an episode of diabetic coma in a patient with diabetes) is often treated as an acute disease.

ADC: See *average daily census*.

addict: An individual habituated to drugs, alcohol, or another habit-forming substance and who cannot voluntarily refrain from use.

addiction: See *drug addiction, abuse,* and *drug dependence*.

adequate and well-controlled studies: The type of investigations, including clinical investigations, that must be conducted by a new drug sponsor to demonstrate that a *new drug* is effective. As amended in 1962, the Federal Food, Drug, and Cosmetic Act (the Act) requires that drug sponsors provide substantial evidence of *effectiveness* and gives this term a special definition: "evidence consisting of adequate and well-controlled investigations, including clinical investigations, by experts qualified by scientific training and experience to evaluate the effectiveness of the drug involved, on the basis of which it could fairly and responsibly be concluded by such experts that the drug will have the effect it purports or is represented to have under the conditions of use *prescribed*, recommended, or suggested in the *labeling* or proposed labeling thereof" (Section 505(d) of the Act). FDA *rules* further specify the types of studies that must be conducted to satisfy this requirement, and permit waiver in certain cases. The study protocol must minimize bias and must assure comparability between test and control groups. Generally, four types of control are recognized: comparing treated and untreated *patients*, comparing results of new drug use with a *placebo*, comparing results of new drug use with results from a regimen of therapy known to be effective, and comparing results of new drug use with experience that is historically derived. The statute and regulations do not explicitly require that *safety* of a new drug be established by adequate and well-controlled studies.

adjudication: The process in health insurance of reviewing claims to determine eligibility of services billed.

adjunct diagnostic or therapeutic unit: A special ancillary unit within a hospital equipped to assist physicians in unusual diagnostic, treatment, or therapeutic procedures.

adjunct disability: In the Veterans Administration health care program, a nonservice-connected disability arising from, associated with, or held to be aggravating a *service-connected disability*.

adjunct staff: Includes credentialed nonphysicians, such as physician's assistants and nurse anesthetists.

adjusted average daily census: The average number of patients who receive care (both inpatients and outpatients) each day during the census period, usually one year.

adjusted expenses per admission: The average daily expenses incurred by a hospital in providing care to an inpatient.

administration: The guidance or management of an undertaking toward the achievement of its purpose. Administration and *management* are so similar that they may be considered synonymous, although they are distinguished by applying administration to public activities and management to private, or by describing the first as concerned with the making of broad *policy* and the second as concerned with the execution of that policy once formulated. See also *planning, goals,* and *objectives.*

administrative agency: A unit of government created to administer legislative laws and executive policies. A medical licensing board is an example of a state agency. The *Department of Health and Human Services (HHS)* is an example of a federal government unit.

administrative law: Set of procedures by which administrative and regulatory agencies must function.

Administrative Procedures Act (APA): A body of law enacted in each state that regulates the conduct of administrative agencies within its jurisdiction. The federal government also has an administrative procedures act governing federal agencies.

administrator: Head of a health care facility responsible for managing its day-to-day affairs under the control or direction of a board of directors or trustees.

administrator, qualified: An individual currently licensed by the state to serve as administrator of a long-term care facility accredited by the *Joint Commission*.

admission: The formal acceptance by a hospital or other *inpatient* health care facility of a *patient* who is to be provided with room, board, and continuous nursing service in the hospital or facility where patients remain at least overnight.

admission certification: A form of medical care review in which an assessment is made of the medical necessity for *admission* of a patient to a hospital or other inpatient institution. Admission certification seeks to assure that patients requiring a hospital level of care, and only such patients, are admitted to the hospital without unnecessary delay and with proper planning of the hospital stay. *Length of stay* appropriate for the patient's admitting *diagnosis* is usually assigned and certified, and payment by any program requiring certification for the assigned stay is assured. Certification can be conducted before (preadmission) or shortly after (concurrent) admission.

admission/discharge/transfer (ADT): An admitting department procedure to collect, store, and distribute *patient* data to the various hospital departments.

admission notice: Verification of a patient's eligibility and benefits under a *health insurance* program.

admission, referred outpatient: Formal hospital acceptance of a *patient* for specific outpatient services upon referral by a *physician* or other health care *provider*.

admission review: The review of a patient's condition and treatment to determine the medical necessity of admission.

admitted assets: Assets of an *insurance* company recognized by a state regulatory body or other examining body in determining the company's financial condition and compliance with net worth requirements.

admitting physician: The *physician* responsible for *admission* of a patient to a hospital or other inpatient *health facility*. The physician may remain responsible for care of the patient after admission (see *private patient*) or the *housestaff* may become responsible for care. Most facilities have all admitting decisions made by a single physician (typically a rotating responsibility) called an admitting physician.

admitting privileges: See *staff privileges*.

adolescent medicine: A branch of medicine that concerns medical and health care problems of the adolescent patient, generally between 11 and 21 years of age.

adult day health services: Special medical and health care services provided during the day to ambulatory patients who do not need continuous (24-hour) care.

advance appropriation: In the federal budget, an *appropriation* provided by the Congress one or more years in advance of the *fiscal year* in which the *budget authority* becomes available for *obligation*. Advance appropriations allow state and local governments and private agencies sufficient time to develop plans with assurance of future federal funding. An advance appropriation is sometimes mistakenly referred to as forward funding, which involves an agency's obligation of funds during the current year for *outlay* to programs that will operate in subsequent fiscal years.

adverse selection: Disproportionate *insurance* of *risks* who are more prone to suffer *loss* (poorer risks) or make claims than the average risk. It may result from the tendency for poorer risks or less desirable *insureds* (sick people) to seek or continue insurance to a greater extent than do better risks (healthy people), or from the tendency for the insured to take advantage of favorable options in insurance contracts. Favorable selection, as compared to adverse selection, is called *skimming* when it is intentional.

advisory group (board): An ongoing formal body of health practitioners (other than staff physicians and hospital representatives) who participate in the *Professional Standards Review Organization*.

aerospace medicine: A relatively new branch of medicine that focuses on the effects of space travel on the human body.

AFDC: See *Aid to Families with Dependent Children*.

affected person: Any person residing or provider practicing within a geographic area likely to be affected by a *certificate of need* or a rate increase.

affiliated hospital: One that has an *affiliation* for some mutual purpose with another health program, usually a medical school. Some definitions, in fact, limit the term to hospitals with close or extensive affiliations with medical schools.

affiliation: An agreement (usually formal) between two or more otherwise independent programs or individuals that defines how they relate to each other in a joint undertaking. Affiliation agreements may specify: procedures for referring or transferring *patients* from one facility to another; joint faculty and medical staff appointments; teaching relationships; sharing of records or services; or provision of *consultation* between programs. See also *affiliated hospital*.

aftercare: Services provided a *patient* after discharge that support and increase the gain made during *treatment*, or a continuing program of *rehabilitation* to help the patient make a transition to self-care.

against medical advice (AMA): The self-discharge of a *patient* who leaves a *health care facility* against the advice of his physician or the medical staff.

age dependency ratio: A demographic measure of those too young or too old to provide for their own financial or social well-being.

age-specific birth rate: The number of live births (usually per 1000) to a selected population in a specified age group.

age-specific death rate: The number of deaths (usually per 1000) to a selected population in a specified age group.

aggregate indemnity: The ceiling or maximum dollar amount payable for any *disability,* period of disability, or covered service under an *insurance policy*.

AHA: See *American Hospital Association.*

AHCA: See *American Health Care Association.*

Aid to the Blind (AB): A federal program to furnish financial assistance to states with approved programs of medical care to the blind.

Aid to Families with Dependent Children (AFDC): A federal program designed to furnish assistance to families with dependent children under age 21.

Aid to the Permanently and Totally Disabled (APTD): A federal program that provides medical care to those permanently and totally disabled who are also medically indigent under federal guidelines.

air quality control region: Designated by the secretary of Health and Human Services. These geographical regions involve two or more communities that share a common air pollution problem.

Alcohol, Drug Abuse, and Mental Health Administration (ADAMHA): A unit of the U.S. Public Health Service that incorporates and coordinates the activities of three agencies: National Institutes of Health, National Institute on Alcohol and Drug Abuse, and National Institute of Mental Health.

Alcoholics Anonymous: This organization, formed in 1935, rehabilitates those with alcohol addiction.

alcoholism: A *chronic disease* evidenced by chronic consumption of alcoholic beverages in excess of the dietary and social uses and norms of the community and to an extent that interferes with *health* or social or economic functioning. The definition of alcoholism in both theory and practice is highly variable, sometimes requiring only excessive drinking or interference with the individual's functioning rather than both; sometimes requiring, in addition to the above, physical signs of *drug dependence,* or being recognized as present without either of the aforementioned conditions. There are many variable systems for separating different types of alcoholism and grading its severity. See also *drug abuse.*

alcoholism rehabilitation center: A specialized facility within a hospital that offers inpatient or outpatient services for the alcoholic.

allergist: A physician who specializes in the diagnosis and treatment of allergies.

allergy immunology technician: A technician trained to administer materials prescribed by an *allergist* and to desensitize patients to various allergens.

allied health personnel: Specially trained and *licensed* (when necessary) health care personnel other than *physicians, dentists, podiatrists,* and *nurses.* The term has no constant or agreed-upon meaning: sometimes being used synonymously with *paramedical personnel;* sometimes meaning all health workers who perform tasks that otherwise must be performed by a physician or tasks that are ancillary to the services of a physician; and sometimes referring to health workers who do not usually engage in independent practice.

allocated benefit provision: A provision in an *insurance policy* under which payment for certain *benefits* (usually including miscellaneous hospital and medical services such as x-rays and drugs) will be made at a rate for each as specified (scheduled) in the provision. Usually there is also a maximum amount that will be paid for all such expenses. An allocated benefit is one subject to such a provision. In an *unallocated benefit* provision no specification is given of the amount that will be paid for each type of service, although the provision sets a maximum amount payable for all listed services.

allopathic physician: Typically used in contrast to the terms *osteopathic* and *homeopathic;* a *physician* practicing a philosophy of medicine that views the role of the physician as an active interventionist who attempts to counteract the effect of a *disease* by using surgical or medical treatments that produce effects opposite to those of the disease. A homeopathic physician, on the other hand, generally uses a drug therapy that reinforces the body's natural self-healing process. Most physicians in the United States would be considered allopathic.

allopathy: Deals with the diagnosis and prevention of illness through intervention that incorporates a preventative approach to health care.

allowable charge: A term referring to the maximum fee that a third party will use in reimbursing a *provider* for a given service. An allowable charge may not be the same as *reasonable, customary,* or *prevailing charges* as the terms are used under the *Medicare* and *Medicaid* programs.

allowable costs: Items or elements of an institution's costs that are reimbursable under a payment formula. Both *Medicare* and *Medicaid* reimburse hospitals on the basis of certain costs, but do not allow reimbursement for all costs. Allowable costs, for example, may exclude noncovered services, luxury accommodations, costs which are not *reasonable,* or expenditures that are unnecessary in the efficient delivery of health services to persons covered under the program in question. See also *Section 223* and *Section 1122.*

ALOS: See *average length of stay.*

alternate delivery system (ADS): New and innovative health care approaches (i.e., *health maintenance organizations*) that emphasize preventative care, cost containment, comprehensive care, and other benefits more so than traditional systems of health care.

alternative birthing center: A specialized *facility* (usually part of a hospital) offering a cheerful and homelike environment for child-birth.

alternatives to long-term institutional care: The range of health, nutritional, housing, and social *services* designed to keep persons, particularly the aged, disabled, and retarded, out of institutions such as *skilled nursing facilities* providing care on a long-term basis. The goal is to provide the range of services necessary to allow the person to continue to function in the home environment. Alternatives to long-term care include day-care centers, foster homes, and *home-maker services.*

ambulatory care: All types of health services provided on an *outpatient* basis, in contrast to services provided in the home or to persons who are *inpatients.* Many inpatients may be ambulatory, but the term ambulatory care usually refers to patients who travel to locations other than their home to receive services and then depart the same day.

ambulatory care center: See *outpatient care.*

ambulatory surgery center: A freestanding unit capable of performing minor surgical procedures on a same-day care or outpatient basis.

American Association for Comprehensive Health Planning (AACHP): A national organization of members of regional comprehensive health planners.

American Association of Health Care Facilities (AAHCF): A national association of owners or managers of proprietary and nonproprietary long-term care facilities.

American College of Healthcare Executives (ACHE): Previously called the American College of Hospital Administrators (ACHA), the organization establishes standards of competence and fosters the professional growth of hospital administrators and related health care executives.

American College of Medical Group Administrators: A society for managers and administrators of medical clinics and medical group practices.

American College of Nursing Home Administrators (ACNHA): An individual society for *long-term care* administrators. Organized in 1962, its overall objective is to improve the quality of care in long-term care facilities by establishing standards for nursing home administrators.

American Dental Association (ADA): The national professional organization for practicing dentists. It accredits dental school internships and residency programs and engages in general organizational activities.

American Dietetic Association (ADA): A professional organization that establishes educational and supervised clinical experience requirements and sets standards of practice in the field of dietetics.

American Group Practice Association (AGPA): Represents private health care group practice practitioners in the United States. It is affiliated with the American Academy of Medical Directors.

American Health Care Association (AHCA): The nation's largest organization of licensed long-term care facilities and nursing homes. Formerly the American Nursing Home Association, the organization consists of *skilled nursing facilities, intermediate care facilities,* and *residential care* facilities, as well as adult day-care, child-care, and mental health facilities.

American Health Planning Association (AHPA): An organization of health planning professionals founded in 1971 to make health care services more responsive to local needs.

American Hospital Association (AHA): A national association consisting of nonprofit and proprietary hospitals. The association represents the interests of the nation's hospitals on legislative and legal matters.

American Medical Association (AMA): The major national physician organization, founded in 1847. The AMA consists of local, county, city, and state medical societies and undertakes a wide variety of legislative, political, and educational programs.

American Medical Records Association (AMRA): The national organization of medical information records professionals and personnel.

American Nurses' Association (ANA): The official national organization of *registered nurses.* It was founded in 1896.

American Nursing Home Association: See *American Health Care Association.*

American Optometric Association (AOA): A national association of doctors of optometry. This organization represents the professional interests of optometrists on legislative matters and offers a wide range of programs to its members.

American Osteopathic Association (AOA): A national association of doctors of osteopathy. This organization represents the professional interests of osteopathic medicine.

American Pharmaceutical Association (APhA): The national organization for the nation's 140,000 practicing pharmacists.

American Psychiatric Association (APA): The national association of physicians qualified to specialize in the practice of psychiatry.

American Public Health Association (APHA): Organized in 1872, this nongovernmental association represents all specialties and disciplines in public health with a membership of over 55,000.

American School Health Association (ASHA): A national professional association concerned with the health of school-age children, including the establishment of comprehensive health programs for public school systems.

American Society of Consultant Pharmacists (ASCP): A national association of pharmacists who specialize in offering consulting and pharmaceutical services to long-term care facilities.

American Society of Law and Medicine (ASLM): A national nonprofit society of professionals and academics with an interest in interdisciplinary health and legal issues.

amortization: The process of extinguishing a debt, usually by equal payments at regular intervals over a specific period of time.

anatomist: An instructor who teaches medical, dental, and other health students about the structure of the human body.

ancillary benefits: Health insurance that pays for ancillary or special services (tests, treatments, and procedures) not included in basic insurance coverage.

ancillary charges: Those extra hospital charges not included as part of the per diem rate (such as drugs, x-rays, and computerized axial tomography).

ancillary expenses: See *miscellaneous expenses*.

ancillary services: Hospital or other inpatient health facility services (excluding room and board) and *professional* services. They may include x-ray, *drug*, laboratory, or other services not separately itemized. See also *miscellaneous expenses*.

anesthesiologist, qualified: A licensed physician who is also certified to practice anesthesiology.

anesthetist: According to Joint Commission standards, this is a generic term to encompass anesthesiologists, other physician anesthetists, and qualified dentist or nurse anesthetists.

annual hospital report: A special form of health care accounting in which costs are grouped and reported according to function and are tied to reimbursement rates.

annual implementation plan (AIP): A plan required by the National Health Planning and Resources Development Act of 1974 (P.L. 93-641) that *health systems agencies* must prepare or update annually. Each plan specifies how to implement and establish priority for short-run *objectives* to achieve the long-range *goals* of the agency detailed in its *health system plan*.

antepartum care: Includes certain prenatal services (i.e., weight and height recording, physical examination, and urinalysis).

antibiotic: *Drug* containing any quantity of any chemical substance produced by a microorganism that has the capacity to inhibit the growth of, or to destroy, bacteria and other microorganisms (or a chemically synthesized equivalent of such a substance). Antibiotics are used in the *treatment* of infectious *diseases*.

antibiotic certification: A *Food and Drug Administration* (*FDA*) program in which each batch of every *antibiotic* drug for human use is certified by FDA as possessing the necessary characteristics of identity, strength, *quality*, and purity to insure adequate *safety* and *effectiveness* in its use. Before an antibiotic is eligible for certification, FDA must approve the drug as safe and effective under procedures that are substantially equivalent to those for approving *new drugs*. Similar procedures exist for batch certification of insulin.

antidiscrimination laws: In *insurance*, state laws which prohibit *insurers* from giving preferential terms or rates not warranted by the rating of the *risks* involved.

antisubstitution laws: Various state laws that require the pharmacist to "dispense as written." The effect is to prohibit a pharmacist from substituting a different *brand name* drug for the one prescribed, or substituting a *generic equivalent* drug in place of a *drug* prescribed by brand name, even if the drug that would be substituted is considered to be *therapeutically equivalent* to the drug prescribed and perhaps is less expensive. Drug reimbursement programs, such as the *Maximum Allowable Cost* (*MAC*) *program,* that limit reimbursement to the lowest cost at which a drug is generally available will be effective only if they override antisubstitution laws.

appropriate: As it applies to a particular person, condition, occasion, or place; proper; fitting. The term is commonly used in making *policy,* usually without specific indication of which aspects of the person or thing to which the term is applied are to be judged appropriate, or how and by what standard those aspects are to be judged. An example is P.L. 93-641, Section 1523(a)(6), which requires *state health planning and development agencies* to review existing *institutional health services* periodically and to make public findings "respecting the appropriateness of such *services.*" No indication is given in the law or *legislative history* of what the agencies are to find either appropriate or inappropriate (the costs, *charges,* necessity, *quality,* staffing, *administration,* or location of the services) or what methods and criteria are to be used.

appropriation: In the federal budget, an act of Congress that permits federal agencies to incur *obligations* and to make payments from the U.S. Treasury for specified purposes. An appropriation usually follows enactment of *authorizing legislation.* An appropriation is the most common form of *budget authority,* but in some cases the authorizing legislation provides the budget authority. Appropriations are also categorized by their period of availability (one-year, multiple-year, no-year), the timing of congressional action (current, permanent), and how the amount of the appropriation is determined (definite, indefinite).

area health education center (AHEC): An organization or system of health, educational, and service institutions whose *policy* and programs are frequently under the direction of a medical school or university health science center and whose prime *goals* are to improve the distribution, *supply, quality, utilization,* and *efficiency* of health personnel in relation to specific *medically underserved areas.* The primary *objectives* are to educate and train the health personnel specifically *needed* by that underserved community and to decentralize *health manpower* education, thereby increasing manpower supplies and providing a linkage between the health and educational institutions in scarcity areas. In practice, each AHEC has one or more public or nonprofit hospitals some distance away from the medical school or university health science center, but the hospitals' educational efforts are under the effective guidance of the medical school or university center. The development of AHECs is assisted by HHS under its *health manpower education initiative* *award* (HMEIA) authority.

areawide comprehensive health planning agency (areawide CHP, or 314(b) agency): A substate (usually multicounty) agency assisted under Section 314(b) of the *Public Health Service Act.* The areawide CHP agencies were created by the Comprehensive Health Planning and Public Health Service Amendments of 1966 (P.L. 89-749). They were charged with the preparation of regional or local plans for the coordination and development of existing and new health services, facilities, and manpower. The agencies were authorized to review and comment upon proposals from hospitals and other institutions for development of programs and expansion of facilities, but they had no significant powers of enforcement. Under the provisions of the new health planning law, P.L. 93-641, existing 314(b) agencies will be replaced by *health systems agencies* that will have expanded duties and powers.

ASHA: American Speech and Hearing Association. See also *American School Health Association.*

AS-SCORE: A multi-attribute clinical index of illness severity. In *diagnosis-related groups (DRGs)* this is a severity of illness classification based on five factors: (1) age, (2) organ or body system, (3) complications, (4) stage of the disease, and (5) patient's response to treatment. The system assigns the patient to one of four classifications based on the aggregate seriousness of the disorder. This system is used to determine if patients in a DRG category are homogeneous or if severity of illness is not being accounted for.

assessment: In health *insurance,* a charge upon *carriers* to raise funds for a specific purpose (such as meeting the administrative costs of a government-required program) made by government (usually state government) or a special organization authorized by government and provided for in law or regulation. It is also applied to all carriers handling a specific line of coverage subject to regulation by the government in question and based upon a formula.

assigned risk: A *risk* that underwriters do not care to insure (such as a chronically ill person seeking health insurance) but that, because of state law or otherwise, must be insured. Insuring assigned risks is usually handled through a group of insurers (such as all companies licensed to issue health insurance in the state), and individual assigned risks are assigned to the companies in turn or in proportion to their share of the state's total health insurance business. Assignment of risks is common in casualty insurance and less common in health insurance. As an approach to providing insurance to assigned risks, this can be contrasted with pooling of such risks (see *insurance pool*) in which the *losses* rather than the risks are distributed among the group of insurers.

assignment: An agreement in which a *patient* assigns to another party, usually a *provider,* the right to receive payment from a *third party* for the service the patient has received. Assignment is used rather than a patient paying directly for the service and then receiving reimbursement from a public or private insurance program. In *Medicare,* for example, if a physician accepts assignment from the patient, he must agree to accept the program payment as payment in full (except for specific *coinsurance, copayment,* and *deductible* amounts required of the patient). Assignment protects the patient against liability for charges which the Medicare program will not recognize as *reasonable charges.* Under some *national health insurance* proposals, physicians must agree to assignment for all of their patients or none of them; under Medicare, physicians may choose assignment for some of their patients but not others, and may do so on a claim-by-claim-basis for some services but not others.

assignment of benefits: The patient assigns all or part of the benefits to be paid to the provider of care, who usually accepts the assignment as full payment for the services rendered.

Assisted Health Insurance Plan (AHIP): A concept contained in former proposals for *national health insurance,* known as the *Comprehensive Health Insurance Plan.* AHIP is designed to provide health insurance coverage for low-*income* and high-medical-risk people. It would be available to anyone electing coverage, at a premium no greater than 150 percent of the average group premium for private health insurance in the state. Premiums and *cost sharing* would be *indexed* to income. AHIP would replace *Medicaid* and be state administered under contract with fiscal *intermediaries*. Benefits under AHIP would be identical to those formerly proposed under the *Employee Health Insurance Plan (EHIP)* and *Federal Health Insurance Plan (FHIP)*. The plan would be financed by premiums and subsidized by state and federal revenues under a matching formula.

associate degree program: A program, for example, which educates *registered nurses* in a junior college. The associate degree is given upon junior college graduation. The student's classroom and laboratory instruction is principally provided in the college, and clinical instruction takes place in an *affiliated hospital*. See also *diploma school* and *baccalaureate degree program*.

associate medical staff: Professional-level health care *providers* who are new to the *hospital* staff and are probationary for regular staff appointment.

association: In *epidemiology*, the general name for a relationship between two variables. Two related variables, such as age and the incidence of diabetes, are said to be "associated." Several different types of association are recognized, such as artifactual, causal, and chance.

Association for the Advancement of Health Education (AAHE): A national professional organization of health educators concerned with health education and health promotion in public and private school systems.

Association for Health Records (AHR): A multidisciplinary organization of professionals in the medical and health information field whose purpose is to exchange professional interest.

Association for Health Services Research (AHSR): An organization representing health services research professionals in a variety of legislative, educational, and professional programs of common interest.

Association of University Programs in Health Administration (AUPHA): An international organization to assist participating colleges and universities in the training of health administration professionals. Its efforts are largely supported by a unique partnership of industry, individuals, organizations, foundations, universities, and government.

assurance: Synonymous with *insurance* or risk bearing.

at risk: Subject to some uncertain event occurring which denotes potential loss. In the financial sense, this refers to an individual, organization (such as an *HMO*), or insurance company assuming the chance of loss by running the risk of having to provide or pay for more *services* than were paid for through *premiums* or per capita payments. If payments are adjusted after the fact so that no loss can occur, then there is no risk. Of course, losses incurred in one year may be made up by increases in premiums or per capita payments in the next year, so the "risk" is somewhat tempered. A firm which is at risk for losses also stands to gain from *profits* if costs are less than premiums collected. For a *consumer,* financially at risk usually means being without insurance or at risk for substantial *out-of-pocket* expenses. A second use of the term relates to the special vulnerability of certain populations to certain diseases or conditions. For example, ghetto children are at risk for lead poisoning and rat bite; workers in coal mines are at risk for *black lung* disease.

attending physician: The physician legally responsible for the care provided a *patient* in a hospital or other health program. Usually the *physician* of a *private patient* is also responsible for the patient's *outpatient* care. The attending physician for a *public patient,* upon the patient's *admission,* is typically chosen by the hospital from its *medical staff* or its *teaching physicians.*

audiologist: An individual trained in *audiology* who evaluates hearing function; performs research related to hearing; and plans, directs, and conducts rehabilitative programs designed to improve the communication efficiency of individuals with impaired hearing. Approximately 32,000 persons are employed as *speech pathologists* and audiologists. *Licensure* generally requires a master's degree in audiology. The *American Speech and Hearing Association (ASHA)* awards a certificate of clinical competence which requires academic training at the master's degree level, one year of experience in the field, and passing a national examination. Nearly half of the ASHA members are employed in elementary or secondary schools, and a large majority are engaged in either diagnostic or therapeutic clinical work.

audiology: The study, examination, appreciation, and treatment of hearing defects, including the use of auditory substitutional *devices* (hearing aids) and other *therapy.* See also *audiologist* and *pathologist.*

audit: An accounting process to verify the accuracy or validity of financial records or the appropriateness of charges under a third-party payment plan.

audit, medical: The retrospective review of medical records by qualified personnel for purposes of evaluating the quality and quantity of medical care in relation to accepted standards.

authorization or authorizing legislation: In the federal budget, legislation enacted by Congress that sets up or continues the legal operation of a federal program or agency indefinitely or for a specific period of time, often three years in the health area. Such legislation is a prerequisite for subsequent *appropriations* or other types of *budget authority* contained in appropriation acts. It may limit the amount of budget authority to be subsequently provided or may instead authorize the appropriation of "such sums as may be necessary"; in a few instances budget authority may be provided in the authorization (see *backdoor authority*). The term is often used more strictly to refer to annual dollar limits specified in authorizing legislation on amounts that may be appropriated for the authorized program.

autogroup: The computerization of medical records by an interactive statistical analysis system which segregates data into groups using patients' medical records.

autopsy: Examination of the body after death (post mortem, therefore also called a "post" or "post mortem") to determine the cause of death. The *autopsy rate* (percentage of deaths involving autopsies in a hospital) is sometimes considered a measure of the *quality* of a hospital. Consent for an autopsy, except where exception is made by law, is required from survivors of the deceased.

autopsy rate: The percentage of bodies examined compared to the number of deaths in a given population for a given time period.

auxiliary services: Those ancillary services in a health care facility (such as pharmacy, x-ray, and laboratory) other than room and board services.

availability: A measure (in terms of type and location) of the *supply* of health resources and services relative to the *needs* (or *demands*) of a given individual or community. Health care is available to an individual when he can obtain it, at the time and place that he *needs* it, from *appropriate* personnel. Availability is a function of the distribution of appropriate resources and services, and the willingness of the *provider* to serve the particular *patient* in need. See also *access* and *acceptability*.

available bed days: The total number of available beds multiplied by the number of days in the time period measured. Hence, a 100-bed facility would have 36,500 available bed days per year.

average daily census (ADC): The average number of inpatients per day over a given time period.

average length of stay (ALOS): The average number of days a person remains in the hospital or other facility over a given time period.

Bb

baccalaureate degree program: In *nursing*, a program combining liberal arts and clinical studies in a four-year college or university that prepares students to become *registered nurses*. A bachelor of arts or science degree is granted upon graduation from the program. Classroom and laboratory instruction is principally provided by the college or university (usually by its nursing school) and clinical teaching by its hospital or an *affiliated hospital*. See also *diploma school* and *associate degree program*.

backdoor authority: In the federal budget, legislative authority for the *obligation* of funds outside the normal *appropriation* process. It is often called backdoor spending. The most common forms of backdoor authority are borrowing authority (authority to spend debt receipts) and contract authority. In other cases (e.g., interest on the public debt), a permanent appropriation is provided that becomes available without any current action by the Congress. *Entitlement authority* is sometimes included as a form of backdoor authority, since the enactment of the basic benefit legislation may effectively mandate the subsequent enactment of the appropriations to pay the statutory benefits. Examples of programs that have backdoor authority are the Environmental Protection Agency's construction grant program and the social security *trust funds*.

backup hospital: A hospital that furnishes *inpatient* care which cannot be obtained in a neighborhood health center.

bacteriologist: A microbiologist or medical technologist specializing in the study of bacteria for medical, scientific, or public health purposes.

bad debts: The amount of *income* lost to a provider because of failure of *patients* to pay amounts owed. The impact of the loss of revenue from bad debts may be partially offset for *proprietary* institutions by the fact that income tax is not payable on income not received. Bad debts also may be recovered by increasing *charges* to paying patients by a proportional amount. Some *cost-related or cost-based reimbursement* programs reimburse certain bad debts (see *reasonable cost*).

bargaining unit: Employees (in a health care *facility*) organized in a group for purposes of collective bargaining as a labor unit.

basic health services: The minimum *supply* of health *services* that should be generally and uniformly available in order to assure adequate *health status* and protection of the population from *disease,* or to meet some other *criteria* or *standards.* Although all possible services cannot be supplied to the entire population, there has been no definition of what set of services constitutes an *appropriate* minimum and of how to assure its availability. A beginning has been made in federal *policy* with the definition of *required services* for *Medicaid* and basic health services required of *HMOs* requesting federal assistance or *qualification.* These include *physician* services, *hospital* services, medically necessary *emergency care, preventive health* services, *home health care* services, up to 20 *visits* of outpatient *mental health* services, medical *treatment* and *referral* services for *alcoholism* and *drug abuse,* and laboratory and radiologic services (Section 1302(1) of the *PHS Act*). Where a minimum is defined, a higher level of service is usually also defined (*supplemental health services* and *optional services* for HMOs and Medicaid, respectively).

BCHS: See *Bureau of Community Health Services.*

bed: Literally, a bed in a *hospital* or other inpatient health facility. Many definitions require that the beds be maintained for continuous (24-hour) use by *inpatients.* Beds are often used as a measure of capacity (hospital sizes are compared by comparing their number of beds). *Licenses* and *certificates of need* may be granted for specific numbers or types of beds, for example, surgical, pediatric, obstetric, or extended care. Facilities may have both licensed and unlicensed beds or have both active and licensed, but unused, beds. Other qualifying adjectives are frequently used to categorize beds, such as available, occupied, *acute care,* or observation beds.

bed capacity: The number of *beds* approved in a *facility* by *accreditation* or other standards. Also known as *licensed* beds.

bed count: The actual number of *beds* available for *patient* use.

bed, swing: A *hospital* bed used either for *acute care* or *long-term care*, depending upon immediate demand.

bed turnover rate: The number of *patients* occupying and vacating the same *bed* in a health care *facility* during a given time period.

behavioral health: Attempts to alleviate problems of *health* or *illness* by attacking self-defeating behaviors (smoking or addiction) through behavioral influences of education and health activation.

beneficiary: A person who is eligible to receive, or is receiving, *benefits* from an *insurance policy* or *health maintenance organization*. Beneficiaries usually include people who have contracted for benefits for themselves and their eligible *dependents.* See also *subscriber* and *insured.*

benefit: In *insurance,* a sum of money provided in an *insurance policy* payable for certain types of *loss* or for covered services defined under the terms of the policy. The benefits may be paid to the *insured* or to others on the insured's behalf. In *prepayment* programs such as *HMOs,* benefits are the services the programs will provide their *members* whenever, and to the extent, *needed.*

benefit-cost analysis: Evaluating the relationship between the *benefits* and *costs* of a particular program or activity.

benefit period: The period of time for which payments for *benefits* covered by an *insurance policy* are available. The availability of certain benefits may be limited over a specified time period. While the benefit period is usually defined by a set unit of time, such as a year, benefits also may be tied to a *spell of illness*.

benefits, health: Outcomes or changes in *health status* that are derived from health care processes. The term also includes medical and dental benefits provided employees as a fringe benefit.

Best's Report: An annual publication that presents the financial stability and rating of health and other insurance *underwriters*.

BHI: See *Bureau of Health Insurance*.

Bill of Patient's Rights: Accepted standards that recognize basic rights of a *patient*. See also *patient's rights*.

binding review: For *peer review organization (PRO)* programs, a review for which determinations are final and which affects payments under *Medicare* and *Medicaid*.

bioavailability: The extent and rate of absorption of a dose of a given *drug*, measured by the time-concentration curve for appearance of the administered drug in the blood. The concept is important in attempting to determine whether different *brand name* drugs, a *generic name* drug as opposed to a brand name drug, or, in some cases, different batches of the same brand name drug will produce the same *therapeutic effect*. The same drug made by two different manufacturers or different batches of the same drug made by the same manufacturer may demonstrate differing bioavailability. There is continued controversy as to whether such differences are therapeutically significant. See also *Maximum Allowable Cost Program, antisubstitution,* and *bioequivalence*.

bioequivalence: Describes drugs that have the same *bioavailability*. Such *drugs* are *chemical equivalents* (indistinguishable by chemical means), although chemically equivalent preparations are not always bioequivalent. Bioequivalence is a function of bioavailability, and the terms are often used synonymously. Chemically equivalent drugs that are bioequivalent are *therapeutically equivalent* (have the same treatment effect), although therapeutically equivalent preparations need not be either chemically equivalent or bioequivalent.

biologics: (Also biological products, biologicals.) Any virus, therapeutic serum, toxin, antitoxin, or analogous product of plant or animal origin used in the prevention, *diagnosis,* or *treatment* of *disease.* Biologics, including vaccines and blood plasma products, are regulated by the *Bureau of Biologics*, a division of the *Food and Drug Administration.* They differ from *drugs* in that biologics are usually derived from living microorganisms and cannot be synthesized or readily standardized by chemical or physical means. Since biologics tend to be chemically less stable than drugs, their *safety* cannot be as easily assured, and they are never as chemically pure as drugs.

biomedical research: *Research* concerned with human and animal biology and with *disease* and its prevention, *diagnosis,* and *treatment.* It differs from *health services research,* which is concerned with the organization, effects, and other aspects of health services.

biostatistician: A person with special training in the application of statistics to health care and health care research.

birth control: The deliberate limiting of childbirth through contraceptive measures. See *family planning*.

birth rate: A fraction whose numerator is the total number of births in a population during a given period and whose denominator is the total number of person-years lived by the population during that period. The latter is generally approximated by the size of the population at the mid-point of the period multiplied by the length of the period in years. The rate is usually stated per 1,000. Like other rates in which the population at the midpoint of the period is used as the denominator of the fraction, this is sometimes called the central birth rate. Where birth rate is used without qualification, it generally refers to the *live birth* rate; only live births appear in the numerator. The total birth rate, based on live births and late fetal deaths, is sometimes calculated. Legitimate birth rates and illegitimate birth rates, using legitimate and illegitimate births respectively, are also computed. The illegitimacy ratio, which indicates the number of illegitimate births per 1,000 total births, is frequently used. To compare the fertility of different populations, standardized birth rates (the definition above being the crude birth rate) are often used to eliminate the effect on the birth rate of differences in structure of the population (most commonly the age and sex structure).

births: The number of children born in a health facility within a given time period.

black lung: Common name for pneumoconiosis, a *chronic,* severely debilitating lung *disease* caused by inhaling coal dust and found principally among coal miners. Certain medical benefits for the victims of the disease are available under Title IV of the federal Coal Mine Health and Safety Act of 1969 (P.L. 91-173), as amended by P.L. 92-303.

blanket medical expense: A provision (usually included as an added feature of a policy providing some other type of coverage, such as loss of income insurance) that entitles the *insured* to collect, up to a maximum established in the policy, for all hospital and medical expenses incurred without limitations on individual types of medical expenses.

blood bank: A special medical unit with responsibility for blood procurement, processing, grouping, typing, and distribution. Many major hospitals maintain their own blood banks; others procure blood from outside blood bank facilities.

Blue Cross Association (BCA): The national nonprofit organization to which the 70 *Blue Cross plans* in the United States voluntarily belong. BCA administers programs of *licensure* and approval for

Blue Cross plans, provides specific services related to the writing and administering of health care benefits across the country, and actively represents the Blue Cross plans in national affairs. Under contract with the *Social Security Administration* (SSA), BCA is the *intermediary* in the *Medicare* program for the majority of the participating *providers*. See also *Health Services, Inc.,* and *Blue Shield plan.*

Blue Cross plan: A nonprofit, tax-exempt health service *prepayment* organization providing coverage for health care and related services. The individual plans should be distinguished from their national association, the *Blue Cross Association.* Historically, the plans were largely the creation of the hospital industry. They were designed to provide hospitals with a stable source of revenues, although formal association between the Blue Cross and the American Hospital Association ended in 1972. A Blue Cross plan is generally a nonprofit community service organization with a governing body whose membership includes a majority of public representatives. Most plans are regulated by state *insurance commissioners* under special enabling legislation. Plans are exempt from federal income taxes and, in most states, from state taxes. Unlike most private insurance companies, the plans usually provide *service* rather than *indemnity benefits,* and they often pay hospitals on the basis of *reasonable costs* rather than *charges.* See also *Health Services, Inc.,* and *Blue Shield plan.*

Blue Sheet: See *Drug Research Reports.*

Blue Shield plan: A nonprofit, tax-exempt plan established in 1939 that provides coverage of physician's services. The individual plans should be distinguished from the National Association of Blue Shield Plans. Blue Shield coverage is commonly sold in conjunction with *Blue Cross* coverage, although this is not necessarily the case. The relationship between Blue Cross and Blue Shield plans has been a cooperative one; it is not uncommon for the two organizations to have a common board, one management, and the same facilities. Most states have enacted special enabling legislation for the Blue

Cross and Blue Shield plans. See also *Medical Indemnity of America, Inc.*

BNDD: Bureau of Narcotics and Dangerous Drugs of the Department of Justice. It is now named the *Drug Enforcement Administration.*

board certified: A *physician* or other health *professional* who has passed an examination given by a medical *specialty board* and has been *certified* by the board as a specialist in that particular subject. The examination cannot be taken until the professional meets requirements set by the specialty board for board eligibility (see *board eligible*). Physicians may be board certified in at least 1 of 22 specialty areas.

board eligible: Describes a *physician* or other health *professional* who is eligible for a specialty board examination (including an individual who may have failed the examination if he or she remains eligible). Each of the *specialty boards* has requirements that must be met before the examination can be taken for specialty *board certification.* These include graduation from an approved medical school, training experience of specified type and length, and specified time in practice or on the job. The minimum time required after graduation from medical school to become board eligible is generally three to five years. Governmental and other types of health programs that define standards for specialists often accept board eligibility as equivalent to board certification, since the only difference is that the board-certified professional has passed an examination.

boarding homes: Informal facilities that provide room and board (often to the aged) for a fee. *Custodial care* is sometimes included. Medical supervision, social activities, and counseling are not normally provided. The homes are not *licensed* as *health facilities* and usually are not subject to any type of licensure.

borrowed servant: An employee temporarily under the supervision or control of one who does not work for the organization. The temporary master of the borrowed servant assumes responsibility for the negligent act of the borrowed servant.

brand name: The registered trademark given to a specific *drug* product or *device* by its manufacturer. It is also known as a *trade name*. As an example, there is a widely prescribed broad-spectrum antibiotic with the *generic name* or *established name* of tetracycline hydrochloride. Its *chemical name* is 4-dimethylamino-1,4,4a,5,5a,6,11,12a-octahydro-3,6,10,12,12a-pentahydroxy-6-methyl-11-dioxa-2-naphthacenecarboxamide hydrochloride. Its chemical formula is $C_{22}H_{24}N_2O_8HCL$. This drug is marketed by Lederle Laboratories under the brand name "Achromycin," by Bristol-Myers under "Bristacycline," by Robins as "Robitet," and by Squibb as "Sumycin." There are no official rules governing the selection of brand names. According to the *Pharmaceutical Manufacturers Association*, the objective is to use a name that is "useful, dignified, easily remembered, and individual or proprietary." Drugs are primarily advertised to practitioners by brand name. When a physician prescribes by brand name, *antisubstitution laws* in most states forbid the pharmacist from substituting either a brand- or generic- name equivalent made by a different manufacturer, although either may be less expensive than the drug prescribed.

budget: A detailed financial plan for carrying out a program of activities in a specified period, usually a *fiscal year*. The budget typically accounts for all the program's proposed income, by source, and expenses, by purposes such as salaries and *capital* costs, for the year. Expenses are sometimes related to the program's *goals* and *objectives*. See also *policy planning, administration,* and *congressional* budget, and *president's budget*.

budget authority (BA): In the federal budget, authority provided by law to enter into *obligations* that will result in immediate or future *outlays* of government funds. It does not include the authority to insure or guarantee the repayment of indebtedness incurred by another person or government. The basic forms of budget authority are *appropriations,* contract authority, and borrowing authority. Budget authority is classified by the timing of congressional action (current or permanent) or by the manner of determining the amount of funds available (definite or indefinite).

Bureau of Biologics: A subdivision of the *Food and Drug Administration* responsible for the control of biologicals, serums, and blood plasma.

Bureau of Drugs: A subdivision of the *Food and Drug Administration* responsible for the regulation and control of *drugs.*

Bureau of Health Insurance (BHI): An agency within the *Social Security Administration (SSA)* that administers the *Medicare* program. Actual operation of the program is carried out through arrangements with *intermediaries* and *carriers,* who operate under contract with BHI and SSA and receive all policy guidance from BHI.

Bureau of Health Manpower: see *Bureau of Health Professions.*

Bureau of Health Professions: A unit within Health Resources Administration, Public Health Service. The bureau projects and monitors the human resources needed to staff the U.S. health care system adequately.

Bureau of Quality Assurance (BQA): An agency within the Health Resources Administration of the *Department of Health and Human Services.* The BQA administers the *peer review organization* program.

bureaucracy: A government or other organization characterized by specialization of functions, adherence to fixed rules, and a hierarchy of authority; a system of administration marked by officialism, red tape, and proliferation (from *Webster's New Collegiate Dictionary*).

Cc

California relative value studies (CRVS): A numbering system used by *physicians* to evaluate difficulty of procedures used in *patient* care.

cancer registry: A system of identifying and keeping data on cancerous tumors. These data are gathered nationally and used for research purposes.

CAPER: Computer Assisted Pathology Encoding and Reporting System. A computerized medical reporting system that functions as a comprehensive pathology information system for hospitals.

capital: Fixed or durable nonlabor inputs or factors used in the production of goods and services, for example, the buildings, *beds,* and *equipment* used in the provision of hospital services. Capital also refers to the value of such factors or money specifically available for their acquisition or development. Capital goods are usually thought of as permanent and durable and should be distinguished from *supplies.* The term refers also to investment in self (human capital). *Preventative care* is purchased because of the positive effect such care may have on one's ability to sustain future earning capacity. See also *capital depreciation* and *working capital.*

capital depreciation: The decline in value of *capital* assets of a permanent or fixed nature, such as goods and plant, over time with use. The rate and amount of depreciation are calculated by a variety of methods (e.g., straight-line, sum-of-the-digits, and declining balance) that give different results. Reimbursement for health *services* usually includes an amount equivalent to the capital depreciation experienced by the *provider* of the services. See also *debt service, Section 1122,* and *funded.*

capital expenditure review (CER): A review of proposed *capital* expenditures of hospitals and other health facilities to determine the *need* for, and *appropriateness* of, proposed expenditures. The review is completed by a designated *regulatory* agency, such as a *state health planning and development agency,* and has a sanction attached that prevents (see *certificate of need*) or discourages (see *Section 1122*) unneeded expenditures.

capitation: A method of payment for health services in which an individual or institutional provider is paid a fixed, per capita amount for each person served without regard to the actual number or nature of services provided to each person. Capitation is characteristic of *health maintenance organizations* but unusual for physicians (see *fee for service*). Also, a method of federal support of health professional schools authorized by the Comprehensive Health Manpower Training Act of 1971, P.L. 92-157, and the Nurse Training Act of 1971, P.L. 92-158 (Sections 770 and 810 of the *PHS Act*), in which eligible schools receive a fixed capitation payment from the federal government for each student enrolled.

captain of the ship: One who assumes complete control over others (i.e., a surgeon in an operating room). See *borrowed servant.*

cardiac care unit (CCU): An *intensive care unit* specializing in the care of *patients* who suffer from severe cardiac disorders.

cardiologist: A *physician* who specializes in cardiovascular *diseases* and disorders.

CARE: Computerized Audit and Record Evaluation System. A computerized record evaluation system for medical records.

care plan: A formal plan of activities or procedures to be performed by health care personnel on behalf of a *patient.*

care team: Members of the health care staff, together with members of the patient's household, who care for a *Medicare* patient under a *home health care* program.

carrier: A commercial health *insurer,* a government agency, or a *Blue Cross* or *Blue Shield* plan which underwrites or administers programs that pay for health services. Under the *Medicare* Part B (*Supplemental Medical Insurance*) Program and the *Federal Employees Health Benefits Program,* carriers are agencies and organizations with which the programs contract for administration of various functions, including payment of *claims.* See also *intermediary* and *third party.*

case-control study: An inquiry in which groups of individuals are selected because they have a specific *disease* (the cases) or do not have that *disease* (the controls) for a study of the cause and other attributes of the disease. The groups are then compared with respect to their past, existing, or future characteristics likely to be relevant to the disease to see which of the characteristics differ, and how, when compared to the controls.

case-fatality ratio: The number of *deaths* from a specific *disease* (per 100 episodes of the disease) within a given time period.

case mix: The diagnosis-specific makeup of a health program's work load. Case mix directly influences the *lengths of stay* in a hospital or other health program and the *intensity,* cost, and *scope* of the *services* provided by the facility.

cases treated: The number of *patients* cared for by a health program during a year. *Inpatient* discharges and *outpatient* visits can be combined into an aggregate weighted index of hospital output.

catastrophe policy: See *major medical* policy.

catastrophic health insurance: Health insurance that provides protection against the high cost of treating severe or lengthy *illnesses* or *disabilities*. Generally such policies cover all or a specified percentage of medical expenses above an amount that is the responsibility of the insured (or the responsibility of another insurance policy up to a maximum limit of liability). For example, protection may begin after an individual (or family unit) has incurred medical expenses equal to a specified dollar amount (e.g., $2,000 within a 12-month period) or a specified percentage of *income* (e.g., 15 percent), or has been in a medical institution for a specified period (e.g., 60 days). The individual is liable for all costs up to the specified limits. However, in the absence of any effective prohibition against additional insurance the individual could be expected to obtain health insurance protection for costs below the catastrophic minimum limits. Generally, there are no maximum limits of coverage under these plans; however, many include *coinsurance*. See also *major medical*.

catchment area: A geographic area defined and served by a health program or institution, such as a hospital or *community mental health center*. The area is delineated on the basis of population distribution, natural geographic boundaries, transportation accessibility, and other factors. It should be contrasted with service, medical market, or *medical trade areas*. All residents of the area needing the services of the program are usually eligible for them, although eligibility may depend on additional criteria (age or *income*). Residents of the area may or may not be *enrolled* in the program or limited to obtaining services from the program. Also, the program may or may not limit services to residents of the area or be required to register, or have the capacity to serve, all residents of the area.

categorical program: Originally, a health program that was concerned with research, education, control, and *treatment* of only one or a few specific *diseases*. The term now generally describes a program concerned with only a part, rather than all, of the population or health system. More specifically, it often refers to an existing program which its sponsors feel the federal government should cease to support.

categorically needy: Persons in certain categories of groups eligible to receive public assistance who are also economically needy. As used in *Medicaid,* this means a person who is aged, blind, disabled, or a member of a family with children under 18 (or 21, if in school) where one parent is absent, incapacitated, or unemployed and, in addition, meets specified *income* and *resources* requirements that vary by state. In general, categorically needy individuals are persons receiving cash assistance under the *AFDC* or *supplemental security income (SSI)* programs. A state must cover all recipients of AFDC payments under Medicaid. However, the state is provided certain options in determining the extent of coverage for persons receiving federal SSI or supplementary state SSI payments. In addition, a state may cover other specified groups, such as foster children, who are categorically needy. A state may restrict its Medicaid coverage to the categorically needy or may cover additional persons who meet the categorical requirements as *medically needy.*

categorically related: In the *Medicaid* program, the requirements (other than *income* and *resources*) that an individual must meet in order to be eligible for Medicaid benefits; also individuals who meet these requirements. Specifically, any individual eligible for Medicaid must fall into one of four main categories of people who are eligible for assistance in the form of cash payments. The individual must be "aged," "blind," or "disabled" (as defined under the *supplemental security income* program, Title XVI of the Social Security Act) or a member of a family with dependent children where one parent is absent, incapacitated, or unemployed (as defined under the *Aid to Families with Dependent Children* program, Title IV of the Social Security Act). After the determination is made that an individual is categorically related, income and resources tests are applied to determine if the individual is poor enough to be eligible for assistance (*categorically needy*). As a result of this requirement, single persons and childless couples who are not aged, blind, or disabled and families headed by males in states that do not cover such groups under their AFDC programs cannot receive Medicaid coverage regardless of poverty.

cause: A factor that, if prevented, removed, or eliminated, will prevent the occurrence of the event in question; or, if permitted, introduced, or maintained, will be followed by the event in question. A necessary cause is one that must exist if a given event is to occur, but may not itself result in the event.

census, inpatient: The actual number of inpatients in the *hospital* receiving health care services for a given time period.

Centers for Disease Control (CDC): An organization within the *Department of Health and Human Services (HHS)* that serves as the national focal point for *disease* control and *public health* activities. The center (formerly the Communicable Disease Center) provides facilities and services for the investigation, prevention, and control of diseases; supports *quarantine* and other activities to prevent introduction of communicable diseases from foreign countries; conducts *research* into the *epidemiology,* laboratory *diagnosis,* prevention, and *treatment* of infectious and other controllable diseases at the community level; provides grants for venereal disease research, immunization against infectious diseases, and disease control programs; and sets standards for laboratories. Activities focus primarily on the improvement of the health care system through emphasis on prevention, investigation, surveillance, and control operations, including training state and local health workers in specific control techniques (rather than direct treatment of disease).

central supply: The service within a *hospital* that sterilizes, packages, and distributes equipment, sheets, wearing apparel, and surgical dressings for use in surgery or where other sterile materials are required.

certificate of insurance: In *group* health *insurance,* a statement issued to a *member* of a group certifying that an insurance contract covering the member has been written and containing a summary of the terms applicable to that member.

certificate of need or necessity: A certificate issued by a governmental body to an organization proposing to construct or modify a *health facility* or to offer a new or different health *service*. The certificate recognizes that the facility or service will be *needed* by those for whom it is intended when it becomes available. A certificate is required, for instance, for all proposals involving more than a minimum *capital* investment or a change in *bed* capacity and is a condition of *licensure* of the facility or service. The certificate-of-need program is intended to serve the public interest by controlling expansion of facilities and services and preventing excessive or duplicative development of facilities and services. All states are required to have the *state health planning and development agency* (designated pursuant to law) administer a state certificate-of-need program, which must apply to all new *institutional health services* proposed or developed in the state. The *health systems agencies* (local planning bodies under P.L. 93-641) are required to make recommendations to the state agencies regarding proposed new institutional health services within their areas.

certification: The process by which a governmental or nongovernmental agency or association evaluates and recognizes an individual, institution, or educational program as meeting predetermined *standards*. One so recognized is said to be certified. Certification is synonymous with *accreditation,* except that certification is usually applied to individuals and accreditation to institutions. Certification programs are generally nongovernmental and do not exclude the uncertified from *practice* as do *licensure* programs. In *PROs* and other *regulatory programs*, certification of services means that provision of the services has been approved and payment for them is assured (see *admission certification*). See also *certificate of need.*

chairside: The dental equivalent of bedside.

CHAMPUS: See *Civilian Health and Medical Program of the Uniformed Services.*

charge nurse: According to *Joint Commission* accreditation of *long-term care* facilities, a registered or licensed practical or vocational *nurse* in charge of a nursing unit. Also, the head nurse of a given nursing shift is called a charge nurse.

charges: Prices assigned to units of medical *service*, such as a visit to a physician or a day in a hospital. Charges for services may not be related to the actual *costs* of providing the services. Further, the methods by which charges are related to costs vary substantially among services and institutions. Various *third-party* payers may require different methods to determine either charges or costs. Charges for one service provided by an institution are often used to subsidize the costs of other services. Charges to one type or group of patients also may be used to subsidize the costs of providing services to other groups. See also *actual charge, allowable charge, customary charge, prevailing charge, reasonable charge,* and *usual charge.*

charitable immunity: In *malpractice,* a doctrine in use in a decreasing number of states that nonprofit, or charitable, hospitals and other nonproprietary health facilities are not subject to suit for malpractice. The doctrine of charitable immunity relies on and involves waiver of the patient's right to sue for negligence by accepting the charity; the basic unfairness, either assumed or stated, of applying a doctrine, such as *respondeat superior* applicable to commercial pursuits, to a nonprofit enterprise; and the increased financial demands on the assets of the charity that might result from adverse judgments. There are exceptions to the rule of charitable immunity. A charity may be held liable to a stranger, that is, one who is not a *beneficiary.* Sometimes, a charity may be held liable only to the extent of its nontrust assets. The trend today is toward abolition of charitable immunity. This is based on the unfairness of forcing the injured party to contribute indirectly to the charity by refusing an opportunity to recover damages, as well as the availability of liability insurance for health facilities. See also *governmental immunity.*

chemical equivalents: *Drug* products from different manufacturers that contain essentially identical amounts of the identical active ingredients in identical dosage forms, meet existing physiochemical *standards* contained in official *compendia,* and are therefore chemically indistinguishable. See also *bioequivalence.*

chemical name: The exact description of the chemical structure of a *drug,* based on the rules of standard chemical nomenclature, such as the tranquilizer with the chemical name 2-methyl-2-propyl, 1-3-propanediol dicarbamate. While cumbersome, this name is also precise, serving as a complete identification of the compound to any chemist. The chemical formula of this drug, known by the *generic name* of meprobamate, is:

$$CH_3$$
$$|$$
$$H_2NCOO - CH_2 - C - CH_2 - OOCNH_2$$
$$|$$
$$CH_2CH_2CH_3$$

The drug is sold by different firms under various *brand names,* such as Miltown, Equanil, Pathibamate, and SK-Bamate.

chief of medical staff: The formal director of the *physicians'* staff at the community *hospital* level.

chief of service: A *physician* who is appointed or elected as the administrative head of a clinical department within a *hospital.*

children and youth project (C&Y): Under the Maternal and Child Health Program.

chiropodist: See *podiatrist.*

chiropractor: A practitioner of chiropractic medicine, a system of mechanical therapeutics based on the principles that the nervous system largely determines the state of *health* and that *disease* results from abnormal spinal nerve function and conformity. Treatment consists primarily of the adjustment or manipulation of parts of the body, especially the spinal column. Some chiropractors also use physiotherapy, nutritional supplementation, and other therapeutic modalities. Radiography is used for *diagnosis* only. *Operations, drugs,* and immunizations are usually rejected by chiropractors as violations of the human body. Chiropractic was founded in 1895 by D.D. Palmer. Chiropractors are licensed by all states, and their services are covered in most state *Medicaid* programs. Manual manipulation of the spine is covered under *Medicare* when subluxation of the spine is demonstrated on x-ray.

Christian Science: A religion and system of healing through prayer and the control of mind over matter. The services of Christian Science are covered under some health insurance programs, including *Medicare* and, in some states, *Medicaid,* often with an exemption from *standards* applied by such programs to traditional medical providers.

chronic disease: A *disease* that has one or more of the following characteristics: (1) it is permanent; (2) it leaves residual *disability*; (3) it is caused by nonreversible pathological alteration; (4) it requires special training of the patient for *rehabilitation*; or (5) it may be expected to require a long period of supervision, observation, and care. See also *acute disease.*

Civilian Health and Medical Program of the Uniformed Services (CHAMPUS): A program administered by the Department of Defense, without *premiums* but with *cost-sharing* provisions, that pays for care delivered by civilian health *providers* to retired members and *dependents* of active and retired members of the seven uniformed services of the United States (Army, Navy, Air Force, Marine Corps, Commissioned Corps of the Public Health Service, Coast Guard, and the National Oceanic and Atmospheric Administration).

Civilian Health and Medical Program of the Veterans Administration (CHAMPVA): A program administered by the Department of Defense for the Veterans Administration, without *premiums* but with *cost-sharing* provisions, that pays for health care provided by civilian *providers* to dependents of totally disabled veterans who are eligible for retirement pay from a uniformed service.

claim: A request to an *insurer* by an *insured* person (or, on his behalf, by the provider of a service or good) for payment of *benefits* under an *insurance policy*.

claim review: A review procedure undertaken by a panel of physicians and administrators employed by an *insurance* underwriter to determine the eligibility of a *beneficiary* or *provider*, the reasonableness of *cost*, and the appropriateness of service.

claims-incurred policy: *Malpractice insurance,* under which the *insured* is covered for any claims arising from an incident that occurred or is alleged to have occurred during the policy period, regardless of when the claim is made. The only limiting factors are the *statutes of limitations* that vary from state to state. An alternative type of malpractice insurance policy is the *claims-made policy.*

claims-made policy: *Malpractice insurance* gaining increasing popularity among *insurers* because it increases the accuracy of rate making. In this type of policy the *insured* is covered for any claim made, rather than any *injury* occurring, while the policy is in force. Claims made after the insurance lapses are not covered as they are by a *claims-incurred policy.* This type of policy was initially resisted by *providers* because of the nature of medical malpractice claims, which may arise several years after an injury occurs (see *discovery rule*). A retired physician, for example, could be sued and not be insured, unless special provisions were made to continue coverage beyond the years of *practice.* There are also retrospective problems for providers who switch from a conventional (claims-incurred) policy to a claims-made policy, since the latter policy would not cover claims arising from events occurring during the years when the conventional policy was in effect. Insurers marketing malpractice insurance policies are now commonly offering providers the opportunity to purchase both types of insurance.

claims review: A review of *claims* by governments, *medical foundations, PROs, insurers,* or others responsible for payment to determine liability and amount of payment. This review may include determination that the claimant or *beneficiary* is eligible to make the claim; that the *provider* of the *benefit* is eligible to receive payment; that the benefit for which payment is claimed is covered; that the benefit is not payable under another policy (see *coordination of benefits*); and that the benefit was *necessary* and of *reasonable cost* and *quality.*

clinic: A *facility* for *diagnosis* and *treatment* of *outpatients.* Clinic is irregularly defined, sometimes either including or excluding *physicians'* offices, sometimes being limited to facilities that serve *poor* or *public patients* or limited to facilities in which medical education is undertaken.

clinical equivalents: See *therapeutic equivalents* and *bioequivalence.*

clinical privileges: See *staff privileges.*

clinical psychologist: A health *professional* specializing in the evaluation and treatment of mental and behavioral disorders. A psychologist does not have a degree in medicine, as does a psychiatrist. A clinical psychologist generally has a doctoral degree in psychology, plus clinical training in treating psychological disorders. Clinical psychologists are *licensed* by most states for independent professional practice, and their services are reimbursed by many health insurance programs. They do not treat physical causes of *mental illness* with *drugs* or other medical or surgical measures, since they are not licensed to practice *medicine.*

closed panel: A health care plan in which the beneficiaries are allowed to obtain *services* from those *providers* specifically approved by the *underwriter*.

cohort study: A study in which a group (the cohort) is chosen for the presence of a specific characteristic at or during a specified time (for example, the independent variable of hypertension). The group is followed over time for the appearance of particular, presumably related characteristics (for example, the dependent variables of heart failure and stroke).

coinsurance (Co): *Cost sharing* under a health *insurance policy* which provides that the *insured* will assume a portion or percentage of the costs of covered services. The health insurance policy, for example, may provide that the *insurer* will reimburse a specified percentage (usually 80 percent) of all, or certain specified, covered medical expenses in excess of any *deductible* amounts payable by the insured. The insured is then liable for the remaining percentage of the costs until the maximum amount payable under the insurance policy, if any, is reached.

Commission on Professional and Hospital Activities (CPHA): A nonprofit, nongovernmental organization in Ann Arbor, Michigan, established in 1955. It collects, processes, and distributes data on *hospital* use for *management,* evaluation, and research purposes. The two main programs of CPHA are the *Professional Activity Study* (*PAS*) and the *Medical Audit Program* (*MAP*), which represent a continuing study of hospital practice. PAS hospitals account for almost 40 percent of all *patients* discharged from short-term general hospitals in the United States and Canada. The system abstracts and classifies information from medical records in a standard format. The computer-accessible data library at CPHA now contains the world's largest collection of such data. CPHA is sponsored by the American College of Physicians, American College of Surgeons, *American Hospital Association*, and Southwestern Michigan Hospital Council. See also *discharge abstract.*

committee report: In the Congress, a formal report by a congressional committee to the House of Representatives, Senate, or both (see *conference*) on a proposed law or other matter. The report is part of the *legislative history* and includes a summary of the proposed law, recommendations as to its passage and amendments, relevant background information, a discussion and defense of its provisions, a detailed section-by-section analysis of the provisions, a demonstration of the changes the proposed law will make in existing laws, cost estimates, and dissenting views from members of the committee. State legislative committees are similarly structured.

community action program (CAP): An agency organized in 1964 by the Economic Opportunity Act to provide funds for social service and health programs for needy and special populations.

community health care: Activities and programs to improve the healthfulness of, and general *health status* in, a specified community. The term is widely used and has many definitions. It is often defined, as above, in a manner similar to *public health*. The term frequently refers to all health services available to a given community. It is also used synonymously with environmental health and with a community's *ambulatory care center*.

community health center (CHC): An *ambulatory* health care program usually serving a *catchment area* with scarce or nonexistent health services or a population with special health needs. It is often called a neighborhood health center. Grant support for these centers was originally provided on a research and demonstration basis from the Community Action Program of the *Office of Economic Opportunity (OEO)*. Subsequently, the funding authority for these projects shifted to Section 314(e) of the *Public Health Service (PHS) Act*. Community health centers attempted to coordinate federal, state, and local resources in a single organization capable of delivering both health care and related social services to a defined population. Other ambulatory centers providing health services in *medically underserved areas* and supported with Section 314(e) funds include family health centers and *community health networks*. P.L. 94-63, the

Health Revenue Sharing and Health Services Act of 1975, incorporates "neighborhood health centers," "family health centers," and "community health networks" under the single term "community health centers" defined in Section 330 of the PHS Act. While such centers may not directly provide all types of health care, they usually take responsibility for arranging for all medical services needed by their patients.

community health network (CHN): A community (state, county or city) health system for delivering medical care to the *poor*. Started by *OEO* in the early 1970's, the program was transferred to the former *Department of Health, Education, and Welfare* and has now become part of the *community health center* program. A CHN usually consisted of several centrally managed community or *neighborhood health centers*.

community medicine: Variously defined as synonymous with *community health care, public health, preventive medicine,* or *primary care*.

community mental health center (CMHC): An organization that provides comprehensive (principally *ambulatory) mental health* services primarily to individuals residing or employed in a defined *catchment area*. The term is defined in the Community Mental Health Centers Act (Section 201), which specifies the services to be provided and requirements for the governance, organization, and operation of the centers. The CMHC Act provides for federal financial assistance for the construction, development, and initial operation of CMHCs, and, on an ongoing basis, for the costs of their *consultation and education services*.

community rating: A method of establishing *premiums* for health *insurance*. The premiums are based on the average cost of actual or anticipated health care used by all *subscribers* in a specific geographic area or industry and do not vary for different groups or subgroups of subscribers or with such variables as a group's *claims* experience, age, sex, or *health status*. The *HMO* Act (Section 1302(8) of the *PHS Act*) defines community rating as a system of fixing rates of payments for health services that may be determined on a per-person or per-family basis. The rates may vary with the number of persons in a family but must be equivalent for all individuals and for all families with similar composition. The intent of community rating is to spread the cost of illness evenly over all subscribers (the whole community) rather than charging the sick more than the healthy for health insurance. Community rating is the less common means of establishing health insurance premiums in the United States today. The *Federal Employee's Health Benefits Program*, for example, is *experience rated*, not community rated.

comparability provision: A *Medicare* provision specifying that the *reasonable charge* for a service may not be higher than *charges* payable for comparable services insured under comparable circumstances by a *carrier* for its non-Medicare *beneficiaries* (see Section 1842(b)(3)(B) of the Social Security Act).

compendium: Official information about *drugs*. Under the federal Food, Drug, and Cosmetic Act, *standards* for strength, *quality*, and purity of drugs are those set forth in one of the official compendia: the United States Pharmacopeia, the Homeopathic Pharmacopeia of the United States, or any supplement to them. See also *formulary*.

Comprehensive Health Insurance Plan (CHIP): A *national health insurance* proposal submitted in 1974 to the Congress and introduced as H.R. 12684. The plan would provide all citizens with identical *benefits* but would do so through three separate plans with varying administration, financing, and *cost sharing:* (1) *Employee Health Insurance Plan, (2) Assisted Health Insurance Plan,* and (3) *Federal Health Insurance Plan.*

comprehensive health planning (CHP): Health planning that encompasses all programs which impact on people's *health*. Federally assisted CHP was geographically based by areawide and *state*

CHP agencies that had authority in areas of environmental and *occupational health,* health education, and personal health behavior, as well as medical resources and services. CHP was initiated by the Comprehensive Health Planning and Public Health Services Amendments of 1966, P.L. 89-749, and replaced by the National Health Planning and Resources Development Act of 1974, P.L. 93-641.

compulsory: Used in connection with coverage under proposed *national health insurance* or other health insurance plans that require coverage to be offered or taken. A plan may be compulsory only for an employer (coverage must be offered to employees and a specified portion of the *premium* paid, if they opt to take it) or for individuals as well. Any universal public plan is necessarily compulsory in that the payment of taxes to support the plan is not optional with the individual.

concurrent resolution on the budget: In the federal budget, a resolution passed by both houses of Congress, but not requiring the signature of the president, that sets forth, reaffirms, or revises the *congressional budget* for the United States government for a *fiscal year.* Two concurrent resolutions must be completed each year, the first by May 15 and the second by September 15.

concurrent review: Review of the medical *necessity* of *hospital* or other health facility *admissions* upon or within a short period following admission of a *patient* and the periodic review of services provided during the course of *treatment.* The initial review usually assigns an appropriate *length of stay* to the admission (using *diagnosis*-specific *criteria*). The length of stay also may be reassessed periodically. Where concurrent review is required, payment for unneeded hospitalizations or services is usually denied. Concurrent review should be contrasted with a retrospective *medical audit,* which is performed for *quality* purposes and does not relate to payment, and a *claims review,* which occurs after the hospitalization is over.

conditions of participation: The conditions that a *provider* (e.g., *hospital* or *skilled nursing facility*) or *supplier* of *services* desiring to participate in the *Medicare* program is required to meet before participation is permitted. These conditions are specified in the statute and *regulations*. They include (1) compliying with Title VI of the Civil Rights Act, (2) signing an agreement to participate that is acceptable to the secretary of HHS, (3) meeting the definition of the particular institution or facility contained in the law (e.g., in order to participate as a hospital an institution must be a hospital within the meaning of Section 1861(e) of the Social Security Act and must further meet standards for health and safety specified in regulations), (4) conforming with state and local laws, (5) having an acceptable *utilization review* plan, and (6) meeting appropriate *PRO* requirements. Investigations to determine whether or not health care facilities meet or continue to meet conditions of participation are made by the appropriate state health agency responsible for certifying that the conditions have been met and that the provider is eligible to participate.

conference: In the Congress, a formal meeting of representatives of the House and Senate at which differences between House and Senate versions of a single piece of legislation or *policy* are resolved. The members of the House and Senate chosen to conduct the conference are called managers and together form the conference committee. The managers jointly recommend a compromise version of the legislation; the text is called the conference report. Attached to the report is an explanation of how the differences were resolved (the equivalent of a *committee report,* called the joint statement of managers) that becomes part of the *legislative history.* Since the compromise version is different from the House and Senate versions originally passed, the conference report must be enacted by both the House and Senate before being sent for presidential signature.

confidential: Private or secret information, practices, or procedures. Confidentiality of a *medical record* refers to the degree and circumstances in which information in such a record is private or secret. Information that is held confidential may include medical, financial, or other information about *patients* obtained in the course of medical practice and information about the cost, *quality,* and nature of the practices of individual and institutional *providers* obtained through payment and *regulation* programs. Confidentiality can be difficult to protect; various detailed efforts to do so in the health field already have become law (see Section 333 of the Comprehensive Alcohol Abuse and Alcoholism Prevention, Treatment, and Rehabilitation Act of 1970 and Title XI, Part B, of the Social Security Act). The circumstances under which information should be confidential are often controversial. Confidentiality may keep secret the inappropriate acts of patients or providers, but its absence may limit the freedom and confidence with which *medicine* is practiced.

congressional budget: The federal *budget* as set by the Congress in a *concurrent resolution on the budget.* The resolution includes the appropriate level of total budget *outlays* and of total new *budget authority*; an estimate of budget outlays and new budget authority for each major functional category, for contingencies, and for undistributed intragovernmental transactions (based on allocations of the appropriate level of total budget outlays and of total new budget authority); the amount, if any, of the surplus or deficit in the budget; the recommended level of federal revenues; and the appropriate level of the public debt.

consultation: In a *medical practice* or dental practice, the act of requesting advice from another *provider,* usually a *specialist,* regarding the *diagnosis* or *treatment* of a *patient.* The consultant usually reviews the history, examines the patient, and then provides a written or oral opinion to the requesting practitioner. *Referral* for consultation should be distinguished from referral for services, because responsibility for patient care is not usually delegated to the consultant. This definition distinguishes a consultation between providers from a *visit* between a provider and *consumer.*

consultation and education services: Services required of each *community mental health center* (*CMHC*) by section 201 of the CMHC Act. They consist of consultation with, and education for, the staffs of programs and institutions in the CMHC's community that are likely to be responsible for people with *mental illness* (such as schools, prisons, and courts). These services are subsidized by section 204 of the CMHC Act, because they are high-priority *preventative care* not usually reimbursed by the recipient institutions or covered under health insurance (which rarely covers services not directly delivered to *insured* individuals).

consumer: An individual who may receive or is receiving health services. While all people at various times consume health services, a consumer, as the term is used in health legislation and programs is usually someone other than a *provider*. The consumer is not associated in any direct or indirect way with the provision of health services. The distinction has become important in programs where a consumer majority on the governing body is required, as in the case of *community health centers* and *health systems agencies* assisted under the *PHS Act*. See also *patient*.

Consumer Price Index (CPI): An economic index prepared by the Bureau of Labor Statistics of the U.S. Department of Labor. It measures the change in average prices of the goods and services purchased by urban wage earners and their families. It is widely used as an indicator of changes in the cost of living, as a measure of inflation (and deflation, if any) in the economy, and as a means for studying trends in prices of various goods and services. The CPI consists of several components that measure prices in different sectors of the economy. One of these, the medical care component, gives trends in medical care *charges* based on specific indicators of hospital, medical, dental, and drug prices. The medical care component of the CPI, as well as other service components, characteristically rises faster than the CPI itself. However, since the CPI measures charges, which are not always related to *costs,* the CPI may fail to reflect accurately changes in medical or health care costs.

contingency fees: Fees based or conditioned on future occurrences or on the results of services to be performed. Contingency fees are used by lawyers representing patients as plaintiffs in *malpractice* cases and are usually a set fraction (commonly a third) of any settlement awarded the patient. If no settlement is awarded, the lawyer is not paid. Such fees are said to give lawyers incentives to try cases with full vigor, choose only cases that are likely to succeed, choose only cases that will have large settlements, and seek to increase the settlement amounts.

contingency reserves: Funds set aside by an *insurance* company for unforeseen or unanticipated circumstances and expenses other than normal *losses* incurred by *risks* insured by the company.

continued stay review: Review during a *patient's* hospitalization to determine the medical *necessity* and *appropriateness* of continuation of the patient's stay at a *hospital* level of care. The review may also include assessment of the *quality* of care being provided. Occasionally, the term is used for similar reviews of patients in other health facilities (see *medical review*).

continuing education: Formal education obtained by a health *professional* after completing degree and postgraduate training. Such education is usually intended to improve or maintain the professional's competence. Some, but not all, states require a specified number of hours of recognized continuing education per year as a condition of continued *licensure*.

continuing resolution: In the federal *budget*, legislation enacted by the Congress to provide *budget authority* for specific ongoing activities during a *fiscal year* in cases where the regular *appropriation* for such activities has not been enacted by the beginning of that fiscal year. The continuing resolution usually specifies a maximum rate at which the agency may obligate funds, based on the rate of the prior year, the *president's budget* request, or an appropriation bill previously passed by either the House of Representatives or the Senate.

contributory insurance: *Group insurance* in which all or part of the *premium* is paid by the employee; the remainder, if any, is paid by the employer or labor union. In this context, noncontributory insurance is insurance in which the employer pays all the premium. Contributory insurance is so called because the *risk* (employee) contributes to the cost of the insurance as well as the *insured* (employer or union). See also *enrollment period*.

contributory tax: See *payroll tax.*

controllability: In the federal *budget,* the ability of the Congress or the President under existing law to control *outlays* during a given *fiscal year.* Uncontrollable and relatively uncontrollable are terms used to describe outlays and the programs in which they occur (such as *Medicare*) that cannot be increased or decreased without changes in existing substantive law. This type of spending is usually the result of open-ended programs and fixed costs, such as social security and veterans benefits and payments due under *obligations* incurred or commitments made during prior years.

controlled substance: A drug regulated by the *Controlled Substances Act.*

Controlled Substances Act: A federal law enacted in 1970 to control the manufacture and distribution of narcotics and other dangerous or addictive *drugs.*

convalescent centers: Health care *facilities* that provide care for convalescing patients for a short-term, intermediate, or long-term stay. They are licensed as either skilled or intermediate care facilities.

conversion privilege: In *group* health *insurance*, conversion to some form of individual insurance, without medical examination, upon termination of the group insurance (usually upon termination of employment or other source of membership in the group). Group insurance does not always offer a conversion privilege. When it does, the available individual insurance is usually more expensive and may not compare in scope of benefits.

Cooperative Health Statistics System (CHSS): A program sponsored by the National Center for Health Statistics in which federal, state, and local governments cooperate in collecting health statistics. Any particular item of data is collected by the level best equipped to collect and distribute it to other levels. When CHSS becomes fully operable, it will collect data in the following subject areas: (1) *health manpower* (inventories and surveys), (2) *health facilities* (inventories and surveys), (3) hospital care, (4) household interviews, (5) *ambulatory care*, (6) *long-term care,* and (7) *vital statistics.* Legislative authority for CHSS is found in Section 306(e) of the *PHS Act.*

Coordinated Transfer Application System (COTRANS): A system established in 1970 by the *Association of American Medical Colleges* (*AAMC*) in which the AAMC evaluates U.S. citizens who receive *undergraduate medical education* outside the United States and sponsors those it deems qualified for Part One of the *national board examinations* (boards). Students who take and pass the boards with this sponsorship may then apply to a U.S. medical school for completion of their training with advanced standing. Some students obtain sponsorship for the boards from an individual school without using COTRANS.

Coordinating Council on Medical Education (CCME): A supervisory body established in 1972 to coordinate *policy* matters and *accreditation* at all levels of medical education. Among its members are the *American Medical Association*, the American Board of Medical Specialties, the *Association of American Medical Colleges*, the *American Hospital Association,* and the Council of Medical Specialty Societies. The council also has public and federal members. See also *Liaison Committees on Medical Education* and *graduate medical education.*

coordination of benefits (COB): Procedures used by *insurers* to avoid duplicate payment for *losses* insured under more than one *insurance policy*. For example, some people have a *duplication of benefits* for medical costs arising from an automobile accident in their automobile and health insurance policies. A coordination of benefits or antiduplication clause in one or the other policy will prevent double payment for the expenses by making one of the insurers the *primary payer* and assuring that no more than 100 percent of the costs are covered. There are standard rules for determining which of two or more plans, each having COB provisions, pays its benefits in full and which pays a sufficiently reduced benefit to prevent the claimant from making a *profit*.

copayment: A type of *cost sharing* whereby *insured* or covered persons pay a specified flat amount per unit of service or unit of time (e.g., $2 per visit or $10 per inpatient hospital day) and the *insurer* pays the balance of the cost. The copayment is incurred at the time the service is used. The amount paid does not vary with the cost of the service (unlike *coinsurance,* which is ordinarily payment of some percentage of the cost).

coronary care unit (CCU): See *cardiac care unit.*

cosmetic surgery: Any *operation* to improve appearance, except when required for the prompt repair of accidental *injury* or to improve the function of a malformed body member. The term does not apply to surgery in connection with treatment of severe burns, for repair of the face following a serious automobile accident, or for therapeutic purposes that coincidentally result in some cosmetic improvement. Merely reshaping an ugly nose, however, does constitute cosmetic surgery. Most health insurance plans and governmental programs do not cover this type of surgery.

cost center: Accounting device whereby all related *costs* attributable to some "center" within an institution, such as an activity, department, or program (e.g., a hospital burn center), are segregated for accounting or reimbursement purposes. This procedure contrasts with segregating costs of different types, such as *nursing care, drugs,* or laundry, regardless of which center incurred them.

cost containment: The control or reduction of overall *costs* within the health care delivery system or as related to a specific *treatment*.

cost of insurance: The amount which a policyholder pays to the *insurer* minus what he gets back from it. This should be distinguished from the *rate* for a given unit of insurance (such as $10 for a $1,000 life insurance policy).

cost, reasonable: The amount a third-party *underwriter* will pay a *provider* using *cost-based reimbursement.* This amount excludes any costs found to be unnecessary for the efficient delivery of services.

cost-related or cost-based reimbursement: one method of payment of medical care programs by *third parties,* typically *Blue Cross plans* or government agencies, for services delivered to *patients.* In cost-related systems, the amount of the payment is based on the *costs* to the provider of delivering the service. The actual payment may be based on any one of several different formulas, such as full cost, full cost plus an additional percentage, *allowable costs,* or a fraction of costs. Other reimbursement methods are based on the *charges* for the services delivered or on budgeted or anticipated costs for a future time period (*prospective reimbursement*). *Medicare, Medicaid,* and some Blue Cross plans reimburse hospitals on the basis of costs.

cost sharing: Provisions of a health *insurance policy* that require the *insured* or otherwise covered individual to pay some portion of covered medical expenses. Several forms of cost sharing are employed, particularly *deductibles, coinsurance* and *copayments.* A deductible is a set amount a person must pay before any payment of *benefits* occurs. A copayment is usually a fixed amount to be paid for each service. Coinsurance is payment of a set portion of the cost of each service. Cost sharing does not refer to or include the amounts paid in *premiums* for the *coverage*. The amount of the premium is directly related to the benefits provided and hence reflects the amount of cost sharing required. For a given set of benefits, premiums increase as cost sharing requirements decrease. In addition to being used to reduce premiums, cost sharing is used to control *utilization* of covered services, for example, by requiring a large copayment for a service likely to be overutilized.

costs: Expenses incurred in providing services or goods. Many types of costs are defined and used (see *allowable costs, direct costs, indirect costs, life costs, marginal costs,* and *opportunity cost*). *Charges,* the prices of services or amounts billed an individual or third party, may or may not be the same as, or based on, costs. Hospitals often charge more for a given service than it actually costs in order to recoup losses from providing other services where costs exceed feasible charges. Despite the terminology, cost control programs are often directed toward controlling increases in charges rather than actual costs. (Also see *actual charge.*)

courtesy medical staff: *Hospital* medical staff privileges given on a temporary basis to *physicians* who are not official members of the staff.

coverage: The guarantee against specific *losses* provided under the terms of an *insurance policy.* The term is frequently used interchangeably with *benefits* or protection. Also, the extent of the insurance afforded by a policy. It is often used synonymously with insurance or an insurance contract.

covered charge: Health care *services* that will be paid by a *third-party payer*.

creaming: See *skimming*.

credentialing : The recognition of *professional* or technical competence. The credentialing process may include *registration, certifica-*

tion, licensure, professional association membership, or the award of a degree. Certification and licensure affect the supply of *health manpower* by controlling entrance into *practice,* and thus influence the stability of the labor force by affecting geographic distribution, mobility and retention of health personnel. Credentialing also determines the *quality* of personnel by providing *standards* for evaluating competence and defining the scope of functions and utilization of personnel.

credentials committee: A committee of *physicians* and administrative personnel that reviews applications for medical staff membership.

criteria: Predetermined elements of health care against which the *necessity, appropriateness,* or *quality* of health services may be compared. For example, criteria for appropriate diagnosis of a urinary tract infection may include performance of a urine culture and urinalysis. The term is often used synonymously with guidelines.

critical care services: The care of medically ill *patients* in medical emergencies who require the constant attention of a *physician.* Critical care includes shock, cardiac arrest, severe bleeding, respiratory failure, and other life-threatening conditions.

critical care unit: A specially equipped and staffed cardiac care, intensive care, or emergency care unit.

current liabilities: As listed on a balance sheet, these include debts and obligations presently due or due within one year.

Current Procedural Terminology (CPT): A system of terminology and coding developed by the American Medical Association used for describing, coding, and reporting medical *services* and procedures.

current services budget: In the federal *budget,* a budget that projects estimated *budget authority* and *outlays* for the next *fiscal year* based on the continuance of existing programs without *policy* changes at the same levels of service as the present fiscal year. The Congressional Budget and Impoundment Control Act of 1974 requires that the President submit a current services budget to the Congress each year. To the extent mandated by existing law, estimates take into account anticipated changes in economic conditions (such as unemployment or inflation), different caseloads, pay increases, and budget changes.

custodial care: Board, room, and other personal assistance services, generally provided on a long-term basis, that do not include medical care. Such services generally are not paid for under private or public health *insurance* or medical care programs, except as incidental to medical care that a *hospital* or *nursing home* inpatient receives. See also *boarding homes*.

customary charge: Generally, the amount that a *physician* normally or usually *charges* the majority of *patients*. Under *Medicare*, it is the median charge used by a particular physician for a specified type of service during the calendar year preceding the *fiscal year* in which a *claim* is processed. Customary charges in addition to *actual charges* and *prevailing charges* are taken into account in determining *reasonable charges* under Medicare.

Dd

daily inpatient census: The number of persons present as *inpatients* at the time the census is taken.

daily recap sheet: The daily census count and summary of the total number of newborns less the number of deaths within a health care *facility*.

data security administrator: A *medical records* specialist who, through education and training, is skilled in the protection and security of medical record information.

data set: A minimum aggregation of uniformly defined and classified statistics that describe an element, episode, or aspect of health care; for example, a hospital *admission* (see *discharge abstract*), ambulatory *encounter*, or a *physician* or *hospital*. Data sets are used for evaluation, research, and other similar purposes.

DEA: Drug Enforcement Administration, a unit of the Justice Department.

death: A permanent cessation of all vital functions; the end of life (often called *mortality*). A natural physiologic concept whose actual occurrence *medicine* has made very difficult to define and measure. A concensus holds that death occurs when all measurable or identifiable brain functioning (electrical or any other kind) is absent for more than 24 hours. See also *hospice* and *euthanasia*.

death rate, disease-specific: The number of *disease*-induced deaths for a given population for a given time period.

death rate, hospital: The number of *inpatient* deaths compared with the total number of inpatients within a given time period.

death rate, index: A ratio calculated by dividing the number of nonmaternity *admissions* by the number of deaths (excluding nonfetal and infant).

death rate: The total number of deaths in a population (per 1,000) for a given time period.

debt service: The payment of interest and principal on debts; the amount of funds needed, supplied, or accrued to meet these payments during any given accounting period; a budget or operating statement heading for such items.

deductible: The amount of *loss* or expense that must be incurred by an *insured* or otherwise covered individual before an *insurer* will assume any liability for all or part of the remaining cost of covered services. Deductibles may be either fixed dollar amounts or the value of specified services (such as two days of hospital care or one physician visit). Deductibles are usually tied to some reference period over which they must be incurred (e.g., $100 per calendar year, *benefit period,* or episode of illness). Deductibles in existing policies are generally of two types: (1) static deductibles that are fixed dollar amounts, and (2) dynamic deductibles that are adjusted periodically to reflect increasing medical prices. A third type, a *sliding scale deductible,* is proposed in some *national health insurance* plans. This deductible, related to *income,* increases as income rises.

deemed status: An official certification by a *peer review organization* (*PRO*), or formerly by a professional services review organization (PSRO), that a hospital complies with the review organization's effectiveness criteria for *admission review*, continued stay review, and medical care assessment.

defensive medicine: An alteration in modes of medical *practice,* induced by the threat of liability, for the principal purposes of reducing the possibility of *malpractice* suits by patients and providing a good legal defense in the event of such lawsuits. While surveys have shown that 50 to 70 percent of physicians say they practice defensive medicine, it is difficult to define and measure specifically and, except for increasing the costs of care, unclear what effects it has.

deferral of budget authority: In the federal *budget,* any action or inaction of the executive branch, including the establishment of reserves under the Antideficiency Act, that temporarily withholds, delays, or effectively precludes the *obligation* or expenditure of *budget authority.* Under Section 1013 of the Congressional Budget and Impoundment Control Act of 1974, the President is required to report each proposed deferral to the Congress in a special message. Deferrals may not extend beyond the end of a *fiscal year* and may be overturned by the passage of an *impoundment* resolution by either house of Congress. See also *rescission.*

deficiency disease: Any *disease* or pathological state, with characteristic clinical signs, that is due to an insufficient intake of energy or essential nutrients; it is usually of dietary origin and often can be prevented or cured by increasing the required intake to adequate levels or by changing the diet.

delegation: In the *peer review organization (PRO)* program, the formal process by which a PRO, based upon an assessment of the willingness and capability of a hospital or other health program to perform effectively PRO review functions, assigns the performance of some or all PRO review functions to the program. Delegation must be agreed upon in a written memorandum of understanding signed by representatives of the PRO and the program. The PRO monitors the program's performance of the delegated functions and retains responsibility for the effectiveness of the review. As used elsewhere, delegation means the grant of authority or assignment of duties from one individual to another.

Delta Dental Plan: The first national dental prepayment program.

demand or demand schedule: In health economics, the varying amount of a good or service sought at various prices, based on the assumption of constant income and other factors. Demand must be distinguished from *utilization* (the amount of services actually used) and *need* (for various reasons services are often sought that either the *consumer* or *provider* feel are unneeded). See also *supply* and *elasticity of demand.*

demonstration grant: An award of funds for the recipient to use in demonstrating the effectiveness or worthiness of a medical or health care procedure or process.

dental assistant: An individual who assists a *dentist* at the *chairside* in a dental office, performs reception and clerical functions, and carries out dental radiography and selected dental laboratory work. The actual number of active dental assistants is not known, because most dentists train and employ dental assistants who are neither *certified* nor registered as members of an official organization. Dental assistants who have completed *accredited* educational programs are eligible for national certification examinations conducted by the Certifying Board of the American Dental Assistants Association. An accredited dental assistant program is usually conducted in a community college or vocational–technical school and must provide at least one year of academic training.

dental health: A state of complete normality and functional efficiency of the teeth and supporting structures, the surrounding parts of the oral cavity, and the various structures related to mastication and the maxillofacial complex.

dental health services: All services designed or intended to promote, maintain, or restore *dental health,* including educational, preventive, and therapeutic services.

dental hygienist: A professionally trained individual who works under the supervision of a dentist in providing services to dental patients. Dental hygienists perform complete oral prophylaxis, apply medication, perform dental radiography, and provide dental education services for *chairside* patients and in community health projects. Dental hygienists are required to obtain a *license* in all states after completion of either a two-year or four-year program at college level.

dental laboratory technician: See *dental technician.*

dental technician: An individual who makes complete and partial dentures, orthodontic appliances, bridgework, crowns, and other dental restorations and appliances, as prescribed by *dentists.* There are an estimated 32,000 dental technicians in the United States. Most dental technicians work in commercial dental laboratories. However, increasing numbers are being employed by private dental practitioners and by federal, state, and private institutions. Dental technicians have been traditionally trained on the job, but the predominant method of training now is through formal programs offered by two-year postsecondary educational institutions. Upon completion of an aggregate of five years in dental technology training and experience, technicians are eligible to apply for examination and *certification* by the National Board for Certification in Dental Laboratory Technology. See also *denturist.*

dentist: A *professional* person qualified by education and authorized by law (usually by having obtained a *license*) to *practice* dentistry. Dentistry includes the promotion, maintenance, and restoration of individual *dental health* and *treatment of diseases* of the teeth and oral cavity.

denturist: A *dental technician* who provides dentures for patients without benefit of a dentist's professional services. Denturists are rarely found in the United States; their practice is illegal in many states. They are becoming increasingly common in Canada.

deontology: The study of acceptable behavior, duty, and ethics. In health care it usually applies to physician-patient and other professional relations.

department: A functional or administrative division or unit of a *hospital,* health program, or government agency. It is sometimes known as a *service.* A department within a hospital or medical school typically is headed by a responsible individual, either a chairman or director. It has its own *budget* and admits its own *patients,* but is not a separate legal entity. Departments are frequently organized by medical *specialty* (i.e., pediatric, radiology, or surgery). There is no standard departmental organization for health programs.

D

Department of Health and Human Services (HHS): The new title for the former Department of Health, Education, and Welfare; a federal cabinet-level department responsible for health matters throughout the United States.

dependence: See *drug dependence.*

dependency ratio: The ratio between the percentage of the population that is self-supporting and the percentage that is dependent on others for support.

dependent: An individual who relies upon another individual for a significant portion of his or her support. In addition to the requirement for financial support, the definition may require a blood relationship. The Internal Revenue Code defines as dependents for the purposes of *tax deductions* any of the following over half of whose support for the calendar year was received from the taxpayer: children (biologic or adopted); grandchildren; stepchildren; brothers and sisters; stepbrothers and stepsisters; half brothers and half sisters; parents, grandparents, and great-grandparents; stepparents; nephews and nieces; uncles and aunts; in-laws (father, mother, son, daughter, brother, and sister); nonrelatives living as members of the taxpayer's household; and a descendant of a brother or sister of the father or mother of the taxpayer who is receiving institutional care and who, before receiving such care, was a member of the taxpayer's household. The Internal Revenue Code provides that if the support of a dependent was furnished by several persons, one may claim the dependency deduction if the others agree. In *insurance* and other programs, the specific definition is quite variable, often being limited to the individual's spouse and children. Other types of dependents recognized by the Internal Revenue Service are sometimes known as sponsored dependents.

dependent nursing function: Activities carried out by a *nurse* under express *physician's* orders.

depreciation: See *capital depreciation.*

dermatologist: A *physician* who specializes in the diagnosis and treatment of diseases and disorders of the skin.

dermatology (D): The branch of medicine concerned with the diagnosis and treatment of diseases and disorder of the skin.

DESI: See *Drug Efficacy Study Implementation.*

detail person: A sales representative of a pharmaceutical manufacturer who promotes *prescription drugs* for use by physicians, dentists, and *pharmacists.* Detailing includes personal presentations, advertising, and provision of drug samples and educational materials prepared by the manufacturers to *professionals* in their offices. Many detail persons are pharmacists.

developmental disability (DD): A *disability* that originates before age 18; can be expected to continue indefinitely; constitutes a substantial handicap to the disabled's ability to function normally in society; and is attributable to *mental retardation,* cerebral palsy, epilepsy, autism, any other condition closely related to mental retardation that results in similar impairment of general intellectual functioning or adaptive behavior or requires similar treatment and services, or dyslexia resulting from one of the above conditions. The term is defined in the Developmental Disabilities Services and Facilities Construction Act (Section 102(7)), which authorizes federal assistance for services and facilities for the developmentally disabled. See also *rehabilitation.*

device: An item or piece of equipment used in the healing arts other than a *drug*. The term is defined in the federal Food, Drug, and Cosmetic Act as including instruments, apparatus, contrivances, and their components, parts, and accessories intended for use in the diagnosis, cure, mitigation, treatment, or prevention of *disease* in man or other animals; or to affect the structure or any function of the body of man or other animals. Among the products that are regulated as devices are crutches, bandages, wheelchairs, artificial heart valves, cardiac pacemakers, intrauterine devices, eyeglasses, hearing aids, and prostheses. The definition of device distinguishes it from a drug in that a device does not achieve any of its principal intended purposes through chemical action within or on the body and is not dependent on being metabolized for the achievement of any of its principal intended purposes. Legislation also provides detailed authority for *regulation* of the marketing of devices to assure that they are *safe* and *effective* when properly used. See also *premarket approval.*

diagnosis: The art and science of determining the nature and *cause* of a *disease* and differentiating among *diseases* or *illnesses*.

diagnosis code: A numerical classification of diseases, conditions, and illnesses. The most frequently used code is the *International Classification of Diseases adopted for use in the United States* (ICD-9-CM). It provides a uniform system of recording statistical data covering health services.

diagnosis-related groups (DRGs): Classifications of patient illnesses in terms of expected lengths of hospital stay. There are presently 470 group-related classifications. Under the DRG system, a hospital is compensated for a predetermined number of days per patient; the hospital is required to absorb the costs of extended patient stays. DRGs first used with Medicare patients were partially based on a social security amendment in 1983, which set a provision for a prospective payment system for hospitals' Medicare inpatient services. DRG classifications are considered innovative and effective cost-containment measures, particularly as they provide incentives to reduce needless hospital *utilization*.

Diagnostic and Statistical Manual of Mental Disorders (DSM): A standardized handbook for the classification of mental illness.

diagnostic studies: Any test, CT scan, x-ray, or visual examination ordered by a *physician* to determine the nature of a *patient*'s pathological condition.

dictionary: A malevolent literary device for cramping the growth of language. This dictionary, however, is a most useful work. (From *The Devil's Dictionary*.)

dietitian: For American Dietetic Association purposes, a professional who is responsible for the nutritional care of individuals and groups, including the selection of food most appropriate to nourish properly their bodies throughout the life cycle.

diploma school: A program of education in a *hospital* setting for those who wish to become *registered nurses*. A diploma is given upon completion of the program and *licensure* as a registered nurse. Classroom and laboratory teaching may be offered under an arrangement with a college, but the entire program is the responsibility of the hospital. No college-level degree is awarded. See also *associate degree program* and *baccalaureate degree program*.

diplomate: An individual who is awarded a diploma; sometimes used to describe a *board-certified* physician, because a diploma is given with *certification*.

direct cost: A *cost* that is directly identifiable with a particular activity, service, or product of the program experiencing the cost. See also *indirect cost*.

director of nursing: According to *Joint Commission* long-term care accreditation, a *registered nurse* responsible for the full-time direct supervision of nursing services.

disability: Any limitation of physical, mental, or social activity of an individual, compared with other individuals of similar age, sex, and occupation. The term frequently refers to limitation of usual or major activities, most commonly vocational. Disabilities vary according to type (functional, vocational, learning), degree (partial, total), and duration (temporary, permanent). Disability benefits are often available only for specific disabilities, such as total and permanent (requirements for social security and *Medicare* benefits). See also *rehabilitation.*

disability income insurance: A form of health insurance that provides periodic payments to replace *income* when the *insured* is unable to work as a result of *injury* or *disease.* See also *workers' compensation programs.*

discharge abstract: A summary description of an *admission* prepared upon a *patient*'s discharge from a *hospital* or other health *facility.* The abstract records selected data about the patient's stay in the hospital, including *diagnosis,* services received, *length of stay,* source of payment, and demographic information. The data are usually obtained from the patient's *medical record* and abstracted in standard, coded form. See also *Uniform Hospital Discharge Data Set.*

discharge planning: Planning that prepares a *patient* for a continuum of care and arranges for the patient's release from the current health care setting.

discharge status: The manner in which the *patient* left the facility and the intended destination.

discovery rule: In *malpractice,* a rule in use in some jurisdictions under which the statute of limitations does not commence until the wrongful act is discovered or, with reasonable diligence, should have been discovered. The statute of limitations is the period of time, ordinarily beginning with the wrongful act, during which an injured party may sue for recovery of damages arising from the act. Application of the discovery rule is limited in some jurisdictions to cases involving a foreign object left in the body of a *patient*. Some states have adopted statutory rules in malpractice cases that impose double time limits within which a malpractice action may be brought. Typically these statutes provide that the action must be brought within a limited time after its discovery, as well as within a limited time from the date the negligent act occurred.

disease: A condition that may be defined as a failure of the adaptive mechanisms of an organism to counteract adequately, normally, or appropriately the stimuli and stresses to which it is subject, resulting in a disturbance in the function or structure of some part of the organism. This definition emphasizes that disease is multifactorial and may be prevented or treated by changing any of the factors. Disease is a very elusive and difficult concept to define. It is often socially defined. Thus, criminality and *drug dependence* presently tend to be perceived as diseases, whereas they were previously considered to be moral or legal problems. See also *health, injury, acute disease, chronic disease,* and *illness.*

dispensing fee: A fee charged by a *pharmacist* for filling a *prescription*. With this fee system, the *pharmacist* charges for the actual service of filling a prescription. A second fee system utilizes a percentage markup on the *acquisition cost* of each *drug*. A dispensing fee is the same for all prescriptions, thus representing a larger markup on the cost of an inexpensive drug than on an expensive drug or large-quantity prescription. However, it reflects the fact that a pharmacist's service is the same whatever the cost of the drug. Some pharmacists combine the two approaches, using a percentage markup with a minimum fee.

Division of Emergency Medical Services: A unit of the U.S. Health

Service Administration administering programs at state and local levels that are supported by federal grants to develop local emergency care plans.

doctor: Usually considered synonymous with *physician* or *dentist* but actually extends to any person with a doctoral degree.

doctor of osteopathy (DO): A physician trained to practice osteopathic medicine. See *osteopathy*.

doctor of pharmacy (PharmD): A professional degree in pharmacy offered by some colleges of pharmacy as a six-year program or in place of a five-year bachelor of science in pharmacy.

doctor of veterinary medicine (DVM): A physician trained to practice veterinary medicine and to treat diseases and ailments in animals.

domiciliary facility: A residence for people in need of some personal care, such as hygiene care or nutritional assistance.

double-blind technique: A method of studying a *drug* or other medical procedure in which both subjects and investigators are kept unaware of (blind to) who is actually receiving which specific *treatment*. This method eliminates bias, whether conscious or unconscious, in subjects and investigators. Classically, in drug studies the method involves the use of a look-alike *placebo*. In "triple-blind" studies the people analyzing the data also are unaware of the treatment used.

double indemnity (DI): An insurance policy that pays twice the claim value upon certain occurrences, usually death.

dread disease insurance: See *specified disease insurance*.

DRG: See *diagnosis-related groups*.

DRG rate: A fixed amount of money for which a *diagnosis-related group (DRG)* reimbursement is made. The rate is based on the average cost for patients in the specific DRG during the base year and adjusted for inflation, other economic factors, and bad debts.

drug: Any substance (excluding food) or component of a substance intended for use in the diagnosis, cure, mitigation, treatment, or prevention of disease or intended to affect the structure or function of the body. Substances classified as drugs are recognized in the official U.S. Pharmacopeia or the official Homeopathic Pharmacopeia of the United States. See also *device, biologic, effectiveness, compendium, formulary, new drug, not new, "me too" drug, over-the-counter drug, prescription drug, labeling, package insert, established name, brand name, new drug application, Maximum Allowable Cost Program, Drug Efficacy Study Implementation, investigational new drug, drug monograph,* and *drug dependence.*

drug abuse: Persistent or sporadic *drug* use inconsistent with or unrelated to acceptable medical or cultural practice. The definition of drug abuse is highly variable; sometimes it includes excessive use of a drug, unnecessary use (thus incorporating recreational use), *drug dependence,* or the use of illegal drugs. See also *alcoholism.*

drug addiction: Generally used synonymously with *drug dependence.* It is often used to mean physical drug dependence and also often wrongly assumed to be synonymous with *drug abuse.* Interpretation of the term is very irregular.

drug compendium: See *compendium.*

drug dependence: A state, usually psychic and sometimes also physical, resulting from the interaction between a person and a *drug.* It is characterized by behavioral and other responses that include a compulsion to take the drug on a continuous or periodic basis in order to experience its psychic effects and sometimes to avoid the discomfort and other physical effects of its withdrawal or absence. Tolerance for the drug may or may not be present. A person may be dependent on more than one drug. The characteristics of drug dependence will vary with the agent involved, and this must be made clear by designating the particular type of drug dependence in each specific case, for example, *narcotics,* cannabis, barbiturate, or amphetamine. As defined here, drug dependence may or may not be dangerous to the dependent individual or the public or be severe or illegal. Psychic and physical dependence may be separate, although this is difficult to define and to determine in practice. Psychic dependence is some- times called habituation and physical dependence called addiction, but both terms are irregularly used, as are all terms involving drug dependence. See also *drug abuse* and *alcoholism.*

Drug Efficacy Study Implementation (DESI): The plan of the *Food and Drug Administration (FDA)* for implementing the evaluations and recommendations of the Drug Efficacy Study Group of the National Academy of Sciences and the National Research Council about the *effectiveness* of *drugs* marketed prior to 1962 under approved *new drug applications.* The Drug Efficacy Study was undertaken in 1966 to evaluate all of the drugs the FDA had approved as *safe* prior to 1962, when Congress first required that drugs also be proved effective before marketing. The Drug Efficacy Study Group evaluated nearly 4,000 individual drug products and found many of them ineffective or of only possible or probable effectiveness.

drug habituation: Generally used synonymously with *drug dependence.* It is also sometimes used to mean psychic drug dependence, which is often wrongly assumed to be synonymous with *drug abuse.*

drug history: A delineation of the *drugs* used by a *patient,* including prescribed and unprescribed drugs and alcohol.

drug monograph: A *rule* which prescribes the kinds and amounts of ingredients that a *drug* or class of related drugs may contain, the conditions for which it may be offered, directions for use, warnings, and other information to be included in the labeling. Drug monographs established by the *Food and Drug Administration (FDA)* state conditions under which drugs may be marketed as *safe, effective,* unadulterated, and correctly labeled without approval of a *new drug application.* FDA establishes monographs for both non-prescription (*over-the-counter*) drugs and established *prescription drugs.* Special statutory provisions also authorize use of monographs for antibiotic drugs. After a monograph is promulgated, anyone who meets its requirements can market the product (absent patent protection) without seeking approval of a new drug application.

drug room: A facility within a *hospital* or *long-term care* institution used for the storage and dispensing of a limited supply of *drugs* for *patient* use.

druggist: Often synonymous with *pharmacist,* but the term is not always limited to people with a pharmacy degree (or even to operators of drug stores in which *prescription drugs* are dispensed). It is usually applied only to pharmacists who operate or work in drug stores.

dual choice: The practice of giving people a choice of more than one *health insurance* or *health* program to pay for or provide their health *services.* The term usually refers to employers who offer employees the choice of more than one *group health insurance program* or the choice between a health insurance program and a *prepaid group practice* as an employment benefit. This practice is characteristic of the *Federal Employees Health Benefits Program.* Dual choice is required by the *HMO* Act, P.L. 93-222, of employers with respect to *qualified* HMOs (Section 1310 of the *PHS Act*).

duplication of benefits: Duplication occurs when a person covered under more than one health or accident *insurance policy* collects, or may collect, payments for the same hospital or medical expenses from more than one *insurer*. Individual health insurance policies, under state laws, sometimes include antiduplication clauses to prevent overinsurance resulting from two similar policies issued by the same insurer; loss-of-time coverage in excess of the insured's monthly earnings; and duplicate coverage with other insurers, if the insurer has not been given written notice of such duplicate coverage prior to the date of *loss*. Because of this notice limitation, many individual insurance policies do not include antiduplication clauses. The limitation does not apply to *group insurance,* which usually contains similar clauses, especially in *major medical* policies. However, most states will not allow group policies to apply such clauses to individual insurance. Where duplication exists with a group antiduplication clause, the group insurer responsible for paying its benefits first is the *primary payer*. See also *coordination of benefits*.

duration of visit: The actual time a *physician* and *patient* are in contact with each other pursuant to medical care.

Ee

Early and Periodic Screening, Diagnosis, and Treatment Program (EPSDT): A program mandated by law as part of the *Medicaid* program. The law (Section 1905(a)(4)(B) of the Social Security Act) required that by July 1, 1969, all states were to have a program in effect for eligible children under age 21 "to ascertain their physical or mental defects, and such health care, treatment, and other measures to correct or ameliorate defects and chronic conditions discovered thereby, as may be provided in *regulations* of the Secretary." Issuance of regulations implementing the program was delayed until November 1971, and states were allowed to phase in their programs by age groups until July 1, 1973. By law (Section 403(g) of the Social Security Act), states that did not have a program in effect in any fiscal quarter after June 30, 1974, for all children in families receiving AFDC payments were subject to a financial penalty. The state programs were not intended just for payment of services but also were to include an active outreach component to inform eligible persons of the benefits available to them, actively to bring them into care for screening, and, if necessary, to assist them in obtaining appropriate treatment.

Economic Stabilization Program (ESP): A federal program established to control wages and prices. For example, on August 15, 1971, all wages and prices were frozen for a period of 90 days. During that period a system of wage and price controls administered through a Cost of Living Council was implemented. Controls continued, with periodic changes in the flexibility and the intensity with which they were enforced, until their legislative authority ultimately expired in April 1974. Wages and prices in the health care industry were controlled through a specialized series of regulations. That period of 32-1/2 months when the controls were in effect is the only period in which medical care price increases have slowed markedly since the enactment of *Medicare* and *Medicaid.* During the price control period, increases in medical care prices were limited to 4.3 percent. Price controls are generally enacted to curb inflation.

economies of scale: *Cost* savings resulting from growth in resources or mass production. In particular, the term refers to decreases in average cost when all factors of production are expanded proportionately. For example, *hospital* costs for a unit of service are generally less in 300-bed than 30-bed hospitals. (There is some evidence that they may be greater in 1,000-bed than 300-bed hospitals, a diseconomy of scale.) The term is also frequently used, although less accurately, to refer to savings achieved when underused resources are used more efficiently; for example, when many individuals use the same product, or when health care facilities share in the costs and use of expensive equipment (such as automated laboratory equipment) or otherwise underused and highly trained personnel (such as open-heart surgery teams).

Education Resources Information Center (ERIC): A national computerized clearinghouse of information and materials related to health care educational programs.

Educational Commission for Foreign Medical Graduates (ECFMG): an organization sponsored by the American Medical Association, American Hospital Association, Association of American Medical Colleges, Association for Hospital Medical Education, and Federation of State Medical Boards of the United States that operates a program of educating, testing, and evaluating *foreign medical graduates* who seek *internships* and *residencies* in the United States. The ECFMG was formed in 1974 by merger of the Educational Council for Foreign Medical Graduates, incorporated in 1956, and the Commission for Foreign Medical Graduates. *Certification* of foreign medical graduates is granted by the ECFMG after their education is documented and they have passed an examination that verifies medical competence and comprehension of spoken English. See also *Federation Licensing Examination.*

educational therapist: An individual who works with mentally ill or disabled *patients* to instruct them in academic subjects as part of therapy.

effectiveness: The degree to which diagnostic, preventive, therapeutic, or other action achieves the intended result. Effectiveness requires a consideration of *outcomes* to be measured. It does not require consideration of the *cost* of the actions, although one way of comparing the effectiveness of actions with the same or similar intended results is to compare the ratios of their effectiveness to their costs. For example, the federal Food, Drug, and Cosmetic Act requires prior demonstration of effectiveness for most *drugs* marketed for human use. No similar requirement exists for most other medical action paid for or *regulated* under federal or state law. The term is usually synonymous with *efficacy* in common use. See also *safety, quality, efficiency,* and *Drug Efficacy Study Implementation.*

efficacy: Commonly used synonymously with *effectiveness,* but may be usefully distinguished by using efficacy for the results of actions undertaken under ideal circumstances and effectiveness for their results under usual or normal circumstances. Actions thus cen be efficacious and effective, or efficacious and ineffective, but never the reverse.

efficiency: The relationship between the quantity of inputs or resources used in the production of medical *services* and the quantity of outputs produced. Efficiency has three components: input productivity (technical efficiency), input mix (economic efficiency), and the scale of operation. Efficiency is usually measured by indicators, such as output per man-hour or cost per unit of output. However, such indicators fail to account for the numerous relevant dimensions (such as *quality*) of both inputs and outputs and are, therefore, only partial measures. Colloquially, efficiency measures the "bang for the buck" or cost/benefit relationship but, as the above suggests, it is a difficult concept to define and quantify. Ultimately, efficiency probably should be measured in terms of the costs of achieving various health outcomes. Defining it in terms of productivity assumes that what is produced is efficacious and used in an effective manner.

elasticity of demand: In (*health*) economics, a measure of the sensitivity of demand for a product or *service* to changes in its price (price elasticity) or the *income* of the people demanding the product or service (income elasticity). Price elasticity is the ratio of the resulting percentage change in demand to a given percentage change in price. Price elasticity of demand for health services allows one to predict the effect on demand of different *cost-sharing* provisions in present or proposed programs and thus aids in predicting the differing stress their enactment would place on the health system.

elective benefit: An *insurance* benefit payable in lieu of another.

elective surgery: *Surgery* that *need* not be performed on an emergency basis, because reasonable delays will not affect the *outcome* of the surgery unfavorably. It should be understood that elective surgery may be necessary and may be considered *major surgery*.

elephant policy: See *trolley car policy*.

eligibility: To be eligible for *benefits* under a particular program whether it is a private *health insurance* policy or a public program, such as *Medicare* or *Medicaid*.

emergency care: Care for *patients* with severe, life-threatening, or potentially disabling conditions that require intervention within a very short time period. Most hospitals and programs providing emergency care are also asked to provide care for many conditions that *providers* would not consider emergencies. This suggests that *consumers* define the term almost synonymously with *primary care* and often use emergency care programs as *screening clinics*. See also *emergency medical service system*.

emergency kit: A kit that includes pharmaceuticals required for *emergency care*. The kit is usually maintained at convenient locations within a *long-term care* facility pursuant to state guidelines.

emergency medical services system (EMSS): An integrated system of *health manpower, facilities,* and equipment that is *appropriate* in providing all necessary *emergency care* in a defined geographic area. The development of these systems is federally assisted under the Emergency Medical Services Systems Act of 1973, P.L. 93-154, in which the term is defined and the necessary components of the system listed (Sections 1201 and 1206 of the *PHS Act*). One characteristic of the system is a central communications facility using the universal emergency telephone number 911 and having direct communications with all components of the system to facilitate proper dispatching of cases.

emergency medical technician (EMT): An individual trained in *emergency care* who responds to and provides immediate care to critically ill or *injured* persons and provides emergency transport to a hospital. See also *paramedic.*

emergency medical technician, ambulance (EMT-A): A classification granted to an individual who completes the basic 81-hour course as defined by the U.S. Department of Transportation.

emergency medical technician, intermediate (IEMT or EMT-II): Various states recognize different competency levels among EMTs. This level is more advanced than an EMT but less qualified than a paramedic. This type of EMT, however, can administer injectibles under a physician's instruction.

emergency medical technician, paramedic (EMT-P): A classification granted individuals who have completed advanced training in life support beyond that required of an EMT-intermediate. Paramedics are the highest level of nonphysician emergency care personnel.

Employee Health Insurance Plan (EHIP): One of the three parts of a *national health insurance* proposal, the *Comprehensive Health*

Insurance Plan, providing health insurance for full-time employees and their dependents. The plan would operate by requiring employers to offer comprehensive health insurance with *cost sharing* and pay 75 percent of the *premium* cost (65 percent for the first three years). The *benefits* would be underwritten by private *insurers* and financed entirely by premiums. Premiums could be *experience rated* for large employers (over 50 employees), but would have to be *community rated* for small employers.

employee health services: Health care services provided employees that can include pre-employment screening programs, medical care services, or participation in wellness programs.

encounter: A contact or visit between a *patient* and health *professional* in which care is given. Some definitions exclude either telephone contacts or home *visits*.

endemic: A disease or disorder that is native to or restricted to a particular area.

endocrinology: The branch of medicine specializing in disorders of the endocrine glands.

endorsement: Recognition by a state of a *license* issued by another state, when the qualifications and standards required by the original licensing state are equivalent to or higher than those of the endorsing state. The licensee is consequently relieved of the full burden of obtaining a license in the endorsing state. There is not necessarily any *reciprocity* between the two states.

enroll: To agree to participate in a contract for *benefits* from an *insurance* company or *health maintenance organization*. A person who enrolls is an enrollee or *subscriber* (see also *member* and *beneficiary*). The number of people (and their *dependents*) enrolled with an insurance company or HMO constitutes its enrollment. See also *open enrollment*.

enrollment period: A period during which individuals may *enroll* for *insurance* or *health maintenance organization* benefits. For example, there are two types of enrollment periods for the *supplementary medical insurance program* of *Medicare:* the initial enrollment period (the seven months beginning three months before and ending three months after the month a person first becomes eligible, usually by attaining age 65); and the general enrollment period (the first three months of each year). Most group *contributory insurance* has an annual enrollment period when members of the group may elect to begin contributions and become covered. See also *open enrollment.*

entitlement authority: In the federal *budget,* legislation that requires the payment of benefits or entitlements to any person or government meeting the requirements established by such law. Mandatory entitlements include social security benefits and veterans' pensions.

environmental health: The process of health *hazard* identification, detection, management, and control involving environmental factors that influence health.

epidemic: The occurrence of *disease* that affects significant numbers of persons in a specific population at a given time. An epidemic is any number of cases of disease above the expected amount.

epidemiology: The study of the nature, *cause,* control, and determinants of the frequency and distribution of *diseases* and *disability* in human populations. This involves characterizing the distribution of *health status,* diseases, or other health problems in terms of age, sex, race, geography, and other classifications; explaining the distribution of a disease or health problem in terms of its causal factors; and assessing and explaining the impact of control measures, clinical intervention, and health services on diseases and other health problems. The epidemiology of a disease is the description of its presence in a population and the factors controlling its presence or absence. See also *incidence, prevalence, morbidity,* and *mortality.*

episode of care: The continuous stay of a person as an *inpatient* in a health care facility.

episode of illness: A continuous period of ailment or disability for a particular disease.

eponyms: *diseases* or *illnesses* named for persons.

equivalency testing: Tests to equate an individual's knowledge, experience, and skill, however acquired, with the knowledge, experience, and skill acquired by formal education or training. Successful completion of equivalency tests may be used to obtain course credits toward an academic degree without taking the courses, or to obtain a *license* requiring academic training without undergoing the training. See also *proficiency testing*.

established name: A name given to a *drug* or pharmaceutical product by the *United States Adopted Names Council* (*USAN*). This name is usually shorter and simpler than the *chemical name* and is most commonly used in the scientific literature. It is the name by which most physicians and pharmacists learn about a particular drug product. An example would be penicillin, a well-known antibiotic. The established name is also known as the *generic name* or official name. Established names for drugs are required by Section 502(e) of the federal Food, Drug, and Cosmetic Act.

ethical drug: A *drug* that is advertised only to *physicians* and other health *professionals* who write *prescriptions*. Drug manufacturers who make only (or primarily) such drugs are referred to as the ethical drug industry. The term is synonymous with *prescription drug* or *legend* drug.

ethics: A system of moral behavior and professional expectations for health care *providers*; professional *standards* of conduct.

etiology: See *cause*.

euthanasia: For reasons of mercy, the act or practice of terminating the lives of individuals (active euthanasia) or allowing them to die without giving all possible *treatments* for their *diseases* (passive euthanasia) because they are hopelessly *sick* or *injured.* See also *hospice* and d*eath.*

evidence of insurability: Any proof of a person's physical condition or occupation affecting his or her acceptability for *insurance.*

excise tax: A single-stage commodity tax (i.e., a tax levied on a commodity only once as it passes through the production process to the final consumer). An excise tax is narrowly based; enabling legislation specifies precisely which products are taxed, as well as the tax rates. A sales tax is more broadly based; its tax base comprises many commodities, and legislation designates those commodities not subject to tax. Excise taxes are commonly assessed on automobiles, cigarettes, liquor, and gasoline. They are sometimes levied in hopes of discouraging the use of the product taxed. Revenues from such taxes may be set aside from general revenues and used for some purpose related to the taxed product. For example, an excise tax on cigarettes might discourage smoking by raising their cost. Cigarette tax revenues might be used to fund cancer screening programs and thus be useful in health enhancement programs.

exclusions: Specific *hazards, perils,* or conditions listed in an *insurance* or medical care coverage *policy* for which the policy will not provide benefit payments. Common exclusions may include *pre-existing conditions,* such as heart disease, diabetes, hypertension, and a pregnancy which began before the policy was in effect. Because of such exclusions, persons who have a serious condition or disease are often unable to secure insurance coverage, either for the particular disease or in general. Sometimes conditions are excluded only for a defined period after coverage begins, such as nine months for pregnancy or one year for all exclusions. Exclusions are often permanent in *individual health insurance,* temporary (e.g., one year) for small groups in *group insurance,* and uncommon for large groups capable of absorbing the extra risk involved.

executive session: A meeting open only to the committee members, their staffs, and others specifically invited, but closed to the general public. Sometimes the term is used synonymously with markup, especially in the House of Representatives, where markups are now rarely held in private.

expected morbidity or mortality: Expected incidence of *illness* (morbidity) or *death* (mortality) within a given population during a given time period.

expenses: In *insurance,* the cost to the *insurer* of conducting its business (other than paying *losses),* including *acquisition* and administrative costs.

experience rating: A method of establishing *premiums* for health insurance in which the premium is based on the average cost of actual or anticipated health care used by various groups and subgroups of *subscribers.* The rating can vary with the health experience of groups and subgroups or with such variables as age, sex, or health status. It is the most common method of establishing premiums for health insurance in private programs. See also *community rating.*

experimental health service delivery system (EHSDS): A system developed under a program supported by the *Health Services and Mental Health Administration* under general health services research authorities to develop, test, and evaluate the organization and operation of coordinated, communitywide health service *management* systems (EHSDS) in various kinds and sizes of communities. EHSDS sought to improve *access* to services, moderate their *costs,* and improve their *quality.*

experimental medical care review organization (EMCRO): An organization assisted by a program initiated in 1970 by the National Center for Health Services Research and Development (now the *National Center for Health Services Research*). The program, a forerunner of the *PSRO* program, was set up to help medical societies create formal organizations and procedures for reviewing the *quality* and use of medical care in hospitals, nursing homes, and offices throughout a defined community. The use of explicit *criteria* and standard definitions were required of all EMCROs, but the particular approach to organizing the review was determined by the individual organization. Ten such organizations were initially supported (only some of which actually reviewed services), and the program was phased out after enactment of the PRO program.

extended benefits: Insurance coverage supplemental to basic hospital coverage. It usually covers x-ray, *drugs*, and other ancillary services.

extended care facility (ECF): Previously used in *Medicare* to mean a *skilled nursing facility* that qualified for participation in Medicare. In 1972, the law was amended to use the more generic term skilled nursing facility for both Medicare and *Medicaid*. Medicare coverage is limited to 100 days of posthospital *extended care services* during any *episode of care;* Medicare coverage in a skilled nursing facility is limited in duration, must follow a hospital stay, and must be for services related to the cause of the hospital stay. These conditions do not apply to skilled nursing facility benefits under Medicaid. Thus, the continued use of the term "extended care facility benefits" refers to the benefit limitations on skilled nursing facility care under Medicare.

extended care services: As used in *Medicare,* services in a *skilled nursing facility* that provide for a limited duration (up to 100 days during an *episode of care*) after a hospital stay, and for the same condition as the hospital stay. As defined under Medicare the following items and services are furnished to an *inpatient* of a skilled nursing facility: (1) *nursing care* provided or supervised by a *registered professional nurse;* (2) bed and board associated with the nursing care; (3) *physical therapy, occupational therapy,* or *speech therapy* furnished by the skilled nursing facility or by others under arrangements with the facility; (4) medical social services; (5) *drugs, biologics, supplies,* appliances, and *equipment* ordinarily used in care and treatment in the skilled nursing facility; (6) medical services provided by an *intern* or *resident* of a hospital with which the facility has a transfer agreement; (7) and other services necessary to the *health* of the patients or mandated under federal conditions of participation and state regulation.

extended duration review: See *continued stay review*.

externality: In (health) economics, an activity between a *consumer* and *provider* that confers benefits or imposes *costs* on others and is not considered in making the transaction (its value, the external cost, not being reflected in any *charge* for the transaction). Pollution is the classic example. In health, an externality of immunizations is the protection that they give the unimmunized, since that protection is not considered when an individual immunization is obtained or priced.

extra cash policy: An *insurance* policy that pays cash *benefits* to hospitalized individuals in fixed amounts unrelated to the individual's medical expenses or *income*. These policies are usually sold to individuals separately from other health insurance they may have.

Ff

facilities: Buildings, including physical plant, equipment, and *supplies*, used in providing *health* services. Major types of health facilities include *hospitals, nursing homes,* and *ambulatory care centers.*

factoring: The practice of an organization selling its accounts receivable (unpaid bills) to another at a discount. The latter organization, called the "factor," usually, but not always, assumes full risk of loss if the accounts prove uncollectible. In health services delivery, the expression generally refers to a hospital's or *physician's* sale of unpaid bills to a collection agent. Factoring has been used sometimes in *Medicaid* because of the delays that hospitals and physicians experience collecting from the state Medicaid agency. In these cases, the improved cash flow justifies the discount in the amount received by the *provider.* Because factoring is subject to *fraud* and *abuse,* Congress has sought to prohibit its use in relation to receivables due from the government.

faith cure: A religious or folklore approach to healing through confidence and prayer.

false negative: A test result whereby a person is wrongly diagnosed as not having a *disease* or condition that, in fact, he or she does have. See also *false positive.*

false positive: A test result whereby a person is wrongly diagnosed as having a *disease* or condition when, in fact, he or she does not. When assessing a medical *screening* or other *diagnostic* procedure, it is important to know how many false positives and *false negatives* the procedure gives in normal use. See also *sensitivity* and *specificity.*

family: For U.S. census purposes, a group of two or more persons related by blood, marriage, or adoption who are living together in the same household. *Group insurance* and some *national health insurance* proposals offer coverage for eligible individuals and their families. In this context family usually refers to an individual and his or her *dependents,* which is quite a different definition since dependents do not necessarily have to be related to or live with the individual.

family-centered maternity: Health care designed to help the *family* adapt to the needs of a newborn child.

family and community services: Educational and social programs that focus on the cultural, social, and psychological influences on the *family* in a changing society.

family ganging: The practice of requiring or encouraging a *patient* to return for care to a health program with the entire *family,* even if the other family members do not *need* care, so that the provider can charge the patient's *third party* for care given to each member of the family. The practice and term originated and are most common in *Medicaid mills* that frequently have the mother of a sick child bring in her other children for unneeded care.

Family Health Insurance Plan (FHIP): A comprehensive insured plan of health coverage ordinarily extended to the parents and dependent children of a family unit.

family numbering: A medical record-keeping system where the *family* is assigned a number and each family member a separate subnumber.

family physician: A *physician* who assumes continuing responsibility for supervising the health and coordinating the care of all *family* members, regardless of age. Previously viewed as low-level generalists by some specialties, family physicians are now trained as *specialists* or *internists* whose work demands specific skills. These skills include functioning as medical managers, advocates, educators, and counselors for their patients. See also *personal physician, primary care,* and *general practitioner.*

family planning: The range of methods of fertility technique to help individuals or couples avoid unwanted births, to bring about wanted births, to produce a change in the number of children born, to regulate the intervals between pregnancies, and to control the time at which births occur in relation to the age of parents. Family planning may include an array of activities ranging from birth planning, the use of contraception, and the management of infertility to sex education, marital counseling, and even genetic counseling. Family planning has succeeded the older term, birth control, which is now felt to be too negative and restrictive in meaning. Birth control can be separately defined as the prevention of pregnancy by contraception, *abortion,* sterilization, or abstinence from coitus.

family practice: A medical specialty that has replaced general practice. Family practitioners undergo a three-year residency with emphasis on diagnosis of diseases common to the family.

family practitioner: A *physician* who accepts responsibility for providing primary care to a *family.* Such practitioners are now considered *specialists* whose skills include that of medical manager and health coordinator for the family unit. (See *family physician.*)

favorable selection: See *skimming.*

Federal Employees Health Benefits Program (FEHBP): The *group* health *insurance* program for federal employees. It is the largest employer-sponsored *contributory* health insurance program in the world. Participation is voluntary for the employees; about 80 percent of those eligible are covered. Established under the Federal Employees Health Benefits Act of 1959 (P.L. 86-382, codified in chapter 89, Title V, U.S. Code), the program began operation in July

1960. It is administered by the U.S. Civil Service Commission. Each employee may choose between two governmentwide plans, a *service benefit* plan administered by *Blue Cross* and *Blue Shield* or an *indemnity benefit* plan offered by the insurance industry through the Aetna Life Insurance Company. In addition to the two governmentwide plans, there are 15 employee organizations offering indemnity-type plans to their members. An additional choice is available to employees residing in certain geographic areas where *prepaid group practice* plans are in operation. There are now 7 *individual practice plans* and 19 group practice plans participating in the program. A plan operating as part of the FEHBP is referred to as an FEHB Plan.

Federal Health Insurance Plan (FHIP): One of three health insurance plans making up part of a prior proposal for *national health insurance* called the *Comprehensive Health Insurance Plan*. This plan would replace *Medicare* and provide health insurance coverage for persons aged 65 and older. Although many of the features of FHIP are the same as Medicare, changes were made in the *benefits* structure and *cost-sharing* provisions. Among the more significant changes are combining the hospital and medical portions of the benefits package and adding *drugs* as a covered service.

Federal Register: An official, daily publication of the federal government providing a uniform system for making available to the public proposed and final *rules*, legal notices, and similar proclamations, and orders and documents having general applicability and legal effect. The register publishes material from all federal agencies and is available by subscription.

Federation Licensing Examination (FLEX): A standardized *licensure* test for *physicians* developed by the Federation of State Medical Boards of the United States for potential use on a nationwide basis. In fact, some 48 states now use the FLEX as their test for licensure, although they vary in the score required for licensure. The FLEX examination is based on test material developed by the

National Board of Medical Examiners. See also *national board examinations.*

fee schedule: A listing of accepted *charges* or established allowances for specified medical or dental procedures. It usually represents either a *physician*'s or *third party*'s allowable standard or maximum charges for the listed procedures. See also *relative value scale.*

fee for service: A method of charging whereby a *physician* or other practitioner bills for each *encounter* or *service* rendered. This is the usual method of billing by the majority of the country's physicians. Under a fee-for-service payment system, expenditures increase not only if the fees themselves increase but also if more units of service are charged for or more expensive services are substituted for less expensive ones. This system contrasts with salary, per capita, or *prepayment* systems, where the payment is not changed with the number of services actually used or if no services are used. While the fee-for-service system is now generally limited to physicians, dentists, podiatrists, and optometrists, a number of other practitioners, such as *physician assistants,* have sought reimbursement on a fee-for-service basis. See also *fee schedule, fractionation,* and *capitation.*

fee splitting: The unethical and often illegal act of a *physician* who pays a *referral* fee to another physician who makes the referral.

fertility rate: Computed by dividing total live births occurring in one calendar year by the midyear population of women aged 15 to 44.

fetal death: See *stillbirth.*

fetus: The unborn child from the third month of pregnancy until birth.

fiduciary: A term that means relating to or founded upon a trust or confidence. A fiduciary relationship exists where an individual or organization has an explicit or implicit obligation to act in behalf of another person's or organization's interests in matters that affect the latter person or organization. For example, a *physician* has a fiduciary relationship with a *patient*, and a hospital trustee with a hospital. A fiduciary relationship with a *provider* obligates one to act in the interests of the provider. Therefore, people with fiduciary relationships are defined as providers by P.L. 93-641, rather than as *consumers,* for such purposes as determining whether a *health systems agency* governing board has a consumer majority.

fifth pathway: One of the several ways that an individual who obtains all or part of his *undergraduate medical education* abroad can enter *graduate medical education* in the United States. The fifth pathway provides a period of supervised clinical training to students who obtain their premedical education in the United States, receive undergraduate medical education abroad, and pass a screening examination approved by the the *Coordination Council for Medical Education.* After these students successfully complete a year of clinical training sponsored by a U.S. medical school, they become eligible for an American Medical Association-approved *internship* or *residency.*

first-dollar coverage: *Coverage* under an *insurance* policy that begins with the first dollar of expense incurred by the *insured* for the covered benefits. Such coverage, therefore, has no *deductibles,* although it may have *copayments* or *coinsurance.* See also *last-dollar coverage.*

fiscal agent or intermediary: A contractor that processes and pays *provider claims* on behalf of a state *Medicaid* agency or *insurance* underwriter. Fiscal agents are rarely *at risk,* but rather serve as *administrative* units for the state or underwriter and handle the payment of bills. Fiscal agents may be insurance companies, management firms, or other private contractors. Medicaid fiscal agents sometimes are also *carriers* or *intermediaries* for *Medicare.*

fiscal year (FY): Any 12-month period for which annual accounts are kept (sometimes, but not necessarily, the same as a calendar year). The federal government's fiscal year previously extended from July

1 through the following June 30, but was changed in 1976 to October 1 through the following September 30.

flat maternity: A single, inclusive *maternity benefit* for all *charges* incurred as a result of pregnancy, childbirth, and complications arising therefrom. A limit (such as $1,000) may be applied per pregnancy or per year. See also *switch maternity* and *swap maternity*.

FLEX: See *Federation Licensing Examination.*

Flexner Report: A 1910 study of U.S. and Canadian medical schools conducted by Abraham Flexner of Johns Hopkins University. In evaluating medical education, the report found the quality of education below acceptable standards. Many medical schools closed as a result of the Flexner Report. The report gave rise to modern medical education, new standards curriculum, and procedures for training physicians.

float nurse: A *nurse* available for assignment to duty on a per-diem basis. Float nurses are often used to fill in during absences, vacations, and periods of heavy nursing demand. Float nurses also may be regular employees who are assigned to different units as needed.

fluoridation: The addition of controlled, small amounts of fluoride to public water supplies for the purpose of reducing the *incidence* of dental cavities.

Food and Drug Administration (FDA): An agency of the Department of Health and Human Services that assures the safety and efficacy of drugs and drug-related products. The agency is also responsible for protecting the public from health hazards in foods.

foreign medical graduate (FMG): A *physician* who graduated from a medical school not located in the United States and, usually, also not located in Canada. U.S. citizens who attend medical schools outside this country are classified as foreign medical graduates (sometimes distinguished as USFMGs) in addition to foreign-born persons who are not trained in a medical school in this country. Native Americans represent only a small portion of the group. There are more than 75,000 graduates of foreign medical schools in the United States. They constitute more than 20 percent of active physicians in this country. The term is occasionally defined as, and nearly synonymous with, any graduate of a school not *accredited* by the *Liaison Committee on Medical Education*. See also *Coordinated Transfer Application System*, *Educational Commission for Foreign Medical Graduates*, *fifth pathway*, *J visa*, *labor certification*, and *Schedule A*.

forensic medicine: The combination of medical knowledge and legal knowledge used to solve legal issues through the application of medical science. Forensic medicine, for example, is often used in criminology and the detection and prosecution of crimes.

formula grant: A grant of federal funds, usually to states but sometimes to other governmental units or private organizations, authorized by law for specified purposes. The amount of the grant is based on a formula that divides the total funds available among the eligible recipients according to such factors as the number and average income of the population to be served.

formulary: A *compendium* of *drugs*, usually by their *generic names*. A formulary is intended to include a sufficient range of medicines to enable *physicians* or *dentists* to prescribe medically *appropriate* treatment for all reasonably common *illnesses*. A hospital formulary normally lists all the drugs routinely stocked by the hospital *pharmacy*. *Substitution* of a chemically equivalent drug in filling a prescription for a *brand-name* drug listed in the formulary is often permitted. A formulary also may be used to list drugs for which a *third party* will or will not pay or drugs that are considered appropriate for treating specified illnesses. (See *chemical equivalents* and *compendium*.)

forward funding: See *advance appropriation*.

foundation for medical care (FMC): See *medical foundation*.

fractionation: The practice of charging separately for several *services* or components of a service that were previously subject to a single charge or not charged for at all. The usual effect is that the total *charge* is increased. The practice is most commonly seen as a response to limiting increases in the charge that is fractionated.

fraud: Intentional misrepresentation by either *providers* or *consumers* to obtain services, obtain payment for services, or claim program eligibility. Fraud may include receiving services obtained through deliberate misrepresentation of *need* or eligibility; providing false information concerning costs or conditions to obtain *reimbursement* or *certification*; or claiming payment for services that were never delivered or received. Fraud is illegal and typically carries a penalty. See also *abuse*.

free clinics: Neighborhood clinics or health programs that provide medical services in relatively informal settings and styles, often to students and minority groups. Care is given at no *charge* or for a nominal charge by predominantly volunteer staffs. The first such clinic is considered to be the Haight-Asbury Free Clinic that was organized in San Francisco in 1967.

free noncontractual patient: A patient for whom a *physician* or health care *facility* agrees to provide free *services*.

freestanding support center: A *facility* that provides *ancillary* health services (i.e., a pharmacy or clinical laboratory) but does not provide direct patient care.

F.R.S.H.: Fellow in the Royal Society of Health.

function or functional classification: In the federal *budget*, a means of presenting *budget authority, outlay,* and *tax expenditure* data in terms of the principal purposes that federal programs are intended to serve. Each specific account is generally placed in the single function (e.g., national defense or health) that best represents its major purpose, regardless of the agency administering the program. The Congressional Budget and Impoundment Control Act of 1974 requires the Congress to estimate outlays, budget authority, and tax expenditures for each function. Functions are subdivided into narrower categories called subfunctions.

funded: In *insurance,* having sufficient funds to meet future *liabilities.* It also can be used in speaking of *trust funds* for *social insurance* programs. *Capital depreciation* is said to be funded if the amounts included in an institution's reimbursements for capital depreciation are set aside in a fund used for capital purposes rather than spent on current operating costs.

F

Gg

Galen [Plaudius Galenus] (130-200 A.D.): A celebrated Greek *physician* and medical writer, born at Pergamum (Asia Minor), who practiced in Rome and was physician to Emperor Marcus Aurelius. Although he did not dissect the human cadaver, he made many valuable anatomical and physiological observations on animals, and his writings on these and other subjects are extensive. His influence on medicine was profound for many centuries. His teleology ("nature does nothing in vain") was particularly attractive to the medieval mind, although it was inconsistent with advances in medical thought and practice.

General Accounting Office (GAO): The federal agency responsible for all *health* and other expenditures of the United States government.

general duty nurse: A *nurse* who provides general nursing care in a medical or nursing care unit.

general medical and surgical unit: A special area within a *hospital* staffed to provide acute medical and nursing care to *patients* following *surgery* or while under the care of an attending *physician*.

general practice: See *family practice*.

general practitioner (GP): A *practicing physician* who does not specialize in any particular field of *medicine* (i.e., not a *specialist*). The term should be contrasted with a *family physician*, who has specialized, and is subject to *specialty board* examination, in the care of families or a *primary care* physician, who may be a *specialist* in any of several specialties, particularly internal medicine.

general revenue: Government revenues raised without regard to the specific purpose for which they might be used. Federal general revenues come principally from personal and corporate *income* taxes and some *excise* taxes. State general revenues come primarily from personal income and sales *taxes.* Most proposed *national health insurance* programs would be financed in part from general revenues in addition to whatever financing might be obtained from *premiums, cost sharing,* and revenue from *payroll taxes* used only for the program. The expenditure of general revenues is determined by legislative *authorizations* and *appropriations.*

generally recognized as effective (GRAE): One of the conditions that a *drug* must fulfill if it is not to be considered a *new drug,* and thus not subject to the premarket approval requirements of the federal Food, Drug, and Cosmetic Act. To be generally recognized as effective, the drug must be so considered by "experts qualified by scientific training and experience to evaluate the *safety* and *effectiveness* of drugs" and have been "used to a material extent or for a material time." The *Food and Drug Administration (FDA)* determines that a drug is GRAE, subject to judicial reversal if its determination is arbitrary or capricious. The Supreme Court has held that for a drug to be generally recognized as effective, its sponsor must supply the FDA with the same kind of evidence consisting of adequate and well-controlled investigations by qualified experts that the law requires for approval of a *new drug application.* See also *generally recognized as safe.*

generally recognized as safe (GRAS): One of the conditions that a *drug* must fulfill if it is not to be considered a *new drug* or that a food must fulfill if it is not to be considered a food additive. A drug that is GRAS and *GRAE* need not go through the premarket approval procedures prescribed in the federal Food, Drug, and Cosmetic Act for new drugs. General recognition of safety of a drug must be "among experts qualified by scientific training and experience to evaluate the *safety* and *effectiveness* of drugs"; to acquire general recognition of safety and effectiveness a drug must be "used to a material extent or for a material time."

generic equivalents: Drug products with the same active chemical ingredients sold under the same *generic name* but often with different *brand names*. Generic equivalents are often assumed to be, but are not necessarily, *therapeutic equivalents*.

generic name: The *established,* official, or nonproprietary name by which a drug is known as an isolated substance, regardless of its manufacturer. Each drug is *licensed* under a generic name and also may be given a *brand name* by its manufacturer. The generic name is assigned by the *United States Adopted Names Council (USAN).* There have been recent attempts to encourage *physicians* to *prescribe* drugs by generic names, whenever possible, rather than by brand names. This allows considerable cost savings. Much controversy has arisen over whether drugs sold by generic names are in fact *therapeutical equivalents* of their brand-name counterparts. In some cases usually because of differing *bioavailability,* two versions of the same drug manufactured by the same or different manufacturers may not be therapeutically equivalent. Advocates of generic prescriptions question whether such differences are universal or always significant. See also *Maximum Allowable Cost Program* and *antisubstitution.*

generic screen: In the medical care process, a set of questions designed to uncover underlying deficiencies in the delivery of *patient* care that may cause a persistent future problem.

genetic counseling: A counseling service that provides information to prospective parents concerned with their genetic makeup and the possibility of transmitting genetic defects to their offspring.

geriatric care: Providing care to infirm elderly *patients*; administering to the various physical and social needs of the elderly patient in an institutional setting.

geriatrics: The specialty of health care for the aged that commonly includes social emphasis as well as medical care.

gerodontics: A dental specialty that focuses on the dental needs of geriatric or elderly *patients*.

gerontology: The social, psychological, health, and biological study of aging; the social and health problems associated with growing old.

GHHA: See *Group Health Association of America.*

goal: In health *planning,* a quantified or specific statement of a desired future state or condition; for example, an infant mortality of less than 20 per 1,000 live births, a physician-to-population ratio greater than 4 per 1,000, or an average access time for emergency medical services of less than 20 minutes. Health planning formulates goals and seeks to achieve them. A goal differs from an *objective* by lacking a deadline and usually by being long-range (five to ten years) rather than short-range (one to two years).

going bare: An expression indicating a health care *provider* practicing without *malpractice* or liability *insurance*.

Good Samaritan Act: A type of law enacted by most states that protects physicians, nurses, and often others from *malpractice* or *negligence* claims arising from their rendering first aid to a person in an emergency situation.

governing body: In health agencies, an assembly of persons that is legally constituted and must be composed of 50 percent providers and 50 percent consumers. In other organizations, the governing body, usually a board of directors or board of trustees, is defined by the bylaws or charter of the organization.

governmental immunity: In *malpractice*, a doctrine providing that, despite the general proposition that a negligent act gives rise to tort liability for that act, the government, subject to certain qualifications, cannot be sued for the negligent acts of its officers, agents, or employees unless it consents to such a suit. This concept of governmental immunity had its origin in common law doctrine, and the principle has been firmly established that a state cannot be sued without its consent. As with *charitable immunity,* the trend is toward an increasing willingness of the courts to impose liability as the states and the federal government enact statutes to waive their immunity in tort suits.

GP: See *general practitioner.*

grace period: A specified period, after a *premium* payment is due on an *insurance policy,* in which the policyholder may make such payment and during which the protection of the policy continues.

graduate medical education: Medical education given after receipt of the Doctor of Medicine or equivalent degree, including the education received as an *intern, resident,* or fellow and as *continuing education.* This use contrasts with that in general education where graduate education refers to graduate school education leading to a master's, doctoral, or equivalent degree (called *undergraduate medical education* in medicine). It is sometimes limited to education required for certification *by a specialty board* Education at this level usually includes supervised practice, research, and even teaching, as well as didactic learning.

graduate nurse: An individual who has graduated from a nursing program but has not yet passed the registry examination and, therefore, is not a registered nurse.

grand rounds: The process in medical education whereby students review and discuss clinical cases in a *hospital* setting for educational purposes.

grandfather clause or provision: A clause or provision of law that permits continued eligibility or coverage for individuals or organizations receiving program benefits under the law, despite a change in the law that would otherwise make them ineligible; or in some other manner exempts a person, organization, or thing from a change in law that would otherwise affect it. For example, the federal Food, Drug, and Cosmetic Act exempts certain *drugs* from the Act's premarket approval requirements on the basis of their long-standing use.

gross autopsy rate: The ratio of all *inpatient* autopsies to all inpatient *deaths* for a given period of time.

gross premium: A charge for an *insurance policy* that includes anticipated losses, overhead, and profit for the underwriter.

G

group: In *group insurance,* a body of *subscribers* eligible for group insurance by virtue of some common identifying attribute, such as employment by a common employer or membership in a union, association, or other organization.

Group Health Association of America (GHAA): Organized in 1959 to represent *health maintenance organizations* and assist them in numerous *management* areas.

group health plan: Comprehensive, prepaid (usually *HMO*-based) health care services for members of a definable group who have enrolled in the plan.

group insurance: Any *insurance* plan by which a number of employees of an employer (and their *dependents*) or members of a similar homogeneous *group* are *insured* under a single policy issued to their employer or the *group* with individual *certificates of insurance* given to each insured individual or *family.* Individual employees may be insured automatically by virtue of employment only on meeting certain conditions (employment for over a month) or only when they elect to be insured (and usually elect to make a contribution to the cost of the insurance). Group health insurance premiums are usually based on *experience rating,* except for small groups insured by an individual company in the same area that are given the same rate by that company (see *community rating*). Group insurance is usually less expensive than comparable individual insurance (partly because an employed population is generally healthier than the general population, and partly because of lower administrative costs, especially in marketing and billing). Note that the policyholder or *insured* is the employer, not the employees. See also *contributory insurance.*

group practice: A formal association of three or more *physicians* or other health *professionals* providing services with income from medical *practice* pooled and redistributed to the members of the group according to some pre-arranged plan (often, but not necessarily, through partnership). Multispecialty groups offer advantages to the *patient* by their ability to provide several kinds of services on an integrated basis. Groups vary a great deal in size, composition, and financial arrangements. See also *solo practice, private practice*, and *prepaid group practice.*

guardian: One who has legal right and authority to take care of, and act on behalf of, another person because that person legally cannot take care of himself of herself. A "guardian ad litem" is usually a lawyer appointed by a court to manage the affairs of another (usually a child).

guidelines: See *criteria* and *policy.*

gynecology (GYN): The medical specialty that deals with the female reproductive tract and related conditions.

Hh

habeas corpus (Lat.): A court order to obtain the release of a person unlawfully held or detained.

habilitation: See *rehabilitation*.

habituation: See *drug habituation, drug abuse,* and *drug dependence*.

HAC: See *Health Advisory Council*.

halfway house: A local *facility* for *patients* with mental problems who no longer require full institutionalization and yet are unable to care fully for themselves.

halo effect: The effect (usually beneficial) that the manner, attention, and caring of a *provider* have on a *patient* during medical *treatment* regardless of what medical procedures or services the encounter actually involves. See also *Hawthorne effect* and *placebo*.

handicapped: Any physical or mental condition limiting a person from life's normal functions as defined under the Vocational Rehabilitation Act of 1973.

HANES: Health and Nutrition Examination Survey.

hardship case: A situation where a *patient* cannot afford necessary medical *treatment* and is eligible for assistance under one or more social service programs.

Harrison Narcotic Act: Enacted in 1916 as the first federal legislation to control the manufacture and distribution of narcotics. The law was superseded in 1965 by the more contemporary controlled substances laws.

Hawthorne effect: The effect (often beneficial, almost always present) that an *encounter* with a *provider,* health program, or other part of the health system has on a *patient* independent of the medical content of the encounter. The Hawthorne effect is similar to the *placebo* effect but is not obtained intentionally. It is the effect on the patient of the encounter with a provider or program rather than the effect of services performed for the patient. The effect may be changed (intentionally or not) by alterations in the provider or program (for instance, by painting a *clinic* or changing its appointments system). Since *health services research* usually changes the services being studied simply because the research is being conducted or in other unintentional ways, the resulting change in the Hawthorne effect may well confound the results of the research. The name comes from classic industrial management experiments at the Hawthorne plant of the Western Electric Company, New York.

hazard: a situation that introduces or increases the probability of occurrence of a *loss* arising from a *peril* or that increases the extent of a loss (such as slippery floors, unsanitary conditions, or congested traffic).

hazardous procedures: According to *Joint Commission* accreditation requirements for *alcoholism*, psychiatric, and *drug abuse* facilities, these are procedures that place a *patient* at needless or excessive psychological or physical *risk*.

HB: See *House Bill*.

health: Defined by the *World Health Organization* as "a state of complete physical, mental, and social well-being and not merely the absence of *disease* or infirmity." Experts recognize, however, that health has many dimensions (anatomical, physiological, and mental) and is often culturally defined. The relative importance of various *disabilities* will differ depending upon the cultural factors and the role of the affected individual in that culture. Most attempts at measurement have taken a negative approach in that the degree of ill health has been assessed in terms of *morbidity* and *mortality*. In general, the detection of changes in *health status* is easier than the definition and measurement of the absolute level of health.

health administration: (1) The process of planning, organizing, directing, controlling, and coordinating the *resources* and methods by which the *needs* and *demands* for health care are met; (2) the work of administrators in *hospitals*, *HMOs*, health care centers, and other organized bodies that deliver health care.

Health Advisory Council (HAC): A community-based advisory council to the *health systems agency*. These councils are sometimes called subarea advisory councils (SAC).

health appraisal clinic: A preventative health unit, usually within an *HMO*, *clinic*, or *hospital*, that provides health *screening*, including multiphasic health testing and *health risk appraisal*.

health card: An identification card similar to a credit card, proposed in several *national health insurance* bills, that would be issued to each covered individual or *family* unit. This card would be presented at the time services were rendered in lieu of any cash payment. The individual would subsequently receive a bill for any *cost sharing* not covered under the insurance plan. Health cards, it is argued, would simplify eligibility determination, billing, accounting, and the study of use of services. The idea presents interesting *confidentiality* problems (see *confidential*), particularly under the Federal Credit Disclosure Act.

health care corporation (HCC): An organization included in the *American Hospital Association's national health insurance* proposal that would assume overall *management* responsibility for the provision of all *needed* personal health services in a defined *catchment area*.

Health Care Financial Management Association (HFMA): A national organization primarily interested in the financial *management* of hospitals and other health care organizations.

Health Care Financing Administration (HCFA): A federal agency within the *Department of Health and Human Services* that oversees policy relating to payments under the *Medicare* program.

health care management: The function of coordinating and managing activities within a health care *facility* or institution for purposes of achieving its goals.

health care practitioners: (1) All *providers* (other than *physicians*) who furnish health care services under *Medicare* or *Medicaid*; (2) all persons who work as health care providers.

health economics: The discipline within health care administration that studies *supply* and *demand* and the economic consequences of health *policy* on health delivery systems.

health facilities: Collectively, all buildings and *facilities* used in the provision of health *services*. Usually limited to facilities built for the purpose of providing health care, such as *hospitals* and *nursing homes*. Health facilities and *health manpower* are the principal *health resources* used in producing health services. See also *beds, boarding homes, capital, capital depreciation, certificate of need, clinic, Hill-Burton, institutional health services, institutional licensure, Joint Commission, inpatient, length of stay, Life Safety Code, modernization, outpatient, per diem cost, and proprietary hospital.*

health insurance: *Insurance* against loss by *disease* or accidental bodily *injury*. This type of insurance usually covers some or all of the medical costs of treating the disease or injury. It may cover other losses (such as loss of present or future earnings) associated with disease or injury and may be either *individual insurance* or *group* insurance.

Health Insurance for the Aged and Disabled: The *social insurance* program authorized by *Title XVIII* of the Social Security Act and known as *Medicare.*

Health Insurance Benefits Advisory Council (HIBAC): An advisory council to *HHS* whose primary role, pursuant to section 1867 of the Social Security Act, is to provide advice and recommendations on matters of general *policy* in the administration of *Medicare* and *Medicaid.* The council consists of 19 nongovernmental experts in health-related fields who are selected by the secretary of Health and Human Services and hold office for terms of four years. In recognition of the broad impact of Medicare and Medicaid on health care delivery throughout the country, the management and staff support for the council has been transferred to the Office of the Assistant Secretary for Health. Organizationally, this is said to enable information on policy issues to be more directly channeled to the council and to provide the assistant secretary ready access to, and analysis of, HIBAC issues.

Health Insurance Claim Number (HIC): An identification number assigned to a *Medicare* beneficiary.

health interview survey: An information retrieval system used by the *U.S. Public Health Service* to accumulate data on health-related issues.

health maintenance organization (HMO): An entity with four essential characteristics:
   1. an organized system for providing health care in a geographic area, which entity accepts the responsibility to provide or otherwise assure the delivery of

2. an agreed upon set of basic and *supplemental health* maintenance and treatment *services* to
3. a voluntarily enrolled group of persons, and
4. for which services the HMO is reimbursed through a predetermined, fixed, periodic *prepayment* made by or on behalf of each person or *family* unit *enrolled* in the HMO without regard to the amounts of actual services provided. (From the report of the Committee on Interstate and Foreign Commerce on the HMO Act of 1973, P.L. 93-222, in which the term is legally defined, Section 1301 of the *PHS Act*.)

The HMO is responsible for providing most health and medical care services required by enrolled individuals or families. These services are specified in the contract between the HMO and the enrollees. The HMO must employ or contract with health care *providers* who undertake a continuing responsibility to provide services to its enrollees. The prototype HMO is the Kaiser-Permanente system, a *prepaid group practice* located on the West Coast. However, *medical foundations* sponsored by groups of physicians are included under the definition. HMOs are of public policy interest because the prototypes appear to have demonstrated the potential for providing high *quality* medical services for less money than the rest of the medical system. Specifically, rates of hospitalization and surgery are considerably less in HMOs than those in the system outside such prepaid groups, although some feel that earlier care, *skimping,* or *skimming* may be better explanations. See also *prepaid health plan (PHP)*, *individual practice association*, and *group practice.*

health manpower: Collectively, all men and women working in the provision of *health* services whether as individual practitioners or employees of health institutions and programs, whether or not professionally trained, and whether or not subject to public *regulation.* *Facilities* and manpower are the principal health *resources* used in producing health services. It is often difficult to agree on which occupations are health occupations. See also *capitation, Coordinating Council for Medical Education, foreign medical graduate, graduate medical education, undergraduate medical education,* *professional, practice, credentialing, internship, residency, proficiency testing,* and *equivalency testing.*

health manpower education initiative award (HMEIA): A grant or contract under Section 774 of the *PHS Act* (added by the Comprehensive Health Manpower Training Act of 1971, P.L. 92-157) that authorizes awards to health or educational entities for *health manpower* programs to improve the distribution, *supply, quality, utilization,* and *efficiency* of health personnel and the health services delivery system. Support has been provided for the development of *area health education centers* (AHECs), the training of *physician assistants,* the identification and encouragement of disadvantaged students with a potential for training in the health professions, and other activities.

health manpower plan: A plan that projects the *health manpower* needs of a particular state.

health and medical care system: The combination of institutions, agencies, *facilities,* and *resources* used to achieve delivery of health care services on a short-term, long-term, or *preventative care* basis.

health outcomes: Any changes in *health status* of a defined population resulting from specified health programs.

health planning: *Planning* concerned with improving health, whether undertaken comprehensively for a whole community (see *comprehensive health planning*) or for a particular population, type of health service, or health program. Some definitions include all activities undertaken for the purpose of improving health (such as education, environmental control, and nutrition) within the scope of responsibility of the planning process; others are limited to the inclusion of conventional health services and programs, *public health,* or *personal health services.* See also *goals, objectives, state health planning and development agency, health systems agency, policy, management,* and *budget.*

health policy: The course of action selected to influence or determine present and future health activities.

health professional: See *professional*.

health promotion: Preventative and *health* education activities designed to improve health *quality* and well-being by providing consumers informed choices about health matters with the objective of improving *health status*.

health record: Documents used by health care providers that contain a patient's health information including diagnosis and treatment of injuries and diseases.

health resources: *Resources*, whether human, monetary, or material, used in producing health care and services. They include money, *health manpower, health facilities, equipment,* and *supplies*. Available or used resources can be measured and described for an area (see *medically underserved area* and *catchment area*), a population (see *medically underserved population*), and an individual program (see *HMO*) or service.

health risk appraisal: A recent preventative aid that helps identify and reduce major risks to continued good health. The objective of such an appraisal (based on physical examination) is to determine an individual's health risks and to assist in life-style changes.

health service area (HSA): A geographic area appropriate for the effective *planning* and development of health services. Section 1511 of the *PHS Act* requires that health service areas be delineated throughout the United States. The governors of the various states designate the areas by using requirements specified in the law concerning geography, political boundaries, population, *health resources,* and coordination with areas defined for other purposes. See also *catchment area* and *locality*.

Health Service, Inc. (HSI): A *stock insurance company* organized in Illinois by *Blue Cross plans* to serve as a national enrollment agency, to assist individual plans in negotiating contracts, and to serve large national accounts in which two or more plans are involved. While HSI and *Medical Indemnity of America, Inc.,* are separate companies with separate boards of directors, they have operated with an integrated administration and a common president.

health services research: Research concerned with the organization, financing, administration, effects, and other aspects of health *services* rather than with human biology or *disease* prevention, diagnosis, and treatment. Conceptually, health services research concerns itself with process or form, and *biomedical research* with the content of *medicine.*

health status: The state of *health* of a specified individual, group, or population (such as *HMO* membership or an employer's employees). It is difficult to measure the health of an individual. It may be measured through subjective assessment of health or with one or more indicators of *mortality* and *morbidity* in the population, such as longevity, maternal and *infant mortality,* and the *incidence* or *prevalence* of major *diseases* (communicable, coronary, malignant, and nutritional). These are, of course, measures of *disease* status, but they can be used as proxies in the absence of measures of either objective or subjective health. Conceptually, health status is the proper *outcome measure* for the *effectiveness* of the specific population's medical care system, although attempts to relate variations in health status and the effects of available medical care have proved difficult and generally unsuccessful. It cannot be measured with measures of *available* health *resources* or *services* (such as physician-to-population ratios) that, in this context, would be *process measures.* See also *vital statistics* and *National Health Survey.*

health status indicator: A quantitative measure used to reflect the health status of a community. Common indicators include *morbidity, mortality,* and *longevity* rates.

health survey: A program for studying a group or population to assess its *health status,* the conditions influencing or influenced by its *health,* and the health services and medical care available to and used by it. See also *National Health Survey.*

health systems agency (HSA): A *health planning* and resources development agency designated under the terms of the National Health Planning and Resources Development Act of 1974, P.L. 93-641. The designation of an HSA in each of the *health service areas* in the United States is required by P.L. 93-641. HSAs must be nonprofit private corporations, public regional planning bodies, or single units of local government. They are charged with performing the health planning and resources development functions listed in Section 1513 of the *PHS Act.* The legal structure, size, composition, and operation of HSAs are specified in Section 1512 of the Act. HSA functions include (1) preparation of a *health system plan* (HSP) and an *annual implementation plan* (AIP), (2) the issuance of grants and contracts, (3) the review and approval or disapproval of proposed uses of a wide range of federal funds in the agency's health service area, and (4) review of proposed new and existing *institutional health services* and submission of recommendations respecting them to *state health planning and development agencies.* HSAs replaced existing areawide *comprehensive health planning* (*CHP*) agencies and were granted expanded duties and powers.

health systems plan (HSP): A long-range health plan prepared by a *health systems agency* for its *health service area* specifying the health *goals* considered appropriate by the agency for the area. The HSPs are to be prepared after consideration of national guidelines issued by *HHS* and study of the characteristics, resources, and special needs of the health service area. Section 1513 of the *PHS* Act requires and specifies the nature of an HSP. See also *annual implementation plan.*

hematologist: A *physician* who specializes in the study, diagnosis, and treatment of blood and bone marrow disorders.

HEW: Formerly, the Department of Health, Education, and Welfare.

See *Department of Health and Human Services.*

HHS: See *Department of Health and Human Services.*

HIAA: See *Health Insurance Association of America.*

high option: In a *Federal Employees Health Benefits Program* and certain other insurance policies, denotes one of two or more levels of insurance that may be chosen by the *subscriber*. Under such options the *benefits* covered are usually comparable except that the high option provides lower *deductibles* and other *cost-sharing* requirements and more favorable time or quantity limits than the low option. The *premium* for the high option is usually higher than the low option to reflect the more generous coverage.

Hill-Burton: Legislation, and the programs operated under the legislation, for federal support of construction and *modernization* of hospitals and other *health facilities,* beginning with P.L. 79-725, the Hospital Survey and Construction Act of 1946. The original law, which has been amended frequently, provided for the survey of state *needs,* development of plans for construction of hospitals and public health centers, and assistance in constructing and equipping them. Until the late 1960s, most of the amendments expanded the program in dollar amounts and scope. Under P.L. 93-641, the National Health Planning and Resources Development Act of 1974, the Hill-Burton program is administered by each *state health planning and development agency.* The purpose of the existing Hill-Burton programs was modified by P.L. 93-641 to allow assistance in the form of grants, loans, or loan guarantees for the following purposes only: (1) modernization of health facilities; (2) construction of outpatient health facilities; (3) construction of inpatient facilities in areas that have experienced recent rapid population growth; and (4) conversion of existing medical facilities for the provision of new health services.

Hippocrates of Cos (late 5th century B.C.): A famous Greek physician who is generally regarded as the father of medicine. Many of the writings of Hippocrates, the so-called "Corpus Hippocraticum," have survived but it is not certain which portions were written by Hippocrates himself. These writings are usually characterized by the stress placed on treatment and prognosis. An oath that appears in the body of work attributed to Hippocrates and his school, known as the Hippocratic oath, has been the ethical guide of the medical profession since those early days.

Hippocratic oath: See *Hippocrates of Cos.*

HMO: See *Health Maintenance Organization.*

hold harmless provision: A legal provision that prevents a governmental entity, institution, or other party from suffering additional expenses or loss of benefits as a result of a change in a statute or *regulations.* Without this provision, an entity or institution would be responsible for expenses not previously anticipated due to an expanded caseload, increased coverage provisions, or both. On the other hand, the use of hold harmless provisions often creates substantial confusion, heterogeneity, and inequity in eligibility, coverage, and responsibilities under a statute. In *insurance,* the provision offers the *insured* protection in disputes between the *insurer* and the *provider* of a covered service.

holism: A medical theory in which the physical, spiritual, social, mental, and emotional parts of a person must be treated as having equal importance.

holistic: See *holism.*

home for the aged: *Facilities* ranging from private homes to skilled care facilities that provide *custodial care* for the elderly.

home health agency: An agency that provides *home health care.* To be certified under *Medicare* an agency must provide skilled nursing services and at least one additional therapeutic service (*physical therapy, speech therapy, occupational therapy,* medical social services, or home health aide services) within the patient's home.

home health care: Health services rendered to an individual as *needed* within the home. Such services are provided to aged, disabled, sick, or convalescent individuals who do not require institutional care. The services may be provided by a *visiting nurse association* (VNA), *home health agency, hospital,* or other community organization. These services may be quite specialized or comprehensive (such as nursing services; speech, physical, occupational, and rehabilitation therapy; homemaker services; and social services). Under *Medicare,* the services must be provided by a home health agency. Under *Medicaid,* states may, but do not have to, restrict coverage of home health care to services provided by home health agencies.

home visit: See *house call* and *visit.*

H

homemaker services: Primarily nonmedical support services (e.g., food preparation and bathing) given a homebound individual who is unable to perform these tasks himself or herself. Such services are not covered under the *Medicare* and *Medicaid* programs or most other health insurance programs, but may be included in the social service programs developed by the states under Title XX of the Social Security Act. Homemaker services are intended to preserve independent living and normal family life for the aged, disabled, sick, or convalescent. See also *alternatives to long-term institutional care.*

homeopathic: A system of medicine where cure of disease is believed to be effected by minute doses of drugs that produce the same symptoms in a healthy person as are present in the disease for which they are administered. Homeopathic medicine is no longer actively practiced in the United States.

Homeopathic Pharmacopeia of the United States: One of the two official *compendia* in the United States recognized in the federal

Food, Drug, and Cosmetic Act. See also *United States Pharmacopeia.*

homeopathy: A system of *medicine* originally expounded by Samuel Hahnemann based on the simile phenomenon (similia similibus curantur"). Cure of *disease* was said to be effected by minute doses of *drugs* that produce the same signs and symptoms in a healthy person as are present in the disease for which they are administered. This was said to stimulate bodily defenses against the signs and symptoms. This system of medicine is no longer practiced in the United States. The Hahnemann Medical College, originally founded to train homeopathic *physicians*, now trains *allopathic* physicians. See also *osteopathy.*

H

hometown medical and dental care: the Veterans Administration (VA) health care program that pays for outpatient medical and dental treatment for eligible veterans that is provided by VA-approved doctors and dentists of the veterans' choice in their own communities. Such treatment is furnished when the care cannot be provided by VA clinic facilities, or when the health of the patient or distance to be traveled gives sufficient justification.

hospice: A program that provides both palliative and supportive care for terminally ill *patients* and their *families,* either directly or on a consulting basis with the patient's *physician* or another community agency such as a *visiting nurse association.* The word was originally a medieval name for a way station where crusaders were replenished, refreshed, and cared for; it is now used for an organized program of care for terminally ill people going through life's last station. The entire family is considered the unit of care, and care extends through the mourning process. Emphasis is placed on control of pain and other disease symptoms, preparation for *death*, and support before and after death. Hospices originated in England (where there are about 25) and are now prevalent in the United States. Some consider the hospice a worthwhile alternative to *euthanasia.*

hospital: An institution whose primary function is to provide diagnostic and therapeutic *inpatient* services for a variety of medical conditions, both surgical and nonsurgical. In addition, most hospitals provide some *outpatient* services, particularly *emergency care*. Hospitals are classified (1) by *length of stay* (short-term or long-term); (2) as teaching or nonteaching; (3) by major type of service (psychiatric, tuberculosis, general, and other specialties, such as maternity; children's; or ear, nose, and throat); and (4) by control (government, federal, state, or local; for-*profit* [or *proprietary*]; and nonprofit). The hospital system is dominated by the short-term, general, nonprofit community hospital, often called a voluntary hospital.

hospital, accredited: The status granted by the *Joint Commission on Accreditation of Healthcare Organizations* (*Joint Commission*) certifying that the hospital meets the criteria and standards set forth by the commission.

H

hospital-based physician: A *physician* who spends the major part of *practice* time within one or more hospitals rather than within an office setting while providing services to one or more hospitals or their *patients*. These physicians sometimes have a direct financial arrangement with the hospital (salary or percentage of fees collected). They commonly include directors of medical education, pathologists, anesthesiologists, and radiologists, as well as physicians who staff emergency rooms and *outpatient* departments.

hospital district: Several hospitals grouped together on a regional basis for purposes of raising tax revenue directly from the population and independent of other governmental bodies.

Hospital Insurance Program (Part A) (HI): The *compulsory* portion of *Medicare* that automatically enrolls all persons age 65 and over who are entitled to benefits under the Old Age, Survivors, Disability, and Health Insurance Program or railroad retirement; persons under age 65 who have been eligible for *disability* for over two years; and insured workers (and their *dependents*) requiring renal dialysis or kidney transplantation. After various *cost-sharing* requirements are met, the program pays for *inpatient* hospital care and care in *skilled nursing facilities* and *home health agencies* following a period of hospitalization. The program is financed from a separate *trust fund* that is funded by a contributory tax (*payroll tax*) levied on employers, employees, and the self-employed. Each hospital nominates an *intermediary* to review and pay the hospital's *claims* under the program.

Hospital International Classification of Diseases adopted for use in the United States (H-ICDA): See *International Classification of Diseases adopted for use in the United States.*

hospital privileges: See *staff privileges.*

House Bill (HB): A bill pending in a federal or state house of representatives. (Bill number may be preceded by HR, rather than HB.)

house call: A *visit* by a *physician* or other *provider* to a *patient's* home. It is now considered by some to be an obsolete and unprofitable practice with respect to physicians.

house officers: See *housestaff.*

housestaff: The *physician* staff in training at a hospital. It is principally composed of the hospital's *interns, residents,* and fellows. Members of the housestaff are called house officers. Occasionally, the term also applies to physicians who are salaried by a hospital but not in a *graduate medical education* program.

HR: See *House Bill* (*HB*).

human subject research: Used for purposes of *Joint* Commission accreditation of psychiatric, alcoholism, and drug abuse *facilities*. Patients receiving *services* in these facilities are utilized as subjects in the systematic study, observation, and evaluation of factors related to the prevention, assessment, treatment, and understanding of an *illness.*

humanistic medicine: Medical *practice* and culture that respects and incorporates several significant concepts: (1) The *patient* is more than the *disease,* the *professional* more than a scientifically trained mind using technical skills; both are whole human beings interacting in the healing effort. (2) A person is more than a body; a person is a unique, interdependent relation of body, mind, emotions, culture, and spirit. (3) Each person has the capacity to define and be increasingly responsible for self; the professional seeks to assist the patient in taking and fulfilling this responsibility for self. (4) Health and disease are not matters of the moment but have an intricate past, present, and future. (5) Physical disease, pain, suffering, aging, and even death frequently can be valuable, meaningful events in an individual's life. (6) Effective practice requires not just conventional skills but also effective development and use of human qualities, such as intuition, inventiveness, and empathy.

H

iatrogenic: Resulting from the activity of a *physician*. The term was originally applied to disorders induced in the patient by autosuggestion based on the physician's examination, manner, or discussion (see *halo effect*). It is now applied to any condition in a patient occurring as a result of *treatment* by a physician or surgeon, such as a drug reaction.

ICDA: International Classification of Diseases adopted for use in the United States.

ICD-9-CM Diseases Alphabetical Index: The second volume of the ICD-9-CM manual. As a successor to the first volume, it contains many additional terms, including an index to *diseases* and *injuries*, a table of *drugs* and chemicals, an index to external causes of injury, and a table of neoplasms.

ICD-9-CM Procedures: A volume containing surgical, investigative, and therapeutic procedures. It is published separately from the ICD-9-CM manual.

IEMT: Intermediate emergency medical technician. See *emergency medical technician, intermediate*.

illness: Often used synonymously with *disease*. It can be differentially defined by saying illness is present when an individual perceives himself or herself as diseased, and disease is present when identifiable by objective, external *criteria*.

immunology (IG): The branch of medicine that specializes in body immune systems.

impaired provider: One who is not capable of safely and adequately performing required *services* due to addiction or some other physical or mental disorder.

implied consent: Consent that is not expressly written or verbally granted but is based on behavioral patterns from which the other party may assume consent is granted.

implied warranty: A legal inference of quality when goods are sold by a merchant.

impoundment: In the federal *budget*, any executive branch action or inaction that precludes the *obligation* or expenditure of *budget authority* provided by the Congress. An impoundment resolution is a resolution of the House of Representatives or the Senate that expresses its disapproval of a proposed *deferral of budget authority* set forth in a special message ordinarily transmitted by the President. Passage of an impoundment resolution by either house of Congress has the effect of overturning the proposed deferral and requires that such budget authority be made available for obligation. See also *rescission.*

IMR: Institution for the Mentally Retarded.

incidence: In *epidemiology,* the rate of occurrence or number of cases of *disease,* infection, or some other event having their onset during a prescribed period of time in relation to the unit of population in which they occur. It measures *morbidity* or other events as they happen over a period of time; for example, the number of accidents occurring in a manufacturing plant during a year in relation to the number of employees in the plant, or the number of cases of mumps occurring in a school during a month in relation to the pupils enrolled in the school. Incidence usually refers only to the number of new cases of *chronic diseases* or communicable diseases. For example, the incidence of common colds is high relative to their *prevalence.*

incident report: According to *Joint Commission* accreditation procedures for *long-term care* facilities, a written report by either a patient or staff member that documents any unusual problem, incident, or other situation for which follow-up action is indicated.

incur: In *insurance,* to become liable for a *loss, claim,* or *expense.* Incurred cases or losses are those occurring within a fixed period for which an insurance plan becomes liable whether or not reported, adjusted, and paid.

IND: See *investigational new drug.*

indemnity, indemnity benefits: Under health *insurance* policies, *benefits* in the form of cash payments rather than *services.* The indemnity insurance contract usually defines the maximum amounts that will be paid for the covered services. In most cases, after the *provider* of service has billed the patient in the usual way, the *insured* patient submits to the insurance company proof that the bills have been paid. The insured is then reimbursed by the company only to the extent of the covered costs. Indemnity benefits are contrasted with *service benefits.*

independent contractor: A contractor hired to perform a specific service who works independently and is not considered an employee of the individual or organization for whom the service is performed.

independent living centers: Apartments or condominiums to accommodate elderly persons who doe not require institutional care. Medical and social support *services* are available for these individuals when needed.

independent medical evaluation: For *Medicare* purposes, a requirement that a *hospital* or *skilled nursing facility* must submit for annual review and audit each patient's medical record to determine the need for continued skilled nursing care.

independent professional review (IPR): Another name for *medical* *review* required by *Medicaid* for *inpatients* in *long-term care* facilities.

indexed: Describes an amount regularly adjusted in proportion to changes in some index. For example, social security payments are now indexed to (or adjusted to reflect changes in) the *Consumer Price Index (CPI)*. Some proposed *national health insurance* plans index *premiums, cost sharing,* catastrophic thresholds, income levels, or reimbursement rates to the CPI.

Indian Health Service: The *HHS* bureau that is responsible for delivering *public health* and medical services to native Indians throughout the country. The federal government has direct and permanent legal obligation to provide health services to most Indian peoples according to treaties written with the Indian Nations during the last two centuries. The Indian Health Service fulfills these obligations within its very severe budgetary restrictions.

indigent patient: A person of poverty status who is unable to pay for necessary health *services*.

indirect cost: A *cost* that cannot be identified directly with a particular activity, product, or program experiencing the cost. Indirect costs are usually apportioned among the program's services in proportion to each service's share of *direct costs*.

individual care plan: A portion of the *patient's* medical record that documents all aspects of care furnished by each health care *provider*.

individual health insurance: Health *insurance* covering an individual (and usually *dependents*) rather than a group. Individual insurance usually offers *indemnity benefits* and has higher *loadings* than *group insurance*.

individual insurance: *Insurance policies* that provide protection to the policyholder and his or her *family* (as distinct from *group insurance*). It is often called personal insurance.

individual practice: See *solo practice.*

individual practice association (IPA): A partnership, corporation, association, or other legal entity that has entered into an arrangement for provision of services by persons who are *licensed* to practice *medicine, osteopathy,* or dentistry. The arrangement usually provides that these persons furnish their professional services in accordance with a compensation agreement established by the entity. The IPA members usually agree, to the extent feasible, (1) to use additional professional personnel, allied health professions personnel, and other health personnel that are available and appropriate for the *effective* and *efficient* delivery of the services; (2) to share *medical* and other records, *equipment*, and *professional*, technical, and administrative staff of the association; and (3) to arrange for and encourage *continuing education* of the association's members in the field of clinical medicine and related areas. The term originated and is defined in the Health Maintenance Organization Act of 1973, P.L. 93-222, Section 1302(5), of the *PHS* Act. IPAs are one source of professional services for *HMOs* and are modeled after *medical foundations.* See also *individual practice plan.*

individual practice plan: Synonymous with a *medical foundation.* Sometimes used to refer specifically to a *health maintenance organization* that obtains professional services from an *individual practice association.*

individual responsibility program (IRP): A private medical relationship between a *patient* and his or her *physician*, under which the patient is directly responsible for compensating the physician.

industrial health services: Health *services* provided by *physicians*, *dentists*, *nurses*, and other health personnel in an industrial environment for the appraisal, protection, and promotion of the health of employees while on the job. *Occupational health services* is now the favored term.

industrial medicine: A medical *specialty* concerned with illness or injury of employees on work sites.

in extremis (Lat.): In the final illness preceding *death.*

infant: Any person under legal age or age of majority, age 18 in most states.

infant mortality: The death rate *(mortality)* of live-born children who have not reached their first birthday, usually measured as the number of infant deaths per 1,000 *live births* in a given area or program and time period. The infant mortality rate is one common measure of *health status.* Infant mortality varies among countries at least partly because the definition is somewhat variable. See also *neonatal mortality* and *perinatal mortality.*

infection control committee: A committee within *hospitals* and *long-term care* facilities responsible for the investigation, control, and prevention of infections within the institution.

infection control nurse: A *registered nurse* assigned responsibility to control the spread of infection within a health care facility.

infectious diseases (ID): Any micro-organism capable of producing infectious disease through a host or environmental condition favorable to the transmission of a pathogenic organism.

infirmary: A historical term to describe any health care *facility, hospital,* or institution where the sick or infirm are treated.

information activity list: Information on the activity of a *patient's* record (i.e., times copied or requested).

informed consent: Consent, preferably in writing, obtained from a *patient* for a specific medical, surgical, or research procedure after the proposed procedure and risks involved have been fully explained in nontechnical terms and are understood by the patient. If the patient is a minor or is incapable of understanding or communicating, such consent must be obtained from a close adult relative, legal guardian, or other person with authority to grant consent.

infringement: A violation of or encroachment on one's rights; a violation of law.

inhalation therapist: One trained in specialized therapies and treatments for *patients* with respiratory disorders. Respiratory therapist is a term more commonly used.

injury: Traumatic (in *insurance*) or *iatrogenic* (in *malpractice*) damage to the body of external origin unexpected by the injured person.

in loco parentis (Lat.): In place of a parent; one acting as a parent as far as legal authority is concerned.

in pari delicto (Lat.): Being in equal fault or sharing the blame.

inpatient: A *patient* who has been admitted at least overnight to a *hospital* or other *health facility* for the purpose of receiving diagnostic, treatment, or other health services. Inpatient care means the care given inpatients. See also *outpatients.*

inpatient, ambulatory: Any *patient* within a health care *facility* who is capable of walking.

inpatient care, unit-mixed: A general nursing or medical care unit that accepts *patients* regardless of *disease* or *treatment* needs.

inpatient census: The total number of inpatients within a *facility* at a particular time.

inpatient programs: Programs that provide services to *patients* who require an intensity of care equivalent to 24-hour nursing supervision.

input measure: A measure of the *quality* of *services* based on the number, type, and quality of *resources* used in the production of the specific services. Medical services are often evaluated by measuring the education and training level of the *provider*, the reputation and *accreditation* of the institution, the number of health personnel involved, or the number of dollars spent, as proxy measures for the quality of the service. Input measures are generally recognized as inferior to *process measures* and *outcome measures,* because they are indirect measures of quality that do not include the actual results, or outcomes, of services. They are often used nonetheless, because people are accustomed to their use and they are easily obtained. See also *output measure.*

inservice education: A program of *continuing education* for health care *providers* within a health care *facility.*

institution for the mentally retarded (IMR): A facility that specializes in the care of the feebleminded and others with mental or learning disabilities or limitations.

institutional health services: Health services delivered on an *inpatient* basis in *hospitals, nursing homes,* or other inpatient institutions and by *health maintenance organizations.* The term may also refer to services delivered on an *outpatient* basis by departments or other organizational units of, or sponsored by, these institutions. The National Health Planning and Resources Development Act of 1974, P.L. 93-6441 (Section 1531(5) of the *PHS* Act) defines the term as services and facilities subject under *HEW* (now *HHS*) *rules* to *Section 1122* review and requires that all institutional, but not noninstitutional, health services be subject to *certificate-of-need* review and periodic review for *appropriateness.*

institutional licensure: A proposed or often recommended *licensure* system (not presently in use in any state) under which medical care institutions would be generally licensed by the state and then be free to hire and use personnel as each saw fit, whether or not the personnel met usual, individual licensure requirements. Using this system, formal education would become only one of many criteria used in assigning employees to particular positions. Institutional licensure is a suggested remedy to the alleged rigidities of the individual personnel licensing and *certification* programs presently in use in health fields. Other criteria could include job experience and inservice training. Arguments in favor of institutional licensure state that it would allow increased job mobility within the health care field and greater institutional efficiency. It would perhaps also foster teamwork and require only one licensing body at the state level rather than the many health licensing agencies presently functioning in each state. From a negative perspective, the system would not end the need for separate licensure of independent *practitioners*. It also assumes that licensure can assure the quality of an institution's services, deprives the *patient* of any assurance that the individual serving the patient has met individual licensure requirements, and indentures individuals providing care to the institutions through which they are licensed.

insurable risk: A *risk* with the following characteristics: (1) it is one of a large homogeneous group of similar risks; (2) the *loss* produced by the risk is definable and quantifiable; (3) the occurrence of loss in individual cases is accidental or fortuitous; (4) the potential loss is large enough to cause hardship; (5) the cost of insuring is economically feasible; (6) the chance of loss is calculable; and (7) it is sufficiently unlikely that loss will occur in many individual cases at the same time so as to constitute an unacceptable risk to the insurer.

insurance: The contractual relationship existing when one party, for a consideration, agrees to reimburse another for loss to a person or thing caused by designated contingencies. The first party is the *insurer;* the second, the *insured;* the contract, the *insurance policy;* the consideration, the *premium;* the person or thing, the *risk;* and the contingency, the *hazard* or *peril.* Insurance characteristically, but not necessarily, involves equitable contributions by the insured, pooling of risks, and the transfer of risks by contract. Insurance may be offered on either a *profit* or nonprofit basis, to *groups* or individuals. See also *social insurance* and *prepayment*.

insurance clause: A clause indicating the parties to a health or other *insurance* contract; setting forth the types of *losses, benefits,* or *services* covered; and defining the *benefits* to be paid.

insurance commissioner: The state official charged with the enforcement of laws pertaining to *insurance* within the state. The commissioner's title, status in government, and responsibilities differ somewhat from state to state, but all states have such an official, regardless of title. The title may be overseer, superintendent of insurance, or director of insurance.

insurance policy: A written contract of *insurance* that defines its terms.

insurance pool: An organization of *insurers* or reinsurers (see *reinsurance*) through which particular types of *risks* are shared or pooled. The *risk* of high *loss* by a particular insurance company is transferred to the group as a whole (the insurance pool) with *premiums,* losses, and *expenses* shared in agreed amounts. The advantage of a pool is that the size of expected losses can be predicted for the pool with much more certainty than for any individual party. Pooling arrangements are often used for catastrophic coverage. Pooling also may be done within a single company by pooling the risks insured under various policies so that high losses incurred by one policy are shared with others. See also *assigned risk*.

insured: The individual or organization protected in case of *loss* under the terms of an *insurance policy*. The insured is not necessarily the *risk,* who is the person protected against risk of loss from *accident* or *sickness* in a health insurance policy. For example, in *group insurance* the employer is the insured; the employees are the risks.

insurer: The party to an *insurance policy* who contracts to pay *losses* or render services to defend the insured.

intensity of service: The quantities of services provided to *patients* in a *hospital.* Intensity can be expressed in terms of a weighted index of services provided or in terms of a set of statistics indicating the average number of laboratory tests, surgical procedures, x-rays, and other services provided per patient or per patient day. Intensity is a function of the type of program and its *case mix.*

intensive care unit (ICU): A specialized *nursing* unit that concentrates in one area within a hospital for seriously ill patients needing constant nursing care and observation. Some intensive care units limit their services to certain types of patients, such as coronary care, surgical intensive care, and newborn intensive care units. See also *progressive patient care.*

intermediary: A public or private agency or organization selected by *providers* of health care that, in turn, enters into agreements with the secretary of Health and Human Services under the *Hospital Insurance Program* (Part A) of *Medicare* to pay *claims* and perform other functions for the secretary with respect to such providers. An intermediary is usually, but not necessarily, a *Blue Cross plan* or private insurance company. See also *carrier* and *fiscal agent.*

intermediary letter (IL): Directive from the *Bureau of Health Insurance* to the *intermediaries* in the *Medicare* program that provides them with *administrative* direction or *policy.* These letters form a numbered series in which the *Social Security Administration* has established much of the policy for the Medicare program.

intermediate care facility (ICF): An institution licensed under state law and recognized under the *Medicaid* program that provides, on a regular basis, health-related care and services to individuals who do not require the degree of care or treatment offered by a *hospital* or *skilled nursing facility,* but who because of their mental or physical condition require care and services (above the level of room and board) available within institutional facilities. Public institutions that care for the mentally retarded (see *mental retardation*) or people with related conditions are also included in this category. The distinction between "health-related care and services" and "room and board" has often proven difficult to make, but it is important because ICFs are subject to quite different *regulation* and coverage than institutions that do not provide health-related care and services. An ICF/MR is an ICF that cares solely or particularly for the mentally retarded.

intern: A medical school graduate completing a one-year program of graduate medical education. Internships are increasingly being replaced by residencies, which lead to specialty certification.

internal medicine (IM): The branch of medicine dealing with diseases or disorders of the internal organs.

International Classification of Diseases adopted for use in the United States (ICDA): A system, as officially adopted by the *USPHS*, for classifying *diseases* and *operations* for the purpose of indexing hospital records that was developed by the *World Health Organization*. It was replaced by ICD-9-CM, International Classification of Diseases, 9th Revision, Clinical Modification. See *ICD-9-CM Diseases Alphabetical Index.*

internist: A *physician* who specializes in the *diagnosis* and *treatment* of *diseases* and disorders of the internal organs.

internship: On-the-job training that is part of a larger educational program. In *medicine,* dentistry, podiatry, and some other health *professions*, it is a one-year program of *graduate medical education* (usually the year following graduation from medical school). Practically all *physicians* take internships, although they are not required for *licensure* in all licensing jurisdictions. An internship usually is required before *staff privileges* are granted by a hospital. *Residencies* are increasingly beginning in the first year after graduation; this practice may gradually eliminate internships.

intravenous team: A group of specially trained *nurses* authorized to administer intravenous therapy under *physician* supervision.

investigational new drug (IND): A *drug* available solely for experimental purposes intended to determine its *safety* and *effectiveness,* but not yet approved by the *Food and Drug Administration (FDA)* for marketing to the general public. *Prescriptions* for the drug are limited to those experts qualified by training and experience to investigate drug safety and effectiveness. Use of an IND in humans requires approval by the FDA of an IND application that provides reports of animal toxicity tests, a description of proposed clinical trials, and a list of the names and qualifications of the investigators. See also *new drug* and *new drug application.*

IOM: See *Institute of Medicine of the National Academy of Sciences.*

isolation bed: A quarantined bed for a *patient* with an infectious or highly communicable *disease.*

Jj

J visa: A special visa category authorized by the U.S. Information and Educational Exchange (Smith-Mundt) Act of 1948. It is a product of the concept of the educational exchange initiated by the Fulbright program. Individuals with J visas may be admitted to the United States for the purpose of pursuing a full-time program of study (such as *residency*), but must be absent from the United States for two years after their studies have ended before they can re-enter as immigrants. In 1970 legislation was passed which eliminated this requirement for *foreign medical graduates* coming to the United States on private funds as long as they are not from a country where their special skills are in short supply. However, waivers may be obtained by these physicians, if their home countries do not object to their immigration to the United States. Waivers are rarely, if ever, denied, primarily for lack of objection from home countries. See also *labor certification* and *Schedule A.*

Joint Commission: See *Joint Commission on Accreditation of Healthcare Organizations.*

Joint Commission on Accreditation of Healthcare Organizations (Joint Commission): A private, nonprofit organization whose purpose is to encourage the attainment of uniformly high *standards* of institutional medical care. Comprising representatives of the *American Hospital Association, American Medical Association,* American College of Physicians, and American College of Surgeons, the organization establishes guidelines for the operation of *hospitals* and other *health facilities* and conducts survey and *accreditation* programs. A staff of medical inspectors visits hospitals and other health organizations by invitation to examine the operation of the hospital, the organization of its medical staff, and its patient records. Hospitals with 25 or more beds are eligible for review. On the basis of inspection reports, the hospital may be granted "full accreditation" (for three years), "provisional accreditation" (one year), or none. Accreditation has been used by, or adopted as a requirement of, specific public programs and funding agencies. Hospitals participating in the *Medicare* program are deemed to have met most *conditions of participation* if they are accredited by the *Joint Commission.*

joint health planning: A collaborative effort of two or more health care organizations to design a strategic plan to provide health care within a geographic area.

joint purchasing agreement: A formal agreement among two or more *health facilities* or programs to purchase professional services, equipment, or *supplies.* The agreements simplify purchasing or result in *economies of scale* intended to lower costs to the programs. The purchased services, equipment, or supplies may be shared or simply distributed among the programs.

J

joint underwriting association (JUA): An association consisting of all *insurers* authorized by a state to write a certain kind of *insurance,* usually some form of liability insurance such as *malpractice insurance.* The association may be required or voluntarily agree to write malpractice insurance on a self-supporting basis. It may write the insurance on an exclusive basis, which means individual carriers cannot write such insurance, or on a nonexclusive basis. The JUA approach has been used in state legislation to assure the availability of malpractice insurance. Examples of the powers given to such associations are included in the medical malpractice insurance legislation enacted in New York where the JUA can issue policies, develop rates, and employ a service company to handle the insurance (including claims adjustment).

jurisdiction: The geographic area within which a court or some other legal or political authority has the right and power to carry out its prescribed activities.

Kk

Kefauver-Harris Amendment: A 1962 amendment to the U.S. Food, Drug, and Cosmetic Act which requires the effectiveness of a new drug to be proven before marketing of the drug is approved. The amendment also applies to medical devices.

Kentucky January: An educational program intended to teach health profession students about the unique problems of providing health care services in a rural community. The project was originally funded by the Division of Associated Health Professions and the Area Health Education System of the Kentucky Council on Higher Education.

Keogh Act plan: A plan, available since 1963, under the Self-Employed Individual's Tax Retirement Act (Keogh Act), which permits a self-employed individual (such as a private physician) to establish a formal retirement plan including himself or herself and to obtain tax advantages similar to those available for qualified corporate pension plans. Self-employed individuals can annually set aside up to 15 percent of earned *income* or $7,500, whichever is less, and take a *tax deduction* for it.

Kerr-Mills: A common name for the Social Security Amendments of 1960 that expanded and modified the federal government's existing responsibility to assist the states in paying for medical care for the aged poor. The Act liberalized federal sharing in *vendor payments* for medical care under the federal/state old-age cash assistance program. It also created a new public assistance category—Medical Assistance for the Aged (MAA). The *medically indigent* eligible for assistance under this program were persons age 65 or older whose incomes were high enough that they were not eligible for old-age assistance but who needed help in meeting the

K

costs of their medical care. The federal share of medical payments ranged between 50 and 80 percent, depending on the per capita income of the states, with no limitation on the maximum amount of payment. The Social Security Amendments of 1965 established the *Medicaid* program, which substituted a single program of federal assistance for medical vendor payments under the categorical cash assistance and MAA programs. The concept of medical indigency was extended to needy disabled and blind persons and to dependent children and their families.

key primary individual: The first health care *professional* who treats for general health care (e.g., *family physician* or *internist*).

kickback: An unlawful or unethical *referral* fee paid by a *provider* or a *supplier* to a person referring the case or deal.

kiting: Increasing the quantity of a *drug* ordered by *prescription.* Either the *patient* or *pharmacist* may kite the quantity of the original prescription, for example, by adding zeros to the number shown on the prescription. When this is done by a pharmacist, he or she provides the patient with the quantity originally prescribed but bills a *third party,* such as *Medicaid,* for the larger quantity. When the prescription is altered by a patient, it is often because the patient abuses the drug in question. See also *shorting* and *fraud.*

K

labeling: All labels and other written, printed, or graphic matter upon or accompanying a food, *drug, device*, or cosmetic, or any containers or wrappers (Section 201(m) of the federal Food, Drug, and Cosmetic Act). Labeling for these products is regulated by the *FDA*; advertising for the products (with the exception of *prescription drugs*) is regulated by the Federal Trade Commission. Labeling must not contain any false or misleading statements and must include adequate directions for use, unless exempt by regulation. Courts have taken a broad view of the term in FDA cases. Labeling includes all written material associated with a product (including leaflets, books, and reprints of journal articles or materials that explain or are designed to be used with the product) and point-of-purchase display material (such as placards and signs). Written material need not have been provided to the purchaser at the same time as the product to be considered labeling. See also *package insert, Physicians' Desk Reference*, and *compendium*.

labor certification: *Certification* by the U.S. Department of Labor required of certain aliens (such as *foreign medical graduates*) seeking to immigrate to the United States in order to work before they may obtain a visa. People in occupations that the Department of Labor considers in short supply throughout the country (such as physicians and nurses, but not dentists) are granted such certification after review of the applicant's qualifications (for example, *Educational Commission for Foreign Graduates* certification). See also *Schedule A* and *J visa*.

labor room: A specially equipped room in a *maternity ward* for women who are in labor.

laissez faire: A political view that government should play little or no role in regulating (health care) markets.

Lanham Act: A 1964 federal law controlling the use of trademarks and copyrights.

lapsed funds: In the federal *budget,* unobligated *budget authority* that by law has ceased to be available for *obligation* due to expiration of its period of availability.

laryngology (LAR): The branch of medicine dealing with diseases or disorders of the larynx or throat.

last-dollar coverage: *Insurance* coverage without upper limits or maximums no matter how great the *benefits* payable. See also *first-dollar coverage.*

latent defect: A defect that is not readily observable and may violate the implied warranty that goods are merchantable.

law: Any enforceable set of rules to control acts or behavior or to define rights and responsibilities.

legal medicine (LM): The branch of medicine dealing with forensic sciences or the use of medical data or findings for use in legal proceedings.

legend: The statement "Caution: Federal law prohibits dispensing without prescription," required by Section 503(b)(4) of the federal Food, Drug, and Cosmetic Act as a part of the *labeling* of all *prescription drugs* (and only such drugs). Legend drug is thus synonymous with prescription or ethical drug.

legislate: To create, enact, renew, or revoke laws.

legislative authority: The act or statute that grants to an *administrative agency* the authority to enact *regulations.*

legislative history: The written record of an Act of Congress. It may be used in writing *rules* or used by courts in interpreting the law and to ascertain or detail the intent of the Congress if the Act is ambiguous or lacking in detail. The legislative history is listed in the *slip law* and consists of the House, Senate, and *conference* committee reports (if any) and the House and Senate floor debates on the law. The history, particularly the committee reports, often contains the only available complete explanation of the meaning and intent of the law.

length of stay (LOS): The length of an *inpatient's* stay in a *hospital* or other *health facility.* It is one measure of the use of health facilities, reported as an average number of days spent in a facility per *admission* or discharge. It is calculated as follows: total number of days in the facility for all discharges and *deaths* occurring during a period divided by the number of discharges and deaths during the same period. In *concurrent review* an appropriate length of stay may be assigned each patient upon admission. Average lengths of stay vary and are measured for people with various ages, specific diagnoses, or sources of payment, such as in setting *DRGs.*

length-of-stay certification: A written *physician's* order certifying that the continued stay in a health care *facility* is within the criteria of being medically necessary, thus justifying the extension of patient care beyond the *DRG* length of stay.

lethal: Capable of causing death.

level of care: The extent or degree of care required for a particular *illness* or patient condition. In *long-term care*, the levels of care are classified as personal care, intermediate care, and skilled nursing care in increasing order of severity.

level-of-care criteria: The standards adopted to determine the acceptable and appropriate level of care for a particular *patient.*

levels of service: The time required for the prevention, diagnosis, and treatment of an *illness*. Seven time periods are recognized: minimal, brief, limited, intermediate, extended, comprehensive, and usually complex.

liability: Something one is bound to do, or an obligation one is bound to fulfill, by law. A liability may be enforced in court. Liabilities are usually financial or can be expressed in financial terms. Also, liability refers to the probable cost of meeting a legal obligation.

Liaison Committee on Graduate Medical Education (LCGME): A subgroup of the *Coordinating Council on Medical Education* that serves as the *accrediting* agency for *graduate medical education*. The committee includes representatives of the American Board of Medical Specialties; *American Hospital Association, American Medical Association, Association of American Medical Colleges*, and Council on Medical Specialty Societies.

Liaison Committee on Medical Education (LCME): A joint committee of the *American Medical Association (AMA)* and the *Association of American Medical Colleges (AAMC)* responsible for *accrediting* medical schools. Established in 1942, the LCME is recognized for this purpose by the U.S. Commissioner of Education and the National Commission on Accrediting. The committee is made up of six representatives of the AMA Council on Medical Education, six representatives of the AAMC Executive Council, two representatives of the public, and one representative of the federal government. All American medical schools are now accredited, but different types and grades of accreditation are not constant among schools. In addition to accreditation the LCME and the two associations it represents also perform advisory functions for the medical schools with respect to their programs. See also *Liaison Committee on Graduate Medical Education, Coordinating Council for Medical Education*, and *Educational Commission for Foreign Medical Graduates*.

license: A permission or right granted to an individual or organization by competent authority, usually public, to engage in a *practice,* occupation, or activity otherwise unlawful. *Licensure* is the process by which the license is granted. A license is needed to begin lawful *practice.* It is generally granted on the basis of examination, proof of education, or both, rather than on measures of performance. A license is usually granted on a permanent basis, but it may be conditioned on annual payment of a fee, proof of *continuing education,* or proof of competence. Common grounds for revocation of a license include incompetence, commission of a crime (whether or not related to the licensed practice), or moral turpitude. Possession of a medical license from one state may (*reciprocity*) or may not suffice to obtain a license from another. See *national board examinations* and *Federation Licensing Examination.* See also *accreditation, certification,* and *institutional licensure.*

licensure: Describes an individual or facility holding authorization from an agency or approving body authorizing certain acts or engaging in certain occupations.

licensed practical nurse (LPN): A *nurse* who has practical experience in the provision of *nursing care* but who is not a graduate of a formal program of nursing education (see e.g., *diploma school*). The education, required experience, *licensure,* and job responsibilities of LPNs are fairly variable and are below the standards set for *registered nurses (RNs).*

licensed vocational nurse (LVN): See *licensed practical nurse.*

lien: A legal encumbrance against property arising from a claim of indebtedness.

life care centers: Retirement communities that furnish residents with housing, meals, housekeeping, recreation, and comprehensive health care for a monthly fee.

life costs: *Mortality, morbidity,* and suffering associated with a given medical procedure or *disease*. Life costs of *diagnosis* and *therapy* may be contrasted with their financial *costs,* the money required for their provision. Life costs of treating a disease can be compared with the mortality, morbidity, and suffering (life costs) resulting from the untreated disease, while financial costs are compared with the various monetary costs of not treating the disease. Use of life costs in assessing the costs of medical procedures avoids the need for assigning dollar values to mortality and morbidity.

life expectancy: The average span of time an individual born at a certain point in time can expect to live, based on statistical extrapolations. See *longevity*.

life review: In *gerontology*, a reappraisal of worth and redefinition of one's purpose in life.

Life Safety Code: A fire safety code prepared by the National Fire Protection Association. The provisions of this code relating to hospitals and nursing facilities must be met (except in instances where a waiver is granted) by facilities certified for participation under *Medicare* and *Medicaid*. The secretary of Health and Human Services may accept a state's fire and safety code in lieu of the most current edition of the Life Safety Code, if it is determined that the state code is imposed by law and will provide adequate protection for *inpatients* of nursing facilities. The national code is based on the Southern Standard Building Code, which contains optimum (not minimum) standards.

life table: In *insurance,* a tabulated statement presenting *mortality* and survivor characteristics of a given population (for example, employed men aged 20 to 25). It is used in *underwriting* to calculate risks.

lifetime disability benefit: A continuing payment to a disabled person under a disability policy to help replace lost income as long as he or she is disabled.

lifetime prevalence: The proportion of a population that has suffered a particular disease or illness at some point in life.

lifetime reserve: In the *hospital insurance program* of *Medicare,* a reserve of 60 days of inpatient hospital care available over an individual's lifetime that the individual may use after using the maximum 90 days allowed in a single *benefit period.* See also *spell of illness.*

limited insurance: A contract that covers only specified accidents or illnesses as opposed to comprehensive insurance covering all, or virtually all, injuries or illnesses.

limits on liability: In *insurance,* limits on dollar coverage contained in an insurance policy. *Malpractice insurance* generally contains such limits on the amounts payable for an individual claim or in the policy year, for example, $100,000 to $200,000, and $300,000 to $600,000, respectively. Excess coverage describes insurance with limits higher than conventional amounts. It also may be used to refer to limits on *professional liability* imposed by law. Several states have enacted legislation, for example, that places a limit on any malpractice award. Such laws are being challenged as to their legality and, in some instances, have been ruled unconstitutional.

lineal relationship: The direct-line relationship of one to his or her ancestors.

liquidated claim or debt: One that is set or fixed by agreement or court order.

listed: A certification that equipment or material used in a health care facility either meets nationally recognized standards or has been tested and found suitable for use in a specified manner.

Lister, Baron Joseph (1827-1912): The last and best known of an interesting line of English Quaker physicians and the father of modern antiseptic surgery. He applied Pasteur's germ theories of disease to surgery and proved that sterile conditions prevent surgical infections.

live birth: The complete expulsion or extraction of the product of conception from its mother, regardless of the duration of the pregnancy, that breathes or shows any other evidence of life after separation, such as beating of the heart, pulsation of the umbilical cord, or definite movement of voluntary muscles, whether or not the umbilical cord has been cut or the placenta is attached. Each product of such a birth is considered live born. It should be noted that this definition includes no requirement that the product of conception be viable or capable of independent life and thus includes very early and patently nonviable fetuses. This has meant that the definition is often not strictly applied, suggesting the need for the addition of viability *criteria* or the use of a different term (e.g., viable birth) that includes such criteria.

live-in unit: A room or facility maintained in a *hospital* for use by parents who desire to be with their hospitalized children.

living will: A legal document expressing wishes that in the event of prolonged and irreversible *illness* or *injury*, the party signing the living will be allowed to die without efforts to prolong life by artificial means.

loading: In *insurance,* the amount added to the actuarial value of the *coverage* (expected or average amounts payable to the *insured)* to cover the expense to the *insurer* of securing and maintaining the business (i.e., the amount added to the pure premium needed to meet anticipated *liabilities* for expenses, contingencies, *profits,* or special situations). Loading costs for *group* health *insurance* range from 5 to 25 percent of premiums; for individual health insurance they often go as high as 50 percent.

lobbying: Efforts, by the provision of information, argument or other means by anybody other than a citizen acting in his or her own behalf, to influence government officials in the performance of their duties. Federal legislation (Title III of the Legislative Reorganization Act of 1946) does not define the terms lobbying or lobbyist. The Act requires registration by any person "who, by himself or through any agent or employee or other persons in any manner whatsoever, directly or indirectly, solicits, collects, or receives money or any other thing of value to be used principally to aid or the principal purpose of which person is to aid . . . the passage or defeat of any legislation by the Congress." Paid lobbyists are required to register with the clerk of the House and the secretary of the Senate and to file quarterly financial reports with the House clerk. The Act has been subject to considerable criticism for apparent loopholes that allow many interests to avoid registering. The term derives from the frequent presence of lobbyists in the lobbies of congressional and other governmental chambers.

locality: In *Medicare,* the geographic area from which a *carrier* derives its *prevailing charges* for the purposes of making *reasonable charge* determinations. A locality is commonly a political or economic subdivision of a state and should include a cross section of the population with respect to economic and other characteristics. See also *catchment area* and *health service area.*

L

locality rule: In *malpractice,* an evidentiary rule that bases the *standard* of care a *physician* owes a *patient* on the standard of care generally attained in the specific locality. The most restrictive form of the rule compares the measurement of a physician's duty of care to a patient with the degree of care, skill, and diligence used by physicians, generally, in the same locality or community. A less restrictive form holds that a physician owes that degree of care to a patient that is exercised by physicians, generally, in the same or similar localities or communities. The rationale for the more expansive rule, being applied more widely by courts today, is that the earlier emphasis on locality is no longer appropriate in light of better communications and standardization of hospital procedures and physician *licensure* brought about by state statutes and regulations.

longevity: The life expectancy of an individual.

longitudinal health record: A patient record containing medical information from date of birth to current date.

long-term care: Health and personal care services required by persons who are chronically ill, aged, disabled, or retarded on a long-term basis in an institution or a home. The term is often used more narrowly to refer only to long-term institutional care, such as that provided in *nursing homes,* homes for the retarded, and mental hospitals. *Ambulatory services* and *home health care* provided on a long-term basis are seen as *alternatives to long-term institutional care.*

LOS: See *length of stay.*

loss: In *insurance,* the basis for a *claim* under the terms of an *insurance policy.* It refers to any diminution of quantity, quality, value of property, or personal health resulting from the occurrence of some *peril* or *hazard.*

low option: See *high option.*

LPN: See *licensed practical nurse.*

Mm

MAC: See *Maximum Allowable Cost Program.*

mail-order insurance: Health and other disability *insurance* purchased in response to solicitation by mail and advertising. It usually requires no physical examination, but rather a statement of health completed by the *insured*, and becomes effective upon return of the application by mail and approval by the mail-order *insurer*. The abbreviated health information required, the complexities of medical histories, and the relative difficulty of excluding *pre-existing conditions* have contributed to relatively high *premiums, loadings,* and low rates of claims recovery.

maintenance services: Continued medical services provided to individuals with chronic physical and mental conditions in order to avoid further medical deterioration.

major diagnostic categories (MDC): A broad diagnosis classification used as a precursor to the present *DRG* classification system.

major medical: *Insurance* designed to offset heavy medical expenses resulting from catastrophic or prolonged *illness* or *injury*. Generally, the policies do not provide *first-dollar coverage,* but do provide benefit payments of 75 to 80 percent of all types of medical expenses above a certain base amount paid by the *insured*. Many major medical policies sold as private insurance contain maximums on the total amount that will be paid (such as $50,000); thus, they do not provide *last-dollar coverage* or complete protection against catastrophic costs. However, there is a trend toward unlimited plans.

major secondary diagnosis: Under *DRGs*, a new *disease* or *illness* associated with the original illness that requires additional *treatment* during the patient's original stay.

M

major surgery: Surgery in which the operative procedure is considered hazardous. Major surgery is frequently distinguished from *minor surgery* according to whether or not it requires a general anesthetic, involves an amputation above the ankle or wrist, or includes entering one of the body cavities (abdomen, chest, or head).

majority: (1) Being of lawful age, beyond the age of infancy; (2) more than half.

malefactor: One who has committed a wrong or a crime.

malfeasance: Committing a negligent, improper, illegal, or wrongful act.

malingering: The willful, deliberate, and *fraudulent* feigning or exaggeration of the symptoms of *illness* or *injury* for the purpose of collecting *insurance* or *some* other types of benefits.

malpractice: *Professional* misconduct or lack of ordinary skill in the performance of a professional act. A practitioner is liable for damages or injuries caused by malpractice. Professional liability can be covered by *malpractice insurance* that pays for the costs of defending suits instituted against the professional and any damages assessed by the court up to a maximum limit set in the policy. Malpractice requires that the patient prove some *injury* and that the injury was negligently caused. See also *professional liability, charitable* immunity, *governmental* immunity, *claims-incurred policy, claims-made policy, contingency fees, defensive medicine, discovery rule, New Jersey rule, locality rule, joint underwriting association, limits on liability, res ipsa loquiter, respondeat superior, screening panels, sponsored malpractice insurance,* and *warranty*.

malpractice insurance: *Insurance* against the *risk* of suffering financial damage because of a *malpractice* claim.

maltreatment: Wrongful *treatment* of a *patient* usually implying neglect or abandonment.

managed care: A comprehensive, planned, and coordinated program of health care with emphasis on preventative care. Managed care is usually associated with *HMO* programs.

management: The organization and control of human activity directed toward specific ends. See *administration* for further discussion of these two closely related terms. Different forms of management are sometimes described, for example, by exception, in which only exceptions from defined *policy* are reported and acted on, and by *objective,* in which clearly stated objectives are used to guide the management process.

management information system (MIS): A system (frequently automated or computer-based) that produces the necessary information in proper form and at appropriate intervals for the *management* of a program or other activity. The system ideally measures program progress toward *objectives* and reports costs and problems needing attention. Special efforts have been made in the *Medicaid* program to develop information systems for each state program.

mandamus: An order from a court to a public official or agency commanding it to perform a responsibility that is its lawful duty to perform.

mandatory licensure: State laws that make professional *licensure* a compulsory requirement for *practice.*

manpower: The level, type, and quantity of personnel needed to achieve set goals.

MAP: See *medical audit program.*

marginal cost: In (health) economics, the change in the total *cost* of producing services that results from a small or unit change in the quantity of services being produced. Marginal cost is the appropriate cost concept to consider when contemplating program expansion or contraction. *Economies of scale* will result from the expansion of a program when marginal cost is less than average or unit cost. Marginal cost is the cost of producing the last item.

marginal tax rate: The tax rate, or percentage, that is applied to the last increment of income for purposes of computing income tax.

markup: In Congress, a meeting of a congressional committee at which the committee itself writes law to recommend to the full Congress, makes decisions on *appropriations,* or otherwise makes *policy.* The meeting usually takes place after public hearings on the subject matter. See also *executive session.* In economics, the term refers to a profit expressed as a percentile of product cost.

Massachusetts General Hospital's Multi-Programming System (MUMPS): One of the first computer languages developed for the health care field. MUMPS was created by the Massachusetts General Hospital to handle voluminous medical data with an easily updated system featuring ease of use and flexibility.

master patient index: A master list or index that helps locate and identify patient health records and charts.

M

matching grants or funds: The equal funding of a project or program between donor and donee.

maternal and child health services (MCH): Organized health and social services for mothers (particularly as they *need family planning* and pregnancy-related services), their children, and (rarely) fathers. Mothers and children are often considered particularly vulnerable populations with special health needs and their health to be a matter of high public priority. They are particularly benefited by *preventive medicine.* Therefore, these services are sometimes separately organized and funded from other health services. One example is the

Maternal and Child Health Program operated by the federal government under the authority of Title V of the Social Security Act.

maternal mortality rate: The number of deaths attributed to the birth process (usually per 1,000).

maternity benefits: Coverage under *insurance* for the costs of pregnancy, labor, and delivery, and, in some cases, *family planning,* postpartum care, and complications of pregnancy. Health insurance policies take different approaches and apply different conditions to maternity benefits. See also *exclusions, flat maternity, swap maternity,* and *switch maternity.*

maternity ward: The unit within a hospital equipped and staffed for birthing. There are many new maternal care concepts; therefore, the term is less often used.

maximization: The manipulation or exaggeration of census data to increase hospital reimbursement; also changing *ICD-9-CM* final diagnosis codes to cause a higher-paying *DRG.* The practice is fraudulent.

Maximum Allowable Cost (MAC) Program: A federal program that limits reimbursement for *prescription drugs* under the *Medicare* and *Medicaid* programs and Public Health Service projects to the lowest cost at which the drug is generally available. Specifically, the program limits reimbursement for drugs under programs administered by *HHS* to the lowest of the maximum allowable cost (MAC) of the drug, if any, plus a reasonable *dispensing fee,* the *acquisition cost* of the drug plus a dispensing fee, or the provider's *usual charge* or *customary charge* to the general public for the drug. The MAC is the lowest unit price at which a drug available from several sources or manufacturers can be purchased on a national basis and without significant inconvenience.

McCarran-Ferguson Act: The act of March 9, 1945 (15 U.S.C.

M

1011-15) declaring a general policy that federal laws regulating or affecting business and commerce are not to be interpreted as affecting the *insurance* business unless specifically provided for. It is also known as the McCarran-Wiler Bill (S. 1508) and Public Law 15. Prior to a Supreme Court decision in 1944, insurance was not considered a matter of commerce and thus not subject to federal law. When the Supreme Court found insurance to be a matter of commerce, it became necessary to clarify the effect on the insurance industry of existing federal law. The act has the effect of leaving regulation of insurance to the states unless specifically undertaken in federal law. The payment of benefits to providers by insurers is not an exempt activity under the federal antitrust laws.

MCHR: Medical Committee for Human Rights.

MD: Doctor of Medicine.

MDC: See *major diagnostic categories.*

"me too" drug: A *drug* that is identical, similar, or closely related to a drug product for which a *new drug application (NDA)* has been approved. Many "me too" drugs on the market are essentially copies of approved *new drugs* but were introduced by their manufacturers without Food and Drug Administration approval on the theory that the NDA holder, or pioneer drug, had become generally recognized as *safe* and *effective.* Other "me too" products are being marketed with abbreviated new drug applications (ANDAs) that require the submission of manufacturing, *bioavailability,* and *labeling* information, but not data relating to safety and effectiveness, which are assumed to be established. See also GRAS and GRAE.

Meals on Wheels: One of several *long-term care* support *services* offered the elderly who are unable to prepare their own meals. Low-cost, nutritional meals are delivered to the individuals' homes on a regular basis.

Medex: *Physician assistant* programs developed specifically for former military medical corpsmen with independent duty experience. They train physician assistants, especially for *general practitioners* in rural areas. Most Medex, as graduates of the programs are called, have been trained to work with specific physicians. The first program was begun in 1969 at the University of Washington in cooperation with the Washington State Medical Association. The programs generally consist of 3 to 12 months of university training and 12 months of preceptorship.

mediation: A third party who attempts to resolve disputes but who has no authority to bind either party by decree.

medic: (1) Jargon for *physician*; (2) a military corpsman trained to administer aid in combat.

Medicaid (Title XIX): A federally aided, state-operated and administered program that provides medical *benefits* for certain low-income persons in need of health and medical care. The program, authorized by Title XIX of the Social Security Act, is basically for the *poor*. It does not cover all of the poor, however, but only persons who are members of one of the categories of people eligible for cash assistance programs—the aged, the blind, the disabled, and members of families with dependent children where one parent is absent, incapacitated, or unemployed. Under certain circumstances states may provide Medicaid coverage for children under 21 who are not *categorically related*. Subject to broad federal guidelines, states determine the benefits covered, program eligibility, rates of payment for *providers*, and methods of administering the program.

Medicaid mill: A health program that primarily serves *Medicaid* beneficiaries, typically on an *ambulatory* basis. The mills originated in the ghettos of New York City and are still found primarily in urban slums. They are usually organized on a for-*profit* basis, characterized by their great productivity, and frequently accused of a variety of *abuses* (such as *ping-ponging* and *family ganging*).

Medi-Cal: California's *Medicaid* program.

Medical Assistance Program: The health care program for the *poor* authorized by Title XIX of the Social Security Act, commonly known as *Medicaid*.

medical audit: Detailed retrospective review and evaluation of selected *medical records* by qualified *professional* staff. Medical audits are used in some *hospitals, group practices,* and occasionally in private, independent practices for evaluating professional performance by comparing it with accepted *criteria standards* and current professional judgment. A medical audit may be concerned with the care given in a specific *illness;* it is undertaken to identify deficiencies prior to establishing educational programs to improve care for the illness. See also *concurrent review* and *medical care evaluation studies.*

Medical Audit Program (MAP): An extension of the *Professional Activity Study (PAS)*, in which data are contained in comprehensive quarterly hospital reports according to department. The reports are primarily used by hospital clinical departments to conduct comprehensive *medical audits* and retrospective *utilization reviews.* See also *Commission on Professional and Hospital Activities.*

medical care evaluation study (MCE study): Retrospective medical care review that involves an in-depth assessment of the *quality* and nature of the use of selected health services or programs. Evaluation of an MCE study assesses the *effectiveness* of corrective actions taken to correct deficiencies identified in the original study, but does not necessarily repeat or replicate the original study. *Utilization review* requirements under *Medicare* and *Medicaid* require *utilization review committees* in *hospitals* and *skilled nursing facilities* to have at least one MCE study in progress at all times. These studies are also required by the *PRO* program.

Medical College Admission Test (MCAT): A nationally standardized test generally required or strongly recommended by nearly all medical schools in the United States as part of their admission

M

process. The results of the test are evaluated along with other evidence of the student's ability to handle medical school course work by the admissions committee. The test, administered by the Psychological Corporation, is designed to provide objective measures of academic ability and achievement by testing of verbal ability, quantitative ability, science knowledge, and general information. It does not measure motivation, the nature or sincerity of interest in the study of medicine, or the personal characteristics that are of basic importance to the practitioner or teacher of medicine.

Medical Committee for Human Rights (MCHR): Generally a standing committee within a hospital responsible for peer review to prevent experimentation on or unwarranted treatment of patients.

Medical Consumer Price Index (MCPI): That portion of the *Consumer Price Index (CPI)* that reflects increased medical costs over the preceding year.

medical deduction: The federal income *tax deduction* for expenditures on health insurance and other medical expenses in excess of three percent of *income*. In effect, this is the only *national health insurance* program in the United States, with a *deductible* of three percent of income and *coinsurance* of one minus the *marginal tax rate*. No standards are set for the type of health insurance that must be purchased if expenditures are to be deductible. Deductible medical expenses are very broadly defined and include the services of physicians, dentists, podiatrists, optometrists, chiropractors, and Christian Science practitioners. The cost of prescribed *drugs, supplies,* and special diets is also deductible.

medical device: See *device*.

medical eligibility: Refers to individuals eligible for *Medicare* Part A hospital *insurance* benefits, generally those age 65 and older.

medical emergency: The sudden and unexpected onset of a severe

M

disorder demanding immediate medical attention.

medical examiner: (1) A coroner or other public official empowered to certify *death*, (2) a *physician* who examines applicants for *insurance*.

medical expense insurance: A *health insurance* policy that provides reimbursement for outpatient medical care and *physician* office visits.

medical foundation: An organization of *physicians,* generally sponsored by a state or local medical association; also may be called a foundation for medical care. It is a separate and autonomous corporation with its own board of directors. Every physician member of the medical society may apply for membership in the foundation and, upon acceptance, participate in all its activities. A foundation's concerns generally consist of delivery of medical services at reasonable cost, the right of free choice of physician and *hospital* by the *patient, fee-for-service* reimbursement, and local *peer review*. Many foundations operate as *prepaid group practices* or as *individual practice associations* for an *HMO*. They are usually prepaid on a *capitation* basis for services to some or all of their patients, but pay their individual members on a fee-for-service basis. Some foundations are organized only for peer review purposes or other specific functions.

Medical Group Management Association (MGMA): The official association for administrators and managers of medical groups, *clinics*, *group practices*, and similar organizations.

Medical Impairment Bureau (MIB): A clearinghouse of information on people who have applied for *life insurance* in the past. Any adverse medical findings on previous medical examinations are recorded in code and used by companies subscribing to the service. Confidentiality questions, especially with respect to information produced by medical examinations, are major objections to MIBs (see *confidential*).

Medical Indemnity of America, Inc. (MIA): A *stock insurance company* organized in Ohio in 1950 by *Blue Shield plans* to serve as a national enrollment agency, to assist individual plans in negotiating contracts, and to serve large national accounts in which two or more plans are involved. See also *Health Service, Inc.*

medical indigency: The condition of having insufficient *income* to pay for adequate medical care without depriving oneself or *dependents* of food, clothing, shelter, and other essentials of living. Medical indigency also may occur when self-supporting individuals, who are able to provide basic maintenance for themselves and their *families* under ordinary conditions, are unable to finance the cost of medical care during catastrophic illnesses. See also *medically indigent, spend down,* and *medically needy.*

medical jurisprudence: See *forensic medicine.*

medical laboratory assistant: An individual who works under the direct supervision of a *medical technologist,* pathologist, *physician,* or qualified scientist in performing routine laboratory procedures requiring basic technical skills and minimal independent judgment in chemistry, *hematology,* and microbiology. *Certification* is awarded by a board of registry following successful completion of an examination. Prerequisites for the examination include a high school diploma or equivalent, either graduation from a school approved by the American Medical Association or completion of a basic military laboratory course, and a year of experience in the field.

M

medical laboratory technology: An educational program that trains individuals to perform bacteriological, biological, and chemical tests under the direct supervision of a pathologist or microbiologist and to provide resultant data to *physicians.*

Medical Literature Analysis and Retrieval System (MEDLARS): A computerized database literature search system tied into Dental Literature, Nursing Index, and Index Medicus.

medical necessity: A term used when it is medically contraindicated under *Medicare* criteria for a *patient* to leave his or her household.

medical practice: Generally the practice of a particular branch of medicine including osteopathic medicine.

medical record: A record kept for each *patient* containing sufficient information to identify the patient, to justify the *diagnosis* and *treatment,* and to document the results accurately. The purposes of the record are to (1) serve as the basis for planning and continuity of patient care; (2) provide a means of communication among *physicians* and other *professionals* contributing to the patient's care; (3) furnish documentary evidence of the patient's course of *illness* and treatment; (4) serve as a basis for review, study, and evaluation; (5) serve in protecting the legal interests of the patient, hospital, and responsible practitioner; and (6) provide data for use in research and education. The content of the record is *confidential.* See also *problem-oriented medical record* and *health record.*

medical record administrator: A *professional* who plans, designs, develops, and manages systems of patient administrative and clinical data and patient *medical records* in all types of health care institutions. The minimum educational requirement for professional registration as medical record administrator is a baccalaureate degree in a medical record science or medical record administration in a program *accredited* by the *American Medical Association* in collaboration with the *American Medical Record Association* (*AMRA*). The AMRA maintains a list of persons who have successfully completed the national registration examination that qualifies them to use the professional designation of registered record administrator. Recent graduates must meet a *continuing education* requirement five years after initial registration. The administrator is the most highly trained of several types of medical records personnel, including the *medical record technician.* See *registered record administrator.*

M

medical record technician: An individual who provides records assistance and ancillary services to a medical record administrator. General duties usually include compilation and maintenance of medical records and coding of symptoms, diseases, operations, procedures, and other therapies according to standard classification systems.

medical review: A review, required by *Medicaid,* conducted by a team of physicians and other appropriate health and social service personnel of the condition and need for care, including a medical evaluation, of each *inpatient* in a *long-term care* facility. By law, the team must review the (1) care provided in the facility; (2) adequacy of the services available in the facility to meet the current health *needs* and promote the maximum physical well-being of the patient; (3) *necessity* and desirability   of the continued placement of the patient in the facility; and (4) feasibility of meeting the patient's health care needs through alternate institutional or noninstitutional services. Medical review differs from *utilization review* in that it requires evaluation of each individual patient and an analysis of the *appropriateness* of his or her specific treatment in the institution, whereas utilization review is often performed on a sample basis with special attention to certain procedures, conditions, or *lengths of stay.* See also *continued stay review.*

Medical Services Administration (MSA): The bureau that *administers* the *Medicaid* program at the federal level. It is part of the *Social and Rehabilitation Service,* which administers most of the social service programs within the *Department of Health and Human Services.* Direct administration of Medicaid programs is carried out by the states.

M

medical social worker: An individual who coordinates social services for patients who need them. The social worker helps to solve or alleviate social and emotional factors of medical problems and usually counsels the patients and their families.

medical staff: Collectively, the *physicians, dentists,* and other *professionals* responsible for medical care in a *health facility,* typically a *hospital.* The staff may be full time or part time and employed or not employed by the hospital. It may include all professionals (open staff) or just those who meet various standards of competence (closed staff). *Staff privileges* may or may not be permanent or conditioned on continued evidence of competence or other criteria of eligibility.

medical staff bylaws: The written rules and regulations that define the duties, responsibilities, and rights of *physicians* and other health *professionals* who are part of a facility's medical staff.

medical technologist: A specially trained individual who performs a wide range of complex and specialized procedures in all general areas of a clinical laboratory. Approximately two-thirds of all medical technologists are employed in hospital laboratories. Others are employed in physicians' private laboratories; clinics; the armed forces; city, state, and federal health agencies; industrial medical laboratories; pharmaceutical houses; and numerous public and private research programs. There are several certification programs in medical technology. Minimum educational requirements may be a baccalaureate degree with appropriate science course requirements, a 12-month structured medical technology program approved by the *American Medical Association,* and an examination, or may be a baccalaureate degree with appropriate science course requirements and experience. The medical technologist is the most highly trained of several types of clinical laboratory personnel, including the medical laboratory technician and *medical laboratory assistant.*

medical trade area: A geographic area from which one or more specified *providers* draw their *patients.* The term is similar to *catchment area* except that it is defined by the patients rather than by the provider.

medically indigent: A person who is too impoverished to meet medical expenses. The term currently refers to persons whose *income* is too low for them to afford routine medical care, although they are able to pay for their basic living costs, or to persons with generally adequate income who suddenly face catastrophic medical bills. See also *medical indigency, medically needy,* and *spend down.*

medically needy: A term used in the *Medicaid* program for persons who have enough *income* and *resources* to pay their basic living expenses (and so do not need public assistance) but not enough to pay for medical care. Medicaid law requires that the standard for income used by a state to determine if someone is medically needy cannot exceed 133 percent of the maximum amount paid to a family of similar size under the *Aid to Families with Dependent Children (AFDC)* program. In order to be eligible as medically needy, individuals must fall into one of the categories of people who are covered under the cash assistance programs; these include the aged, blind, disabled, and members of families with dependent children where one parent is absent, incapacitated, or unemployed. They receive Medicaid benefits if their income after deducting medical expenses (see *spend down*) is low enough to meet the eligibility standard.

medically underserved area: A geographic location (i.e., an urban or rural area) with insufficient *health resources* to meet the medical *needs* of the resident population. For example, *a physician shortage area* applies to an area with an inadequate number of *physicians* for the population. An underserved area also may be defined in relation to the *health status* of the resident population. An area with an unhealthy population is considered underserved. The term is used in several sections of the *PHS Act* and appropriately defined to give priority to these areas for federal assistance.

medically underserved population: The population of an urban or rural area with a shortage of personal health services or another type of population group with a shortage of these services. A medically underserved population may not reside in a particular *medically underserved area* or be defined by its place of residence. Thus migrants, Native Americans, or the inmates of a prison or mental hospital may constitute such a population. The term is defined and used in the *PHS Act* in order to give certain populations priority for federal assistance (e.g., in the *HMO* and *National Health Service Corps* programs).

Medicare (Title XVIII): A nationwide *health insurance* program for people aged 65 and older, for persons who have been eligible for social security disability payments for more than two years, and for certain workers and their dependents who need kidney transplantation or dialysis. Health insurance protection is available to *insured* persons without regard to *income*. Monies from *payroll taxes* and *premiums* from *beneficiaries* are deposited in special *trust funds* for use in meeting the expenses incurred by the insured. The program, called Health Insurance for the Aged, was enacted July 30, 1965, as Title XVIII of the Social Security Act, and became effective July 1, 1966. It consists of two separate but coordinated programs: the *Hospital Insurance Program (Part A)* and the *Supplementary Medical Insurance Program (Part B).*

medication order: A physician's order for a *drug* to be procured from the *pharmacy* or *drug room* and administered to an inpatient within a facility.

medicine: The art and science of promoting, maintaining, and restoring individual *health* and of diagnosing and treating *disease*. See also *diagnosis* and *treatment*.

medicolegal: See *forensic medicine*.

Medicredit: One of several proposed *national health insurance* plans that are designed to encourage the voluntary purchase of qualified private health insurance policies by granting *tax credits* against personal income taxes to finance, in part or in whole, the *premium* cost of such plans. In addition, the proposal would provide for the federal payment of premiums for qualified policies for *poor* individuals or *families* with no tax liability. The plan was originally proposed by the *American Medical Association (AMA)*. See also *medical deduction*.

medigap policy: A *supplemental health insurance* policy designed to supplement *Medicare*.

MEDIHC: See *Military Experience Directed into Health Careers*.

MEDIPHOR: See *Monitoring and Evaluation of Drug Interactions in a Pharmacy-Oriented Reporting System*.

MEDISGRPS: An abbreviated form of "medical groupings"; used in quality assurance and utilization review, this is a commercially available program that uses clinically accepted information to assess the severity of a patient's illness or admitting diagnosis.

MEDLARS: See *Medical Literature Analysis and Retrieval System*.

MEDLINE: A medical library computerized bibliographic search and acquisitions system.

member: A person who is eligible to receive, or is receiving, benefits from a *health maintenance organization* or *insurance policy*. If a member is married, usually both spouses have *enrolled* or subscribed for benefits and membership includes their eligible *dependents*. See also *subscriber* and *insured*.

mental age: A measure of mental ability determined by standard psychological testing.

mental disorder: A term that refers to *mental illness* or *disease* or *mental retardation*; a general term for abnormal functioning or capacity of the mind or emotions; the absence of *mental health*.

mental health: The capacity in an individual to form harmonious relations with others; to participate in, or contribute constructively to, changes in the social and physical environment; and to achieve a harmonious and balanced satisfaction of his other own potentially conflicting instinctive drives. Harmonious satisfaction refers to reaching an integrated synthesis, rather than the denial of satisfaction to certain instinctive tendencies as a means of avoiding the thwarting of others. This attempt at a definition should be compared with that of *health*. Mental health is a concept influenced by both biological and cultural factors and highly variable in definition, time, and place. It is often operatively defined as the absence of any identifiable or significant *mental disorder*. Sometimes, it is perversely used as a synonym for *mental illness* (for instance, in speaking of coverage of "mental health benefits" under *national health insurance*), apparently because it is thought to be a more acceptable term. See also *community mental health center* and *clinical psychologist*.

mental illness: Refers to any form of *illness* in which a psychological, intellectual, emotional, or behavioral disturbance is the dominating feature. The term is relative and variable in different cultures, schools of thought, and definitions. It includes a wide range of types (such as psychic, physical, neurotic, and psychotic) and severities. It is useful to distinguish mental *diseases* (those with an identifiable physical *cause*) and mental *illnesses* (those with no known cause and those with emotional, familial, social, or other causes). See also *mental health* and *mental disorders*.

M

mental retardation: The absence of normal mental development, usually measured by the intelligence quotient, and considered to be present in individuals scoring less than 70 on the Stanford-Binet scale. Many synonyms are used, such as mental deficiency, subnormality, handicap, and disability. Various types (intellectual, emotional) and degrees (borderline, 68 to 85 on the Stanford-Binet; mild, 57 to 67; moderate, 36 to 51; severe, 20 to 35; and profound, under 20) are described. Mental retardation is one type of *developmental disability* and of *mental disorder*.

mentally retarded (MR): The absence of normal mental development, generally measured by a score of less than 70 on the Stanford-Binet scale.

Merck Manual: A popular medical reference on diagnosis and therapy of illness published by Merck, Sharpe and Dohme.

midwife: See *nurse midwife.*

Military Assistance to Safety and Traffic (MAST): An emergency service utilizing military helicopters for transport of persons in need of medical assistance in rural areas.

Military Experience Directed into Health Careers (MEDIHC): A federal program that recruits qualified former military corpsmen for service in civilian populations experiencing health personnel shortages.

minimal care unit: A nursing unit that provides care for ambulatory patients who need only basic or minimal health care assistance.

minor surgery: Surgery in which the operative procedure is not considered hazardous (e.g., repair of lacerations, treatment of fractures, and surface tissue biopsies.) See also *major surgery.*

miscellaneous expenses: In connection with hospital *insurance,* hospital *charges* other than for room and board, such as x-rays, *drugs,* laboratory, and other ancillary charges, that are not separately *itemized* and *billed.*

M

mission statement: A goal statement developed by health care organizations to provide direction and define purposes and objectives of the organization.

mobile intensive care (MIC): Personnel trained at various levels to provide efficient emergency care to the injured at the scene of an accident; care provided by advanced life support teams.

model A: A *Blue Cross Association* computerized system for processing *Medicare* admissions and claim payments.

modernization: Remodeling, renovation, or replacement of *health facilities* and equipment to meet current construction standards, to comply with fire and safety codes, or to provide for contemporary health delivery *needs* and capabilities. The term usually implies no increase in facility capacity; for example, in the case of hospital modernization the total available number of *beds* may not be increased. Ther term is defined and supported under the *Hill-Burton* program (Title XVI of the *PHS Act*).

Monitoring and Evaluation of Drug Interactions in a Pharmacy-Oriented Reporting System (MEDIPHOR): A program developed by the *National Center for Health Services Research* that alerts *pharmacists* and *physicians* to potential adverse *drug* reactions. It also can be utilized for patient *prescription* billing.

morbidity: The extent of *illness, injury,* or *disability* in a defined population. It is usually expressed in general or specific rates of *incidence* or *prevalence*. The term is sometimes used to refer to any episode of *disease*. See also *mortality*.

morbidity incidence vote: The number of reported cases of a specific disease per year per 100,000 population.

M

mortality: *Death*. The term is used to describe the statistical relation of deaths to the population in which they occur. The mortality rate (death rate) expresses the number of deaths in a unit of population within a prescribed time and may be expressed as crude death rates (e.g., total deaths in relation to total population during a year) or as rates specific for *diseases* and sometimes for age, sex, or other attributes (e.g., number of deaths from cancer in white males in relation to the white male population during a year).

mortality table: A graphic visualization of the number of deaths per 1,000 population.

multiphasic screening: The combined use of a group, or battery, of *screening* tests as a preventive measure to attempt identification of any of several *diseases* in an apparently healthy population.

multisource drug: A *drug* that is available from more than one manufacturer, often under different *brand names*. Limits on reimbursement are more feasible for multisource drugs than drugs available from only a single source. A drug is available from only one source when it is protected by a patent or when only one company has obtained marketing approval from the Food and Drug Administration. Sometimes the demand for a drug is not extensive, and only one *supplier* has entered the market. See also *Maximum Allowable Cost Program.*

multispecialty group: A medical group consisting of three or more physicians who represent two or more fields of medical specialization.

mutual benefit associations: Fraternal or social organizations or corporations established for the relief of members of the organization from specified *perils* or costs such as the costs of *illness*. The associations pay *losses* with assessments on their members that are intended to liquidate specific previously incurred losses, rather than with fixed *premiums* payable in advance.

M

mutual insurance company: An insurance company with no capital stock that is owned by the policyholders. Trustees of the company are selected by the policyholders. Earnings over and above payment of *losses,* operating *expenses,* and *reserves* are the property of the policyholders and returned to them in some form, such as dividends or reduced future *premiums*. See also *stock insurance company.*

Nn

NADSP: National Association of Dental Service Plans. See *Delta Dental Plan.*

NAEMT: See *National Association of Emergency Medical Technicians.*

narcotic drug: As defined in the Comprehensive Drug Abuse Prevention and Control Act of 1970, any of the following *drugs,* whether produced directly or indirectly by extraction from substances of vegetable origin or independently by means of chemical syntheses or by a combination of extraction and chemical syntheses: opium, coca leaves, and opiates; a compound, manufacture, salt, derivative, or preparation of opium, coca leaves, or opiates; and a substance (and any compound, manufacture, salt, derivative, or preparation thereof) that is chemically identical to any of the substances listed above. The term is very irregularly used, sometimes meaning any drug that dulls the senses and reduces pain, sometimes meaning any drug whose use is subject to special governmental control. Narcotics include heroin, morphine, demerol, and methadone. They do not, by the first definition, include marihuana, hallucinogens, amphetamines, and barbiturates. Narcotics are among the most common sources of *drug dependence.*

National Association of Blue Shield Plans (NABSP): An association of the individual Blue Shield plans that coordinate various programs and policies and undertake activities of importance to the individual plans.

National Association of Insurance Agents (NAIA): A national association of independent life and health insurance agents representing various underwriters.

National Association of Retail Druggists: A national association of owners of independent retail pharmacies.

national board examinations: Standard national examinations developed and administered by the *National Board of Medical Examiners.* They are given in three parts, generally during the second and finals years of medical school and the *internship* year. Successful completion of the national boards is a requirement for *licensure* as a *physician* in some states and an acceptable alternative to the state's own medical examinations in other states. See also *Federation Licensing Examination.*

National Board of Medical Examiners (NBME): An organization, founded in 1915, that includes among its members representatives from the Federation of State Medical Boards of the United States, Council on Medical Education of the *American Medical Association*, *Association of American Medical Colleges*, *American Hospital Association*, Armed Services, *U.S. Public Health Service*, and Veterans Administration. Members at large are elected from among leaders in medicine throughout the United States. The purposes of the Board are (1) to prepare and administer qualifying examinations of such high *quality* that legal agencies governing the *practice* of *medicine* within each state may, at their discretion, grant successful candidates a license without further examination (see *Federation Licensing Examination* and *national board examinations);* (2) to consult and cooperate with the examining boards of the states; (3) to consult and cooperate with medical schools and other organizations or institutions concerned with maintaining the advancing quality of medical education; (4) to assist medical *specialty boards* and societies in establishing measurement of clinical knowledge and competence for purposes of *certification* and assessment; and (5) to study and develop methods of testing and evaluating medical knowledge and competence. See also *Coordinating Council for Medical Edu-*

N

cation and *Liaison Committee on Graduate Medical Education.*

National Center for Health Care Technology (NCHCT): A federal organization to provide for the assessment of health care and medical technologies.

National Center for Health Services Research (NCHSR): a federal organization established to research and analyze how Americans utilize health care services as a foundation for future policy-making.

National Federation of Licensed Practical Nurses (NFLPN): The national organization for licensed practical and vocational nurses.

National Formulary (NF): A *compendium* of standards for certain *drugs* and preparations now included in the *United States Pharmacopeia (USP).*

national health insurance (NHI): A term not yet defined or enacted in the United States but one of significant political interest. The term generally describes a uniform program of comprehensive health financing. See also *medical deduction, national health service, social insurance,* and *socialized medicine.*

national health service: Often used synonymously with *national health insurance (NHI).* The terms are sometimes usefully distinguished by applying the former to health programs in which the national government directly operates a health system to serve some or all of its citizens and the latter to programs in which the government *insures* or otherwise arranges financing for health care without arranging for, owning, or operating it (although NHI programs usually include some measure of *regulation* of the financed services). See also *social insurance* and *socialized medicine.*

National Health Service Corps (NHSC): A program that places *U.S. Public Health Service* personnel in areas with a critical shortage of health manpower (see *medically underserved population*) for the purpose of improving the delivery of health care and services to persons residing in these areas. The health service corps was established by the Emergency Health Personnel Act Amendments of 1972, P.L. 92-585 (Section 329 of the *PHS Act*). Its first members were assigned in January 1972.

National Health Survey: A continuing *health survey* by the National Center for Health Statistics of *HHS* that includes studies to determine the extent of *illness* and *disability* (*morbidity*) in the population of the United States, to describe the use of health services by Americans and to gather related information. The center conducts a continuing household interview survey of a sample of the population, surveys certain *medical records,* surveys a sample of the population through health examinations, and conducts related developmental and evaluative studies.

National Institute of Mental Health (NIMH): A federal research institute organized to advance research on mental health issues and finance various state and local mental health programs.

National Institutes of Health (NIH): A major health research center under the *Department of Health and Human Services* that has many divisions and departments, including the National Cancer Institute, the National Library of Medicine, and the National Institute on Aging.

National Interns and Residents Matching Program (NIRMP): The official cooperative plan for first-year appointments in *graduate medical education* of the *American Hospital Association*, American Protestant Hospital Association, *Association of American Medical Colleges*, Catholic Hospital Association, *American Medical Association*, American Student Medical Association, and American Board of Medical Specialties. The program operates as a clearinghouse for matching preferences of medical students for *internships* and *residencies* with available positions in accord with hospital lists

N

of preferences among graduating students. To participate in the program, hospital program directors sign the program's hospital agreement commiting the institution to participate in the NIRMP as a corporate entity and listing with the NIRMP all programs and positions available to students. Under the agreement, positions to be offered to physicians presently serving as interns, in military service, and in other postgraduate activities are not required to be listed with the NIRMP. The matching of students and positions is handled on a *confidential* basis.

National League for Nursing (NLN): The official nursing organization open to all *nurses* from registered nurses to nursing assistants. The NLN also accredits schools of nursing and nursing programs.

National Registry of Emergency Medical Technicians (NREMT): The organization that conducts certification examinations for all categories of *emergency medical technicians* and *paramedics*.

naturopathy: A drugless system of *therapy* that uses physical and natural forces, such as air, light, water, diet, heat, and massage.

necessary: See *need.*

need: A thing or action that is essential, indispensable, required, or cannot be done or lived without; a condition marked by the lack or want of some such thing or action. The presence or absence of a need can and should be measured by an objective *criterion* or *standard.* Needs may or may not be perceived or expressed by the person in need. They must be distinguished from *demands,* which are expressed desires not necessarily needed. Like *appropriateness,* need is frequently and irregularly used in health care with respect to *health facilities* and *services* (see *certificate of need*) and people (see *medically needy*). It is thus important to specify what thing or action's need is being considered, by what criteria the need is to be established and by whom (*provider, consumer,* or *third party*), and with what effect (since payment for services by *insurance,* for

N

instance, is usually conditioned upon the necessity of providing the services).

negligence: The failure to exercise reasonable, usual, expected, or ordinary care that can or does result in harm or injury. See *malpractice*.

neighborhood health center: See *community health center*.

neonatal intensive care unit: A specially equipped and staffed nursing care unit with incubator-type cribs and other monitoring equipment to care for premature babies and other infants with serious illness.

neonatal mortality: The *death* rate *(mortality)* of live-born children who have not reached four weeks or one month of age; number of neonatal deaths per 1,000 *live births* in a given area or program and time period. Early neonatal deaths (those occurring in the first week of life) are sometimes also reported. See also *infant mortality* and *perinatal mortality*.

neuropathology (NA): The medical specialty dealing with diseases of the nervous system.

new drug: A drug for which premarketing approval is required by the federal Food, Drug, and Cosmetic Act. A new drug is any drug that is not generally recognized (among experts qualified by scientific training and experience to evaluate the *safety* and *effectiveness* of drugs) as safe and effective for use under its prescribed conditions of use. Since 1962 most new *prescription drugs* have been subject to the *new drug application* and premarket approval process for new drugs. See also *GRAS* and *GRAE, not new,* and *"me too" drug.*

new drug application (NDA): An application that must be approved by the *Food and Drug Administration (FDA)* before any *new drug* is marketed to the general public. The application must provide

N

information designed to demonstrate *safety* and *effectiveness*. After approval of the application, the drug may be *prescribed* by any *physician* or other health *professional* authorized to prescribe under state law. The NDA must include supportive reports of animal and clinical investigations; a list of ingredients, including the active drug and any vehicle, excipient, binder, filler, flavoring, and coloring; a description of manufacturing methods and *quality* control procedures; samples of the drug; and proposed *labeling*. Approval of an NDA must be based on valid scientific evidence that the drug is safe, as well as *adequate and well-controlled studies* (such as *random controlled trials)* demonstrating that it is effective for its intended (i.e., labeled) uses. NDA also commonly refers to the FDA's approval of an application, which acts as the manufacturer's *license* to market the drug. See also *adequate and well-controlled studies* and *investigational new drug*.

New Jersey rule: A ruling by the Supreme Court of New Jersey which held that *contingency fees* must be scheduled according to the size of the award: the percentage of the award that goes to the claimant's lawyer declines as the size of the award increases. For example, in New Jersey lawyers may receive 50 percent of a $1,000 settlement but only 10 percent of any recovered amount over $100,000. A number of states have adopted variations of the New Jersey rule, and others are actively considering it as a way to reduce the number of malpractice claims.

NIH: See *National Institutes of Health*.

nonassigned: Health care *providers* who will not accept patients under certain governmental health programs.

noncontributory insurance: Group *health insurance* for which the employer pays the entire *premium*.

nonparticipating insurance company: See *stock insurance company*.

nonprofit hospital: One chartered as a nontaxable corporation within its state of incorporation and granted tax exemption by the Internal Revenue Service.

nonservice-connected disability: In the Veterans Administration health care program, a *disability* that was not incurred or aggravated in the line of duty during active military service. Care is available from the program for such disabilities on a bed-available basis after patients with *service-connected disabilities* are provided for.

norm(s): Numerical or statistical measure(s) of usual observed performance. For example, a norm for care of appendicitis would be the usual percentage of appendixes removed in cases diagnosed as appendicitis that pathology results confirm are diseased. A norm can be used as a *standard* but does not necessarily serve as one. Both norm and standard imply single, proper, or mean values rather than a range.

nosocomial: Relating to or originating from a *hospital*. For example, nosocomial infection is an infection originating within a hospital.

nosology: The science of the classification of diseases.

notch: A sudden and sharp discontinuity in health or financial *benefits* for individuals with slightly different *incomes*. In certain public and medical assistance programs, an additional dollar of income can mean a partial or total loss of benefits. For example, *families* just below the income eligibility standard of *Medicaid* receive fully subsidized coverage, while families with only slightly more income do not meet eligibility standards and receive no benefits. Substantial incentives for families to restrict their incomes in order to remain eligible may result. *Spend-down* provisions are used to compensate for notches. A notch may also occur when, without change in eligibility, *cost-sharing* requirements increase suddenly with a small change in income.

not-for-profit carriers: Health insurance programs or prepayment

N

plans chartered under state not-for-profit statutes.

notifiable: Applied to a *disease* that *providers* are required (usually by law) to report to federal, state, or local *public health* officials when *diagnosed.* Examples are tuberculosis, diphtheria, and syphilis. Notifiable diseases are those of public interest by reason of their infectiousness, severity, or frequency. See also *registration* and *quarantine.*

not new: A *drug* for which premarketing approval by the *Food and Drug Administration (FDA)* is not, or no longer, required. A drug may become "not new" upon a ruling by the FDA that the safeguards applicable to approved *new drugs,* for example, maintenance of records and submission of reports, are no longer required. See also *"me too" drug.*

notice of proposed rule-making (NPRM): Notice in the Federal Register of a proposed administrative regulation affording parties of interest opportunity to voice opinion or comments.

nuclear medicine (NM): For *Joint Commission* accreditation purposes, the clinical and scientific discipline utilizing radionuclides for diagnostic and therapeutic purposes.

nurse: An individual whose primary responsibility is the provision of *nursing care.* A *registered nurse* can be defined as a *professional* person qualified by education and authorized by law to *practice* nursing. Other nurses do not fit this exact definition. They include nurses' aides, *licensed practical nurses,* and *licensed vocational nurses.* There are many different types, specialties, and grades of nurses whose titles are generally descriptive of their special responsibilities, such as charge or head, hospital, private, private duty, public health, and school nurses. See also *nurse anesthetist, nurse midwife,* and *nurse practitioner.*

nurse anesthetist: A *registered nurse* who works under supervision of an anesthesiologist or *physician* in administering anesthetic agents to *patients* before and after surgical and obstetrical *operations* and other medical procedures.

nurse midwife: A *registered nurse* who, by added knowledge and skill gained through an organized program of study and clinical experience recognized by the American College of Nurse-Midwives, has extended the lawful limits of *practice* into the management and care of mothers and babies throughout the maternity cycle. The nurse midwife must meet certain professional *criteria.*

nurse practitioner (NP): A *registered nurse* qualified and specially trained to provide *primary care,* including primary health care in homes, *ambulatory care* facilities, *long-term care* facilities, and other health care institutions. Nurse practitioners generally function under supervision of physicians, but not necessarily in their presence. They are usually salaried rather than reimbursed on a *fee-for-service* basis, although supervising physicians may receive fee-for-service reimbursement for services performed by nurse practitioners. See also *physician assistant* and *Medex.*

nursing care: Care intended to assist an individual, whether sick or well, in the performance of those activities contributing to *health* or its recovery (or to peaceful *death*) that would not require assistance if that individual had the necessary strength, will, or knowledge. This care includes assisting *patients* in carrying out *therapeutic* plans initiated by *physicians* and other health *professionals* and assisting other members of the medical team in performing the nursing function and understanding health *needs* of patients. The specific content of nursing care varies in different countries and situations. It is important to note that, as defined, nursing care is not provided solely by *nurses* but also by other health professionals. See also *nurse practitioner, nurse anesthetist,* and *nurse midwife.*

nursing care plan: A document used to assess and determine *patient* needs and to manage and coordinate activities for individual patients

N

within a *nursing unit.*

nursing differential: A differential (usually eight and one-half percent of routine *inpatient* nursing salary costs) added to the costs of nursing services to reflect the supposedly above-average costs of providing routine inpatient *nursing care* to *Medicare* beneficiaries. Medicare reimburses hospitals by this amount for nursing services more often than other insurance programs covering the general population.

nursing homes: Generally, a wide range of institutions, other than hospitals, that provide various levels of maintenance and personal or *nursing care* to people who are unable to care for themselves and who may have health problems ranging from minimal to very serious. The term includes freestanding institutions and identifiable components of other *health facilities* providing nursing care and related services, personal care, and residential care. Nursing homes include *skilled nursing facilities, intermediate care facilities,* and *extended care facilities,* but not *boarding homes.*

nursing unit: A physically segregated or defined unit of nursing care within a *hospital* or *long-term care* facility. Nursing units may be divided by type of specialty, such as surgical, recovery, and obstetrics.

N

Oo

objective: In health *planning,* a quantified or specific statement of a desired future state or condition with a stated deadline for achieving the objective, such as an average access time for emergency medical services of less than 30 minutes by 1990. Health planning specifies objectives that will, when implemented, achieve planning *goals.* See also *policy* and *budget.*

obligations: In the federal *budget,* amounts of orders placed, contracts awarded, services rendered, or other commitments of federal *budget authority* made by federal agencies during a given period that will require *outlays* of federal funds during the same or some future period.

obstetrics (OB): The care and treatment of pregnant women through childbirth.

obstretics and gynecology (OB-GYN): A medical specialty that focuses on the study, diagnosis, treatment, and process of the diseases and medical problems of a woman's reproductive system as well as the childbirth process.

occupancy: The ratio of inpatient census to the number of available beds. See also *occupancy rate.*

occupancy rate: A measure of *inpatient* health facility use, determined by dividing *available bed days* by *patient days.* It measures the average percentage of a hospital's *beds* occupied and may be institutionwide, specific for one *department* or service, or industry-wide.

occupational health and safety: The prevention and control of occupational health hazards and diseases; the promotion of the

O

physical and psychological welfare of workers.

occupational health services: Health services concerned with the physical, mental, and social well-being of individuals in relation to their jobs and working environments and with the adjustment of people to work and work to people. Thus, the services relate to more than the *safety* of the workplace and include *health* and job satisfaction. In the United States the principal federal statute dealing with occupational health is the Occupational Safety and Health Act administered by the *Occupational Safety and Health Administration (OSHA)* and the National Institute of Occupational Safety and Health (NIOSH).

occupational medicine (OM): A *specialty* of medical *practice* for the prevention and treatment of occupationally induced disease or illness.

Occupational Safety and Health Administration (OSHA): The federal agency charged with responsibility to enforce the Occupational Health and Safety Act relating to protecting employed persons from occupational health hazards.

occupational therapist (OT): A specially trained individual who evaluates the self-care, work, and leisure performance skills of well and *disabled* clients of all age ranges. The therapist plans and implements programs and social and interpersonal activities designed to restore, develop, and maintain the clients' abilities to satisfactorily accomplish daily living tasks required for specific ages and necessary for particular occupational roles. About four-fifths of occupational therapists work in *hospitals*. Others are employed in *nursing homes, extended care facilities, long-term care* facilities, *rehabilitation* centers, schools and camps for handicapped children, *community health centers*, and educational and research institutions. Formal educational preparation of an occupational therapist requires at least four academic years of college or university work leading to a baccalaureate degree, plus a minimum of 6 months' field work

O

experience. A person with a baccalaureate degree in a field other than occupational therapy may enroll in a postbaccalaureate program leading to a master's degree or a certificate of proficiency in occupational therapy.

occupational therapy (OT): Medically directed *treatment* of physically and mentally *disabled* individuals by means of constructive activities designed and adapted by a *professionally* qualified *occupational therapist* to promote the restoration of useful function.

Office of Professional Standards Review (OPSR): An agency reporting to the unit within the *Department of Health and Human Services* responsible for the activities of *peer review organizations*, formerly called professional standards review organizations.

office visit: See *visit*.

official name: See *generic name* and *established name*.

Old-Age, Survivors, Disability, and Health Insurance Program (OASHDI): A program, commonly known as social security, administered by the *Social Security Administration* that provides monthly cash benefits to retired and *disabled* workers and their *dependents* and to survivors of *insured* workers. The program also provides health insurance benefits for persons age 65 and older and for the disabled under age 65. The health insurance component of OASHDI was initiated in 1965 and is generally known as *Medicare*. Legislative authority for the program is found in the Social Security Act originally enacted in 1935. The program is an example of *social insurance*.

O

oncologist: A *physician* who specializes in cancer research and treatment.

oncology (ON): The branch of medicine that specializes in cancer diagnosis and treatment.

one-to-one nursing care: A nursing arrangement by which a *patient* is assigned a full-time *nurse*.

on-line medical record: The complete computerization of a *patient's* medical record. The medical record is created in the computer throughout the patient's stay in the same manner as a paper medical record would have been created.

open-ended programs: In the federal *budget*, entitlement programs for which eligibility requirements are set by law. (e.g., *Medicaid*). Actual *obligations* and resultant *outlays* are limited only by the number of eligible persons who apply for *benefits* and the actual benefits received. See also *entitlement authority*.

open enrollment: A time period within which new *subscribers* may elect to *enroll* in a *health insurance* plan or *prepaid group practice*. An open enrollment period may be used in the sale of either *group insurance* or *individual insurance* and may be the only period of a year when insurance is available. Individuals perceived as high-risk (perhaps because of *pre-existing conditions*) may be subjected to high *premiums* or *exclusions* during open enrollment periods. In the Health Maintenance Organization Act of 1973 (P.L. 93-222) the term refers to periodic opportunities for the general public, on a first-come, first-served basis, to join an *HMO*. The law presently requires that HMOs have at least one annual open enrollment period when an HMO must accept "up to its capacity, individuals in the order that they apply," unless the HMO can demonstrate to HHS that open enrollment would threaten its economic viability. In such cases, HHS can waive the open enrollment requirement for a period of up to three years.

open shop: A health care *facility* where either union or non-union employees may work.

operation: Any intrusive medical procedure or act performed on the body with instruments by a *physician* or surgeon. See also *major* *surgery, minor surgery,* and *cosmetic surgery.*

ophthalmologist: A *physician* specializing in the *diagnosis and treatment* of all eye *diseases* and abnormal conditions, including refractive errors. An ophthalmologist may prescribe *drugs* and lenses and perform *surgery* or other treatment. A state *Medicaid* plan must provide for an examination by a physician skilled in diseases of the eye or by an *optometrist* when a decision must be made whether an individual is blind according to the state's definition. A state supervising ophthalmologist must review each eye examination report in making the state agency's decision that the applicant does or does not meet the state's definition of blindness and determining if and when re-examinations are necessary.

ophthalmology (OPH): The branch of medicine that specializes in diseases and disorders of the eye.

opportunity cost: In health economics, the value that *resources,* when used in a particular way, would have if used in the best possible or another specified alternative way. When opportunity cost exceeds the value the resources have in the way they are being used, it represents a lost opportunity to obtain value from the resources. One opportunity cost of devoting physician time to *tertiary care,* for example, is the lost value of devoting the same time to *primary care.* Opportunity cost is the appropriate *cost* concept to consider when making resource allocation decisions. Actual costs often, but not always, can be assumed to represent opportunity costs. See also *marginal cost.*

O

opticians: Health workers who fit, supply, and adjust eyeglasses according to *prescriptions* written by *ophthalmologists* or *optometrists* to correct a *patient's* optical or muscular vision defect. In some states opticians also fit contact lenses. They do not examine the eyes or prescribe *treatment.* Licensing laws govern the practice of opticians in most states. Qualification for initial *licensure* usually includes successful completion of written, oral, and practical examinations. Apprenticeships are required in most licensing states, with an alternative being the completion of a one- or two-year training program.

optional services: Services that may be provided or covered by a health program or *provider* and, if provided, will be paid for in addition to any *required services* that must be offered. In addition to the required services under *Medicaid*, matching funds under *Title XIX* are available for states electing to include any optional services in their programs. States may offer the following optional services: (1) *prescribed drugs* and *clinic* services; (2) *dental health services*; (3) eyeglasses; (4) private-duty *nursing care*; (5) *skilled nursing facility* services for individuals under age 21; (6) care for patients under age 21 in psychiatric hospitals; (7) *intermediate care facility* services; (8) prosthetic *devices*; (9) *physical therapy* and related services; (10) other diagnostic, *screening*, preventive, and *rehabilitation* services; (11) *optometrists'* services; (12) *podiatrists'* services; (13) *chiropractors'* services; (14) care for persons age 65 or older in institutions for *mental illness*; and (15) care for patients age 65 or older in tuberculosis institutions. States also may offer any "medical care or any other type of remedial care recognized under state law, furnished by licensed practitioners within the scope of their *practice* as defined by state law" that is not specifically excluded from coverage by Title XIX. Exclusions include care or services for inmates of public nonmedical institutions; *inpatient* services in a mental institution for individuals over age 20 and under age 65; and services for persons under age 65 in a tuberculosis institution. See also *basic health services* and *supplemental health services*.

O

optometrist: A practitioner concerned with problems of vision. Optometrists examine the eyes and related structures to determine the presence of any abnormality and *prescribe* and adapt lenses or other optical aids. They do not prescribe *drugs*, make definitive *diagnosis* of or treat eye *diseases*, or perform surgery. An *accredited* doctor of optometry degree requires a minimum of two years of pre-optometry college education and four years of *professional* training in a school of optometry. The degree and an optometry board examination are required by all states for *licensure* for the practice of optometry. See also *ophthalmologist* and *optician.*

order/entry system (O/E): Software programs that facilitate on-line, real-time ordering of *patient* services by transmitting orders to the appropriate areas of the health care facility.

organ bank: A unit within many major hospitals that maintains a supply of human organs, bone, and tissue for transplant purposes.

organ donor: An individual granting written permission to have organs removed from the donor's body for use by another person or persons through transplant surgery. The transplant may occur either during the donor's life or at death.

orthoptics: A technique of eye exercises designed to correct the visual axes of eyes not properly coordinated for binocular vision. See also *orthoptist.*

orthoptist: A specially trained individual who works under the supervision of an *ophthalmologist* in testing for certain eye muscle imbalances and teaching the *patient* exercises to correct eye coordination defects. Most orthoptists work in the private offices of ophthalmologists; others are employed in *hospitals* and clinics. The American Orthoptic Council is the regulating board for orthoptists. The council administers the national board examination that is required for *certification.* To qualify for the examination, a person needs a minimum of 2 years of college and 15 months of training in a training center or 24 months of preceptorship training.

O

osteopathic: A branch of medicine with emphasis on normal body mechanics and manipulation techniques for diagnosing and correcting disease and faulty body structure. Osteopathic physicians are graduates of schools of osteopathic medicine and generally practice family medicine.

osteopathy: A school of healing based on the theory, originally propounded in 1874 by Dr. Andrew Taylor Still, that the normal body, when in correct adjustment, is a vital mechanical organism naturally capable of making its own responses to and defense against *diseases,* infections, and other toxic conditions. The body is seen as structurally and functionally coordinate and interdependent; abnormality of either structure or function constitutes disease. The *physician* of this school searches for and, if possible, corrects any peculiar position of the joints or tissues or peculiarity of diet or environment that is a factor in destroying natural resistance. Osteopathic measures include physical, hygienic, medicinal, and surgical therapy. Osteopaths are now distinguished from *allopathic physicians* mainly, if at all, by their greater reliance on manipulation. They are licensed to perform medicine and surgery in all states and are eligible for *graduate medical education* in either osteopathic or allopathic programs. They are reimbursed by *Medicare* and *Medicaid* for their services, supported under *health manpower* legislation, and generally treated identically with allopathic physicians. See also *homeopathy* and *naturopathy.*

otology (OT): The branch of medicine that specializes in diseases and disorders of the ear.

otorhinolaryngology (OTO): The branch of medicine that specializes in diseases and disorders of the ear, nose, and throat.

outcome measure: A measure of the *quality* of medical care in which the standard of judgment is the attainment of a specified end result or outcome. The outcome of medical care is measured with such parameters as improved *health,* lowered *mortality* and *morbidity,* and improvement in abnormal states (such as elevated blood pressure). Any disease has a "natural history" that medical care seeks to alter. Measuring the *effectiveness* of a particular medical action to alter a disease's natural history requires out an outcome measure. Such measures are the only valid way to determine the effectiveness of medical care, and some professionals say they are the only way to measure the quality of medical care. Outcome measures are neces-

O

sary to carry out cost-benefit analyses of medical care. However, they are difficult to devise and have not been done often to compare medical settings. It is possible to perform a *random controlled trial* using outcome measures to compare the therapeutic effect of any *drug* or medical procedure on a disease with the "natural history" of a disease without *treatment* or with a treatment already in use. Some argue that this should be done before any new medical procedure is put into use. See also *input measure, process measure,* and *output measure.*

outlays: In the federal *budget,* actual expenditures of federal funds, including checks issued, interest accrued on the public debt, and other payments (minus refunds and reimbursements). Total budget outlays consist of the sum of the outlays from *appropriations* and other funds included in the budget universe less offsetting receipts. Off-budget federal agencies are not included in the budget universe, and their outlays are excluded from total budget outlays.

outlier: In *DRGs,* extremes experienced in receiving health care as compared to the average patient within the DRG classification.

out-of-pocket payments or costs: Those costs incurred directly by a *patient* without benefit of *insurance,* sometimes called direct costs. They also include patient payments under *cost-sharing* provisions of most health insurance policies.

outpatient: A *patient* who is receiving *ambulatory care* at a *hospital* or other *health facility* without being admitted to the facility. The term usually does not designate a person who is receiving services from a *physician's* office or other program that does not also give *inpatient* care. Outpatient care refers to care given to outpatients, often in organized programs.

outpatient care: Health care services provided to patients on an ambulatory basis, rather than on an inpatient basis where the patient is maintained at the hospital.

O

outpatient department (OPD): A hospital department that provides nonemergency ambulatory care.

outpatient medical facility: A facility designed to provide a limited or full spectrum of *health* and medical services (including health education and maintenance, *preventative care*, *diagnosis*, *treatment*, and *rehabilitation*) to individuals who do not require admission to a hospital or institution (*outpatients*).

output measures: Often used synonymously with measures of the productivity of health programs and manpower, *process measures*, or *outcome measures*.

over-the-counter drug (OTC drug): A *drug* that is advertised and sold directly to the public without *prescription* (e.g., aspirin). See also *legend* drug.

ownership disclosure: Disclosure by a health program of all ownership interests in the program. By law, each *skilled nursing facility* participating in *Medicare* and *Medicaid* must supply ownership information to the state survey agency and each *intermediate care facility* must supply this information to the state licensing agency. Full and complete information must be supplied on the identity of each person having (directly or indirectly) an ownership interest of ten percent or more in such facility; in the case of a facility organized as a corporation, each officer and director of the corporation; and in the case of a facility organized as a partnership, each partner. Any changes that affect the accuracy of this information must be promptly reported.

O

Pp

package insert: The *labeling* approved by the *Food and Drug Administration* for a *prescription drug* product. It accompanies the product when shipped by the manufacturer to the pharmacist, but usually does not accompany the dispensed prescription. The package insert is directed at the prescribing *professional,* principally the *physician* and *pharmacist,* and states the *appropriate* uses of a drug, the mode of administration, dosage information, contraindications, and warnings. The legal effect of prescribing the drug in ways not described in the package insert is unclear. See also *compendium* and *Physicians' Desk Reference.*

pandemic: A widespread or worldwide outbreak of a disease.

panel: See *registry.*

panel group practice: *Physicians* authorized to participate in a *third-party* reimbursement plan. (A panel may be either an open panel (open to all physicians who choose to participate) or a *closed panel.*

paramedic: An *emergency care* provider with more advanced training than a basic or intermediate care emergency medical technician. Paramedics provide advanced life support services.

paramedical personnel: *Health* personnel (excluding *doctors).* The term applies to medical technicians, health aides, family health workers, nutritionists, *dental hygienists, physician assistants,* and health associates. Conversely, there is no agreement on occupations that should be included under paramedical personnel. See also *allied health personnel.*

paraprofessional: A person who assists a professional or works

P

closely with a professional. The term implies high-level delegated responsibilities.

parity: In epidemiology, the classification of women by the number of their live-born children (e.g., a woman of parity four has had four live-born children). In medical usage, the term classifies women by the total number of births, including both live births and *stillbirths*, or the total number of times a woman has been pregnant minus the number of *abortions* and miscarriages (occurring within 28 weeks of gestation).

Part A: See *Hospital Insurance Program (Medicare)*.

Part B: See *Supplementary Medical Insurance Program (Medicare)*.

partial hospitalization: A formal program of care in a *hospital* or other institution for periods of less than 24 hours a day that typically involves services usually provided to *inpatients*. There are two principal types: (1) night hospitalization for *patients* who need hospitalization but can work or attend school outside the hospital during the day; and (2) day hospitalization for people who require in-hospital *diagnostic* or *treatment* services but can safely spend nights and weekends at home.

participating insurance company: See *mutual insurance company*.

participation (participating): A *physician* or other *provider* who participates in an *insurance* plan by agreeing to accept the plan's pre-established fee or *reasonable charge* as the maximum amount that can be collected for services rendered. A nonparticipating physician may charge more than the insurance program's maximum allowable amount for a particular service. The patient is then liable for the excess above the allowed amount. The participating system was developed in the private sector as a method of providing the *insured* with specific health care services at no *out-of-pocket* costs. The term is used more loosely in *Medicare* and *Medicaid* to mean any physician who accepts reimbursement from the respective program. Approximately half of Medicare claims are paid to physicians who participate by accepting *assignment.* Any physician accepting Medicaid payments must accept them as payment in full. A hospital or other health program is called a participating *provider* when it meets the various requirements of, and accepts reimbursement from, a public or private health insurance program. See also *conditions of participation* and *penetration.*

Partnership for Health: A synonym for the *comprehensive health planning* program. The first set of amendments to the program were made in 1967 by P.L. 90-174 which was given the *short title,* Partnership for Health Amendments of 1967, and hence the name.

pathologist: A medical doctor who specializes in the study of the etiology of disease and carries out epidemiological research.

pathology: The study of *disease* processes and the etiology of disease and diseased tissue.

patient: One who is receiving health services; sometimes used synonymously with *consumer* or client. See also *inpatient, outpatient, private patient,* and *service patient.*

patient advocate: (1) One who acts on a patient's behalf; (2) an ombudsman employed by the *facility* to mediate grievances with patients.

patient care plan: A specifically designed plan by a *physician* for the care and rehabilitation of a *patient* within a *nursing unit.*

patient days: A measure of institutional use, usually stated as the number of *inpatients* at a specified time (e.g., midnight). See also *occupancy rate.*

patient mix: The numbers and types of *patients* served by a *hospital* or other health program. Patients may be classified according to

P

geographic distribution (see *patient origin study*), socioeconomic characteristics, *diagnoses,* or severity of *illness.* Knowledge of a program's patient mix is important for *planning* and comparative purposes. See also *scope of services.*

patient origin study: A study, usually undertaken by an individual health program or a health *planning* agency, to determine the geographic distribution of the homes of the *patients* served by one or more health programs. The studies help define *catchment area* and *medical trade area* and are useful in locating and planning the development of new services.

patient's rights: Those rights to which an individual is entitled while a patient. In addition to civil and constitutional rights, they include the right to privacy and confidentiality, the right to refuse treatment, and the right of access to the individual's medical information.

pattern analysis: A program that helps to evaluate the effectiveness of *patient* care through comparative medical data and analysis of trends and indicators of health.

payment, cost-based: A method of health care payment by Blue Cross and other *third parties* wherein the amount of payment is based on the costs to the *provider* of delivering the *service.* Actual payment may be predicated on one of several formulas provided it is based to some extent on provider cost.

payment, lump sum: A method of payment to a *provider* based on a negotiated agreement between the *third party* and provider.

payroll deduction: A specified amount taken out of an employee's pay to finance a *benefit.* Payroll deductions may be either a set *payroll tax,* such as the social security tax, or a required payment for a benefit, such as a *group* health insurance *premium.* A payroll deduction also refers to any amount withheld from the earnings of an employee.

payroll tax: A tax *liability* imposed on an employer or employee, that relates to the amount of the company payroll or individual pay, respectively. Revenue from the tax is used to finance a specific *benefit*. In the health field, payroll tax is often used synonymously with the social security tax. That tax, it is important to note, is not applied on total payroll but rather on the wages of each employee up to a set maximum. A government requirement that an employer pay a set portion of the *premium* on *group* health *insurance* benefits for employees also would be a payroll tax on the employer, although it is often not recognized as such. The amount paid by the employer would be a set amount per employee and not related to the amount of an individual's earnings. Consequently, its impact as a tax would be regressive.

PDR: See *Physicians' Desk Reference.*

pediatrics (PD): The medical *specialty* concerned with the *health* care of infants and children.

peer review: Generally, the evaluation by practicing *physicians* or other *professionals* of the *effectiveness* and *efficiency* of services ordered or performed by other practicing physicians or other members of the profession whose work is being reviewed (peers). The term requently refers to the activities of the *peer review organizations (PROs)* that review services provided under the *Medicare, Medicaid,* and *maternal and child health services.* Local PROs receive federal guidance and funding from the *Department of Health and Human Services.* They are staffed by local physicians, osteopaths, and nonphysicians. The duties of *PROs* include (1) establishment of *criteria, norms,* and *standards* for *diagnosis* and *treatment* of *diseases* encountered in the local PRO jurisdiction and (2) review of services that are inconsistent with the established norms, for example, hospital stays longer than the normal *length of stay.* The norms may be *input measure, process measure,* or *outcome measure.* Peer review has been advocated as the only possible form of *quality* control for medical services, because it is said that only a physician's professional peers can judge his or her work. Critics have indicated there is inherent conflict of interest; they say a physician will not

P

properly judge those who will judge the physician in return. They also suggest that the process does not adequately reflect the *patients'* objectives and viewpoints.

peer review organization (PRO): The replacement for the former *Professional Standards Review Organizations (PSROs).* The PSRO program was repealed by the Tax Equity and Fiscal Responsibility Act of 1982. Through PRO programs, the *Department of Health and Human Services* contracts with PROs, usually consisting of a physician group within a PRO area, to review the *quality* and appropriateness (see *appropriate*) of health care services to *Medicare* participants.

penetration: In marketing *insurance* or *HMOs,* the percentage of possible *subscribers* who have in fact contracted for *benefits* (subscribed). *Participation* is sometimes used synonymously. See also *saturation.*

penetration ratio: The actual admissions in a health care facility per 1,000 population in contrast to national averages.

per diem cost: Literally, *cost* per day. It refers, in general, to hospital or other *inpatient* institutional costs per day or for a day of care. Hospitals occasionally *charge* for their services on the basis of a per diem rate derived by dividing their total costs by the number of inpatient days of care provided. Per diem costs, therefore, are averages and do not reflect true costs for each patient. Patients who use few hospital services (typically those at the end of a long stay) subsidize those who need much care (those just *admitted*). Thus the per diem approach is said to give hospitals an incentive to prolong hospital stays.

P

per 100 adjusted census: The ratio of health care personnel to adjusted average daily census, each on a 100 census basis.

percentage participation: The proportion of *loss* (or health care *cost*) borne by an insurer in contrast to the patient or insured under the policy of insurance.

peril: *Cause* of a possible *loss,* such as an *accident, death, sickness,* fire, flood, or burglary. See also *insurance* and *hazard.*

perinatal mortality: *Death (mortality)* during the late prenatal period (variously defined, but conventionally after the 28th week of gestation or with a fetus weighing over 1,000 grams, including *stillbirths*), birth process, and the early *neonatal* period. Mortality is usually measured as a rate, for example, number of perinatal deaths per 1,000 *live births* in a given area or program and time period. See also *health status, infant mortality,* and *neonatal mortality.*

period prevalence: A measure of prevalence for a given disease within a given time period, plus the recurrence of cases during a subsequent time period.

persistency: In *insurance,* the rate at which policies written in a given line of insurance or for *members* of a given *group* are maintained in force until the completion of the policy terms.

personal care facility: A long-term care facility that offers 24-hour general nursing and personal care on a limited basis.

personal health services: Health services provided to specific individuals. The term may be contrasted with *environmental health,* community health, *public health, consultation and education services,* and health education. These services are usually directed at populations, not individuals, and are undertaken to promote healthful environments, behavior, or life styles.

personal health status: Level of health of individuals in a particular group population.

personal physician: The *physician* who assumes responsibility for the comprehensive medical care of an individual on a continuing basis. The physician obtains *professional* assistance, when needed, for services he or she is not qualified to provide and coordinates the care provided by other professional personnel in accordance with personal knowledge and understanding of the *patient* as a whole. While personal physicians will have an interest in the patient's *family* as it affects the patient, the personal physician may not necessarily serve the entire family (e.g., a pediatrician may serve as a personal physician for children, while an *internist* or other *specialist* may serve in this capacity for adults). Personal physician is sometimes more simply defined for any given patient as the physician the patient designates as a primary or principal physician. See also *family physician* and *private patient*.

pharmaceutical: See *drug* and *legend*.

Pharmaceutical Manufacturers Association (PMA): A national association of manufacturers of brand-name pharmaceutical products.

pharmacist: A *professional* person qualified by at least five years of professional education and authorized by law after obtaining a *license* to practice *pharmacy*.

pharmacy: The science, arta, and *practice* of preparing, preserving, compounding, dispensing, and giving *appropriate* instruction in the use of *drugs;* a place where pharmacy is practiced. See also *druggist*.

pharmacy profile system: A medication record of an individual whereby a pharmacist may detect potential contraindications in a patient's therapeutic regimen.

Pharmacy and Therapeutics Committee: A committee of *physicians* and *pharmacists* within a health care facility responsible for developing policies for the distribution of drugs and selecting *drugs* for the *formulary*.

PHS Act: See *Public Health Service Act and U.S. Public Health Service.*

physical medicine (PM): The branch of medicine concerned with the diagnosis and treatment of the disabled and physically handicapped patient.

physical therapist (PT): A specially trained and *licensed* individual who uses physical agents, biomechanical and neurophysiological principles, and assistive devices in relieving pain, restoring maximum function, and preventing *disability* in a *patient* following *disease, injury,* or loss of a body part. It is estimated that approximately 8,000 physical therapists are employed in *hospitals*; others are employed by *rehabilitation* centers, schools or societies for crippled children, and *public health* agencies. A license is required to practice physical therapy in the 50 states, the District of Columbia, Puerto Rico, and the Virgin Islands. To obtain a license, an applicant must have a baccalaureate degree or certificate from an approved school of physical therapy and pass a state board examination, where required.

physical therapy (PT): An allied health profession that uses physical agents, massage, and neurophysical techniques and devices to relieve pain or correct physical defects or disorders.

physician: A *professional* person qualified by education and authorized by law (after obtaining a *license*) to practice *medicine.*

physician assistant (PA): a specially trained and *licensed* (when necessary) or otherwise credentialed (see *credentialing*) individual who performs tasks, otherwise performed by *physicians* themselves, under the direction of a supervising physician. This individual also may be known as a physician extender or use other essentially synonymous titles. Many were paramedics initially trained by the military (e.g., corpsmen and pharmacist's mates) and later further trained in medical schools to assist physicians in civilian health

P

services (see *Medex*). Other examples of similar occupations are *nurse practitioners, nurse midwives,* psychiatric therapy assistants, and rehabilitative personnel.

physician extender: See *physician assistant.*

physician shortage area: A geographic area with an inadequate *supply* of *physicians.* It is usually defined as an area having a physician-to-population ratio less than a particular standard, such as 1 to 4,000. See also *medically underserved area.*

Physicians' Desk Reference (PDR): An annual, nonofficial *compendium* of information concerning *drugs,* primarily *prescription* and *diagnostic* products, published primarily for *physicians* and widely used as a reference document by physicians, other *health personnel,* and patients. The information is primarily that included in the *labeling* or *package insert* for the drug required by the *Food and Drug Administration* and covers indications, effects, dosages, administration, and any relevant warnings, hazards, contraindications, side effects, and precautions. The PDR is distributed free or at reduced cost to many physicians and other *providers* through patronage of the drug manufacturers who have paid by the column inch for information that is printed about their products. It is the only readily available source that contains photographs for identifying drugs. The drugs are listed by *brand name* for each manufacturer and are indexed by manufacturer, brand name, drug classification, *generic name,* and *chemical name.*

physicians' and surgeons' professional liability insurance: See *malpractice insurance.*

physician's profile: Data on each doctor's charges and the payments made by specific patients for services. *Diseases* are classified according to the use of profiles used by hospitals in connection with *DRGs.*

ping-ponging: The practice of passing a *patient* from one *physician* to another in a health program for unnecessary cursory examinations so that the program can charge the patient's *third party* for a physician *visit* to each physician. The practice and term are most common in *Medicaid mills* where they originated.

pink lady: Jargon for a volunteer worker within a health care facility (because of the traditional color of volunteer uniforms).

placebo: An inactive or inert substance, preparation, or procedure (such as an injection of sugar water) used in *random controlled trials* to determine the *efficacy* of another substance, treatment, or preparation used in research or tests (and usually indistinguishable from it), or one given to please or gratify a *patient*. In many controlled trials of pain medicines (such as those involving Darvon), the placebo gives as much relief from pain perceived by the patient as does the active medication. See also *Hawthorne effect*.

planning: The conscious design of a set of desired future occurrences defined as *goals* and *objectives* of a plan. Planning includes the conduct of activities required for the design (such as data gathering and analysis), description and selection among alternative means of achieving the goals and objectives, and the activities necessary to insure that the plan is achieved. There are many definitions of planning and descriptions of plan. Specific types of plans, for example, are referred to as long-range or perspective (covering 15 or more years); mid-range or strategic (5 to 15 years); short-term or tactical (1 to 3 years, see *budget*); *health facilities* or *health manpower;* community or program; categorical or comprehensive health (see *categorical program* and *comprehensive health planning*); normative (based on *norms* or *standards* with legal basis); and inductive or deductive. These last terms are used when the planning takes place at a local level and then is consolidated and implemented at state and federal levels (bubbled up) or vice versa (trickled down). The extent to which planning is responsible, by definition, for

P

implementation of the plans is controversial, as is its relation to *management*. See also *health planning* and *health policy*.

podiatrist: A health *professional* responsible for the examination, *diagnosis,* prevention, *treatment,* and care involving conditions and functions of the human foot and lower leg. A podiatrist performs surgical and other operative procedures, *prescribes* corrective *devices,* and prescribes and administers *drugs* and *physical therapy.* *Medicare* regulations state that the doctor of podiatry is considered a "physician," but only with respect to functions he or she is legally authorized to perform by the state in which they are performed. However, certain types of foot treatment or care are excluded by Medicare, whether performed by a doctor of medicine or a doctor of podiatry.

policy: A course of action adopted and pursued by a government, party, statesman, or other individual or organization; any course of action adopted as proper, advantageous, or expedient. The Congress makes policy principally by writing legislation and conducting oversight activities. The term is sometimes less actively used to describe any stated position on matters at issue, such as an organization's policy statement on *national health insurance.* In *insurance,* a policy is a written contract of insurance between an *insurer* and the *insured.* In the executive branch of the federal government, policies are documents interpreting or amplifying *rules* and are sometimes referred to as guidelines. Policies bear the same relationship to rules (regulations) as rules do to law, except that, unlike regulations, policies do not have the force of law.

policy planning: The process of foreseeing issues that require resolution and defining specific strategies or programs to satisfy defined objectives.

polydrug: A medicinal product containing several different drugs.

pool: See *insurance pool.*

poor: See *poverty*.

postmortem care: The care of the deceased by health care *providers* prior to delivery to the morgue.

postpartum care: Medical care of the mother following the birth of a baby.

poverty: Having inadequate money, *resources*, goods, or other means of subsistence. Poverty is a difficult concept to define in practice; there is no single national definition. Three of the most commonly cited measures are the low-income level developed by the Bureau of the Census, *income* poverty guidelines published by the Community Services Administration (CSA) of the *Department of Health and Human Services* (formerly *Office of Economic Opportunity* guidelines), and the lower budget developed by the Bureau of Labor Statistics. Each of these uses a different method to measure poverty and arrives at a different dollar result. The census low-income level is the measure accepted by the *Office of Management and Budget* for official data on low-income persons. Eligibility for food stamps is based on a formula using these low-income thresholds. CSA poverty guidelines, essentially the same as the census low-income levels but rounded off to the nearest $10 for easier application, are used primarily to determine eligibility for participation in programs initiated under the Economic Opportunity Act. The Bureau of Labor Statistics income levels for an urban *family* and retired couple are based on a budget for a "modest but adequate" standard of living. In essence, the budget represents a detailed listing of items to meet the normal needs of a family or retired couple as judged adequate by the experts drawing up this hypothetical budget. These items are *indexed* to the *Consumer Price Index*. Income eligibility for welfare programs provides a different definition of poverty. Poverty levels used by the *Aid for Families with Dependent Children (AFDC)* program vary significantly by state, while a nationwide standard has been established under the *supplemental security income* (SSI) program. *Medicaid* income levels are based on, but are not necessarily equivalent to, the levels established under AFDC and SSI.

poverty area: An urban or rural geographic area with a high proportion of low-*income families*. Normally, average income is used to define a *poverty* area, but other indicators, such as housing conditions, illegitimate birth rates, and incidence of juvenile delinquency are sometimes added to define geographic areas with poverty conditions. The term is defined in P.L. 93-641 (Section 1633(15) of the *PHS Act.*)

PPO: See *preferred provider organization.*

practical nurse: See *licensed practical nurse.*

practice: The use of one's knowledge in a particular *profession*. For example, the practice of *medicine* is the exercise of one's knowledge in the promotion of *health* and *treatment* of *disease*.

preadmission: The review of patient needs prior to formal inpatient admission.

preadmission certification: Review of the need for proposed *inpatient* service(s) prior to time of *admission* to an institution. See also *concurrent review* and *prior authorization.*

pre-existing condition: An *injury* occurring, *disease* contracted, or physical condition that existed prior to the issuance of a *health insurance* policy. A pre-existing condition usually results in an *exclusion* from coverage under the policy for costs resulting from the condition.

preferred provider organization (PPO): A health care organization formed by a *hospital* or *physician* group to contract with an *insurer* for health care provided to a defined population. The organization is called a preferred provider. PPOs are not exclusive

P

providers of care to insured groups, but they usually offer lower charges to the insured groups in return for the their influence in channeling patients to PPO participants.

premium: The amount of money or consideration paid by an *insured* person or policyholder (or on his behalf) to an *insurer* or *third party* for coverage under an *insurance policy*. The premium is generally paid in periodic amounts. It is related to the actuarial value of the *benefits* provided by the policy plus a *loading* to cover such items as administrative costs and *profit*. Premium amounts for employment-related insurance are often split between employers and employees (see *contributory insurance*). Under current tax law, one-half of the amount spent on premiums by employees up to a maximum of $150 is deductible (see *medical deduction*) for income tax purposes for those who itemize deductions. Premiums paid by the employer are nontaxable *income* for the employee. Premiums are paid for coverage whether benefits are actually used or not; they should not be confused with *cost sharing* that includes *copayments* and *deductibles* paid only if benefits are actually used.

prepaid group practice: An arrangement where a formal association of three or more physicians provides a defined set of services to persons over a specified time period in return for a fixed periodic *prepayment* or *prospective reimbursement* made in advance of the use of service. See also *group practice, medical foundation,* and *health maintenance organization.*

prepaid health plan (PHP): Generically, a contract between an *insurer* and a *subscriber* or group of subscribers whereby the PHP provides a specified set of health *benefits* in return for a periodic *premium.* The term now usually refers to organizational entities in California that provide services to *Medi-Cal* (the name for California's *Medicaid* program) beneficiaries under contract with the State of California. Provision was made under the Medi-Cal Reform Program of 1971 for Medi-Cal administrators to contract with groups of medical providers to supply specified services on a prepaid, per-capita basis. These entities have been the subject of much controversy regarding the *cost* and *quality* of their services (see *skimping*).

prepayment: A term sometimes synonymous with *insurance*; also refers to any advance payment to a *provider* for anticipated *services* (such as an expectant mother paying in advance for maternity care). It may be distinguished from insurance when used in referring to payment to organizations (such as *HMOs, prepaid group practices,* and *medical foundations*) that, unlike insurance companies, accept responsibility for arranging for and providing needed services as well as paying for them.

prescription: A written direction or order for the preparation and dispensing of a *drug* or other remedy. A prescription can be issued only by a *physician, dentist,* or other practitioner licensed by law to prescribe the drug or remedy. It may be written as an order in a *hospital* or other institution for a drug to be given an *inpatient,* or it may be given to an individual *outpatient* to be filled by a *pharmacist.* A prescription properly specifies the drug to be given, the amount of the drug to be dispensed, and the directions necessary for the patient to use the drug.

prescription drug: A *drug* available to the public only upon *prescription.* The availability of a drug is thus limited when the drug is considered dangerous if used without a *physician's* supervision. See also *ethical drug, over-the-counter drug,* and *legend.*

President's budget: The federal *budget* for a particular *fiscal year* specifying proposed *budget authority, obligations,* and *outlays* that is transmitted to the Congress by the President in accordance with the Budget and Accounting Act of 1921, as amended. Certain elements of the budget, such as estimates for the legislative branch and the judiciary, are included without review by the *Office of Management and Budget* or approval by the President. The budget is submitted for congressional approval in January for the fiscal year beginning the following October 1. See also *congressional budget.*

prevailing charge: A *charge* that falls within the range of charges most frequently used in a *locality* for a particular medical *service* or procedure. A *carrier* may consider prevailing charges as a basis for reimbursement to the *provider*. The maximum figure in each range establishes an overall limitation on charges that will be accepted as *reasonable* for the service without requiring special justification. Current *Medicare* rules state that the limit of an area's prevailing charge is to be the 75th percentile of the *customary charges* for a given service by the *physicians* in a given area. For example, if customary charges for an appendectomy in a locality were distributed so that physicians customarily charging $150 for the procedure rendered 10 percent of the total procedures; physicians charging $200 rendered 40 percent; those charging $250, 40 percent; and those charging $300 or more, 10 percent, the prevailing charge would be $250. This is the level that, under Medicare regulations, would cover at least 75 percent of the cases. See also *actual charge* and *fractionation*.

prevalence: The number of cases of *disease,* infected persons, or persons with some other characteristic present at a particular time in relation to the total size of a given population. It is a measurement of *morbidity* at a moment in time; for example, the number of cases of hemophilia in the country on the first of a specified year. Prevalence also equals *incidence* times average case duration (such as the prevalence of arthritis is high relative to its incidence).

preventive medicine: Care that has the primary aim of preventing *disease* or minimizing its consequences. It includes health care programs for prevention of illness (e.g., immunizations), early detection of disease (e.g., Pap smears), and programs and procedures to inhibit further deterioration of the body (e.g., exercise or prophylactic surgery). Preventive *medicine* developed subsequent to bacteriology. During its early history, specific medical control measures against the agents of infectious diseases were primary concerns. With increasing knowledge of nutritional, malignant, and other *chronic diseases,* the scope of preventive medicine has been ex-

P

tended. It is now operatively assumed that most, if not all, problems are preventable at some stage of their development. Preventive medicine also relates to general preventive measures to improve the healthfulness of our environment and our relationship with the environment, such as avoidance of hazardous substances, modified diet, and *family planning*. In particular, promoting basic health by alteration of behavior, especially through health education, is gaining prominence as a component of preventive medicine. See also *public health, consultation and education services,* and *HMO*.

primary care: Basic or general health care that emphasizes the point at which the *patient* first seeks assistance from the medical care system; care of the less complex and more common *illnesses*. The primary care *provider* usually assumes ongoing responsibility for the patient in both *health* maintenance and *therapy* of illness. Primary care is comprehensive in the sense that it takes responsibility for the overall coordination of the care of the patient's health problems, whether biological, behavioral, or social. The appropriate use of *consultants* and community resources is an important part of effective primary care. Such care is generally provided by *physicians,* but is increasingly being provided by other personnel such as family *nurse practitioners*. See also *family physician, personal physician, secondary care, tertiary care,* and *general practice.*

primary payer: The *insurer* obligated to pay *losses* prior to any liability of secondary insurers. For example, under current law, *Medicare* is a primary payer with respect to *Medicaid;* for a person eligible under both programs, Medicaid pays only for *benefits* not covered under Medicare or after Medicare benefits are exhausted. See also *duplication of benefits* and *coordination of benefits.*

primary reserve: That part of an *insurance* company's *reserves* (funds) set aside for *losses* that have been *incurred but not reported.*

prior authorization: Requirement imposed by a *third party,* under some systems of *utilization review,* that a *provider* must justify before a *peer review* committee, insurance company representative, or state agent the *need* for delivering a particular *service* to a *patient* before actually providing the service in order to receive reimbursement. Generally, prior authorization is required for nonemergency services that are expensive (for example, *preadmission certification* required for a hospital stay) or likely to be overused or *abused* (for instance, prior authorization required for all *dental* services by many state *Medicaid* programs).

prior determination: Similar to *prior authorization* but less restrictive in that payment will be made if prior authorization is not sought, provided that the third party would have approved the *service* as *needed.*

private patient: A *patient* whose care is the responsibility of an identifiable, individual health *professional* (usually a *physician*) who is paid directly (by the patient or a *third party*) for the *service* to the patient. The physician is called a *personal physician,* and the patient is his or her private patient. Private patients are contrasted with public, service, or ward patients whose care is the responsibility of a health program or institution. Public patients are often cared for by an individual practitioner paid by the program (such as a member of the *housestaff*), but the program, rather than the individual, is paid for the care. The distinction is important to third-party payers (including *Medicare*), because situations arise in which payment is made to both a program and an individual practitioner for the same services. Private patient occasionally refers to a patient who has sole occupation of a room in an institution. See also *private practice.*

private practice: Medical *practice* in which the practitioner and the practice are independent of any external *policy* control. It usually requires that the practitioner be self-employed, except when salaried by a partnership in which he or she is a partner with similar practitioners. The term is sometimes wrongly used synonymously with either *fee-for-service* practice (the practitioner may offer services by another method, such as *capitation*), or *solo practice* (*group*

P

215

practice also may be private). Note that physicians practice in many different settings; there is no agreement as to which of these does or does not constitute private practice. *Regulation* exerts external control, but it is not generally considered to result in public practice. The opposite of private practice is not necessarily public (as the word is defined to mean employment by government). Practitioners salaried by private *hospitals* are not usually thought to be in private practice. See also *private patient* and *general practice*.

privileged communication: Any statement or communication made in confidence or trust to a person recognized by law as responsible for holding such communication in trust.

PRN: As needed or as required (as it applies to the taking of medication).

probationary period: See *waiting period*.

problem-oriented medical record (POMR): A *medical record* in which the information and conclusions contained in the record are organized to describe each of the *patient's* problems. This description properly includes subjective, objective, and significant negative information, discussion, and conclusions, in addition to *diagnostic studies* and *treatment* plans with respect to each problem. The record has gained increased acceptance. It can be contrasted with the traditional medical record that is less formally organized and usually records together all information from each source (history, physical examination, and laboratory) without regard to the problems the information describes.

procedure: See *service*.

process measure: An indicator of the *quality* of medical care used to assess the activities of *health manpower* and programs in the management of *patients*. Process measures document the process of care used for various populations or diagnoses; for example, the fraction of people with hypertension who receive an intravenous pyelogram, or the percentage of streptococcal infections of the throat in which cultures are obtained before *treatment*. They do not necessarily measure the results of care, although they measure the use of *diagnostic studies* and treatment methods that are thought or proven to be *effective*. Generally, such measures indicate the degree of conformity with *standards* established by peer groups or with expectations formulated by leaders in the profession. See also *input measure, outcome measure,* and *output measure.*

professional: A term with no consistent or agreed-upon meaning. Most occupational groups in the health field aspire to being considered professions. There are several usual professional components: (1) formal education and examination required for membership in the profession; (2) *certification* or *licensure,* reflecting community sanction or approval, required for membership; (3) regional or national professional associations; (4) a code of ethics governing the activities of individuals in the profession; (5) a body of systematic scientific knowledge and technical skill requirements; and the (6) members functioning with a degree of autonomy and authority under the assumption that they alone have the expertise to make decisions in their area of competence. *Medicine* is often considered the occupation that most closely approaches the prototype of a profession.

Professional Activity Study (PAS): A shared-computer *medical record* information system purchased by hospitals from the *Commission on Professional and Hospital Activities (CPHA)*, a nonprofit computer center in Ann Arbor, Michigan. Information flows into the system through a *discharge abstract* completed by the hospital medical record *department* on every discharged *patient.* The patient information is displayed back to the hospital in a series of monthly, semiannual, and annual reports that compare the hospital's *average lengths of stay,* number and types of tests used, and *autopsy* rates for given diagnostic conditions with those of other hospitals of similar size and scope of services. (These reports are good examples of *process measures*). See also *ICDA* and *ICD-9-CM Procedures.*

P

professional liability: Obligation of *providers* or their professional liability *insurers* to pay for damages resulting from the providers' acts of omission or commission in the *treatment of patients.* The term is sometimes preferred by providers to medical *malpractice* because it does not necessarily imply negligence. It is also a term that more adequately describes the obligations of all types of *professionals,* for example, lawyers, architects, and other health *providers*, as well as physicians.

professional liability insurance: See *malpractice insurance.*

Professional Standards Review Organization (PSRO): A physician-sponsored organization responsible for comprehensive and ongoing review of *services* under the *Medicare, Medicaid,* and *maternal and child health services* programs. The review determines for purposes of reimbursement under these programs whether services are medically *necessary;* provided in accordance with professional *criteria, norms,* and *standards;* and, in the case of institutional services, rendered in an *appropriate* setting. The requirement for the establishment of PSROs was added by the Social Security Amendments of 1972 (P.L. 92-603) to the Social Security Act as Part B of Title XI. PSRO areas have been designated throughout the country, and organizations in many of these areas are at various stages of implementing the required review functions. PSROs have been replaced by *peer review organizations (PROs).* See also *peer review* and *medical review.*

proficiency testing: Assessment of technical knowledge and competency skills related to the performance requirements of a specific job, whether such knowledge and skills were acquired through formal or informal means. Section 241 of the Social Security Amendments of 1972 (P.L. 92-603) requires the secretary of Health and Human Services, in carrying out the functions relating to *qualifications* for *health manpower,* to develop and conduct a program to determine the proficiency of individuals in performing the duties and functions of practical *nurses,* therapists, medical technologists, cytotechnologists, *radiologic technologists,* psychiatric technicians, and other health

P

care technicians and technologists. The program uses formal testing of the proficiency of individuals, and cannot deny any individual, who otherwise meets the proficiency requirements for any health care specialty, a satisfactory proficiency rating solely because of failure to meet formal educational or *professional* membership requirements. Proficiency examinations also determine the necessary work qualifications of health personnel (such as therapists, technologists, technicians, and others), who do not otherwise meet formal educational, professional membership, or other specified criteria established under *regulations* of *Medicare,* so that *services* provided by these individuals will be eligible for payment.

profile: A longitudinal or cross-sectional study of medical care data. *Patient* profiles list all of the *services* provided to a particular patient during a specified period of time. *Physician, hospital,* or population profiles are statistical summaries of the pattern of *practice* of an individual physician, a specific hospital, or the medical experience of a specific population. Diagnostic profiles are a subcategory of physician, hospital, or population profiles with regard to a specific condition or *diagnosis.*

profit: The net gain produced by the sale of a good or *service* after deducting the value of the labor, materials, rents, interest on *capital,* and other expenses involved in the production of the good or service. Economists define profit as return to (or on) capital investment and distinguish normal (competitive) and excessive (more than competitive) profit. Profit relating to a profit-making or *proprietary* institution is present when any of the net earnings of the institution inure to the benefit of any individual. The concept of profit is very hard to define operationally or in detail, and unreasonable or excessive profit even more so. It is important to recognize that reasonable profit on investments must vary with the risks involved in the investment. Profit bears a close relationship to the balance of *supply* and *demand*; it is a measure of unmet demand.

progressive patient care: A system under which *patients* are grouped together in units based on their *need* for care as determined by their degree of *illness* rather than by consideration of medical *specialty*. There are three conventional levels or stages of progressive patient care: (1) intensive care, needed for critically ill patients; (2) intermediate care, between intensive and minimal; and (3) minimal care or self-care, which is self-explanatory. Except for the development of *intensive care units,* the concept of progressive patient care does not appear to have had much impact on the organization of *hospitals* and other health programs.

progressive tax: A tax that takes an increasing proportion of *income* as income rises, such as the federal personal income tax. Incremental increases in taxable income are thus subject to an increased *marginal tax rate*. See also *regressive tax* and *proportional tax.*

project grant: A grant of federal funds to a public or private agency or organization for a specified purpose authorized by law, such as development of an *emergency medical services system* or conduct of a *continuing education* program. Awarding project grants is usually discretionary with the *Department of Health and Human Services*. Applicants are chosen on the basis of merit, often competitively, and the amount of the grant is based on *need* (the estimated cost of achieving the purpose). This contrasts with the usual practice in *formula grants.*

ProPAC: Prospective Payment Assessment Commission; the government-appointed panel that reviews *Medicare's* prospective payment system to *hospitals*.

proportional tax: A tax that takes a constant proportion of *income* as income changes. For example, the social security *payroll tax* is proportional up to the limit on income to which it applies. See also *progressive tax* and *regressive tax.*

proprietary: *Profit* making; owned and operated for the purposes of making a profit, whether or not such a profit is, in fact, earned.

proprietary hospital: A *hospital* operated for the purpose of making a *profit* for its owners. Proprietary hospitals are often owned by *physicians* for the care of their own and others' *patients*. There is also a growing number of investor-owned hospitals usually operated by a parent corporation operating a chain of such hospitals.

prospective reimbursement: Any method of paying *hospitals* or other health programs in which amounts or *rates* of payment are established in advance for the coming year and the programs are paid these amounts regardless of the costs they actually incur. These systems of reimbursement are designed to introduce constraint on *charge* or *cost* increases by setting limits on amounts paid during a future period. In some cases, such systems provide incentives for improved *efficiency* by sharing savings with institutions that perform at lower than anticipated costs. Prospective reimbursement contrasts with the method of payment presently used under *Medicare* and *Medicaid,* in which institutions are reimbursed for actual expenses incurred (i.e., on a *retrospective* basis). See also *Section 222.*

prospective study: An inquiry planned to observe events that have not yet occurred; compare with a *retrospective study* planned to examine events that have already occurred.

provider: An individual or institution that gives medical care. In *Medicare,* an institutional provider is a *hospital, skilled nursing facility, home health agency,* or certain providers of outpatient *physical therapy* services. These providers receive *cost-related reimbursement.* Other Medicare providers, paid on a *charge* basis, are called *suppliers.* Individual providers *practice* independently of institutional providers.

provisional staff: *Physicians* or other *professional* health care *providers* who have been only recently accepted for *staff privileges.*

prudent buyer principle: The principle that *Medicare* should not

P

reimburse a *provider* for a *cost* that is not *reasonable,* because it is in excess of the amount that a prudent and cost-conscious buyer would be expected to pay. For example, an organization that does not seek the customary discount on bulk purchases could be reimbursed through the operation of this principle for less than the full purchase price, as it would be considered an *imprudent* buyer.

psychiatry (P); The branch of medicine that specializes in behavioral or mental disorders.

psychoanalysis (PYA): A technique for determining and understanding the mental processes.

psychosomatic illness: A *disease* that shows a physical dysfunction or lesion in which psychological and other nonphysical factors play a causative role, for example, asthma, vasomotor rhinitis, peptic ulcer, colonic disorders, arterial hypertension, coronary disease, and hyperthyroidism. These diseases should be distinguished from *mental disorders* and from the psychic effects of diseases that are not psychically caused.

psychosurgery: *Surgery* that is done for the purpose of changing the *patient's* personality, thought, emotions, or behavior, rather than for the *treatment* of a physical *disease.* The term is used irregularly; for instance, sometimes it refers to all surgery performed on the human brain for whatever purpose.

psychotropic drug: Any *drug* which influences psychic function, behavior, or experience. This classification includes, but is not limited to, any drugs that produce *drug dependence.*

P

public accountability: See *accountable.*

public health (PH): The science dealing with the protection and improvement of community *health* by organized community effort. Public health activities are generally those less amenable to being undertaken individually or less *effective* when undertaken on an individual basis. They do not typically include direct *personal health services*. Immunizations, sanitation, *preventive medicine, quarantine* and other *disease* control activities, *occupational health and safety* programs, assurance of the healthfulness of air, water, and food, health education, and *epidemiology* are examples of recognized public health activities.

Public Health Service Act (PHS Act): One of the principal health-related Acts of Congress providing legislative authority for federal health activities (42 U.S.C. 201-300). Originally enacted July 1, 1944 (and sometimes referred to as the Act of July 1), the PHS Act was a complete codification of accumulated federal *public health* laws in effect at that time. Since then many of the Acts written in the health area, particularly by the Committee on Interstate and Foreign Commerce, have been amendments to the PHS Act and have revised, extended, or added new authority to the Act (for example, the HMO Act of 1973, P.L. 93-222, which added a new Title XIII, and the Health Revenue Sharing and Health Services Amendments of 1975, P.L. 94-63, which revised many existing sections of the Act). A compilation of the PHS Act, as amended, and related Acts is published for public use by the Committee on Interstate and Foreign Commerce. Generally, the Act contains authority for public health programs, *biomedical research, health manpower* training, *family planning, emergency medical services systems, HMOs,* regulation of drinking water supplies, and *health planning* and resources development.

public patient: See *service patient* and *private patient*.

P

Qq

qualification: The meeting of *standards* for program eligibility, *licensure*, reimbursement, or other *benefits*. Thus, a qualified educational program meets *accreditation* standards, a qualified *HMO* (for the benefit of mandated *dual-choice* under Section 1310 of the *PHS Act*) meets the standards imposed by the HMO Act, and a qualified *provider* for reimbursement by an *insurance* program meets the *conditions of participation*.

quality: The nature or character of an item; hence, the degree or grade of excellence possessed by the item. Quality may be measured with respect to individual medical *services*, various services received by individual or groups of *patients* or given by individual or groups of *providers*, or health programs or *facilities;* in terms of technical competence, humanity, *need, acceptability, appropriateness,* inputs, structure, process, or outcomes; using *standards, criteria, norms,* or direct quantitative or qualitative measures. To avoid the frequent vagueness of the term it is thus necessary to specify who or what is being considered, what aspect of it is being measured, and how it is being assessed. See also *efficacy, effectiveness, peer review organizations, Quality Assurance Program for Medical Care in the Hospital (QAP), tissue review, medical review, peer review,* and *utilization review.*

quality assurance: Activities and programs intended to assure the *quality* of care in a defined medical setting or program. The programs must include educational or other components intended to remedy identified deficiencies in quality, as well as the components necessary to identify the deficiencies (such as *peer review* or *utilization review* components) and assess the program's own *effectiveness.* A program that identifies deficiencies in quality and responds only with negative sanctions, such as denial of reimbursement, is not usually considered a quality assurance program, although the latter may include use of such sanctions. Such programs are required of *HMOs* and other health programs assisted under authority of the *PHS Act* (e.g., Section 1301(c)(8)). See also *Quality Assurance Program for Medical Care in the Hospital (QAP)*.

Quality Assurance Program for Medical Care in the Hospital (QAP): A program developed by the *American Hospital Association* for use by *hospital* administrations and medical staffs in the development of a hospital program to assure the *quality* of the care provided within the hospital.

quarantine: The limitation of freedom of movement of susceptible persons or animals that have been exposed to a communicable *disease*, in order to prevent spread of the disease; the place of detention of such persons or animals; or the act of detaining vessels or travelers suspected of having communicable diseases at ports or places of inspection or disinfection. See also *public health*.

quid pro quo: Something required in return for another thing of like value. The concept is used, for example, in *health manpower* legislation that refers to requirements of health *professional* schools considered as conditions for receiving federal *capitation* payments.

quotes: In the Congress, provisions in a law that amends another, earlier act of Congress are placed in quotation marks (quotes); material that refers to new, freestanding legislative authority is not placed in quotes. Thus, material amending another law (such as the *Public Health Service Act*) is said to be "in the quotes."

Q

Rr

radiologic technologist or technician: An individual who maintains and safely uses equipment and supplies necessary to demonstrate portions of the human body on x-ray film or fluoroscopic screen for diagnostic purposes. The individual also may supervise and teach other radiologic personnel. In 1973 an estimated 100,000 radiologic technologists were employed full time or part time, approximately one-third by *hospitals*. The rest worked in independent x-ray laboratories, multispecialty clinics, *physicians'* offices, and government agencies. Radiologic technology programs approved by the *American Medical Association*'s Council on Medical Education are offered by hospitals, medical schools, and community colleges that have hospital *affiliation*. The programs are open to high school graduates, although a few require one or two years of college or graduation from a school of *nursing*. Training varies from a minimum of two years in a hospital radiology *department* or hospital-affiliated junior college that offers an associate degree to a four-year university course.

radiology (R): A branch of medicine that uses ionizing radiation for diagnosis and therapy.

random controlled trial (RCT): An experimental *prospective study* for assessing the effects of a particular *drug* or medical *procedure* in which subjects (human or animal) are assigned on a random basis to either of two groups, experimental and control. The experimental group receives the drug or procedure; the control group does not. A series of laboratory tests and clinical examinations usually using the *double-blind technique* are performed to detect differences between the two groups. In drug studies, researchers attempt to determine how the drug is absorbed, metabolized, and eliminated; levels of the drug that are tolerated; any obvious toxic effects; long-run toxic and

R

carcinogenic effects; the *effectiveness* of the drug in prevention or control of a *disease* or symptom; and the *safe* and *appropriate* dosage of the drug for various categories of *patients*.

rate setting: The process of determining rates to be paid by a governmental body to a health care provider based on actual costs of service.

rating: In *insurance,* the process of determining or classifying rates, or the cost of insurance, for individuals and *groups* or classes of *risks*.

reasonable charge: For any specific *service* covered under *Medicare,* the lower of the *customary charge* by a particular *physician* for that service and the *prevailing charge* by physicians in the geographic area for that service. Reimbursement is based on the lower of the *reasonable charge* and *actual charge*. For example, the prevailing charge in a certain *locality* for a given medical procedure is $100; this represents the 75th percentile of the customary charges for that service by the physicians in that locality. Dr. A's actual charge is $75, although he customarily charges $80 for the procedure; Dr. B's actual charge is his customary charge of $85; Dr. C's is his customary charge of $125; Dr. D's is $100, although he customarily charges $80. There are no special circumstances in any case. The reasonable charge for Dr. A is $75, because the reasonable charge cannot exceed the actual charge even if it is lower than his customary charge and below the prevailing charge for the locality. The reasonable charge for Dr. B is $85, because his customary charge, is lower than the prevailing charge for that locality. The reasonable charge for Dr. C is $100, the prevailing charge for the locality. The reasonable charge for Dr. D is $80, because that is his customary charge which is lower than the actual charge in this particular case. His reasonable charge cannot exceed his customary charge in the absence of special circumstances, even though his actual charge of $100 is the same as the prevailing charge. Generically, the term is used for any charge payable by an *insurance* program that is determined in a similar but not necessarily identical

R

fashion. See also *comparability provision* and *Section 224.*

reasonable cost: Generally the amount that a *third party* using *cost-related reimbursement* will actually reimburse a provider. Under *Medicare*, reasonable costs are costs actually incurred in delivering health *services* excluding any part of such incurred costs found to be unnecessary for the efficient delivery (see *efficiency*) of *needed* health services (refer to Section 1861 of the Social Security Act). The law stipulates that, except for certain *deductible* and *coinsurance* amounts that must be paid by *beneficiaries,* payments to hospitals shall be made on the basis of the reasonable costs of providing the covered services. The secretary of Health and Human Services has prescribed *rules* setting forth the method or methods to be used and the items to be included in determining the reasonable costs of covered care. The regulations require that costs be apportioned between Medicare beneficiaries and other hospital *patients* so that neither group subsidizes the costs of the other. The items or elements of both *direct cost* and *indirect cost* that the regulations specify as reimbursable are known as *allowable costs.* Such costs are reimbursable on the basis of a hospital's actual costs to the extent that they are reasonable and are related to patient care. Under certain conditions the following items may be included as allowable costs: (1) *capital depreciation;* (2) interest expenses; (3) educational activities; (4) research costs related to patient care; (5) unrestricted grants, gifts, and income from endowments; (6) value of services of nonpaid workers and compensation of owners; (7) payments to related organizations; (8) return on equity *capital* of *proprietary* providers; and (9) the *inpatient* routine *nursing differential. Bad debts* may be included only to the extent institutions fail in good faith efforts to collect the debts. See also *Section 223.*

reciprocity: In *licensure* of *health manpower,* the recognition by one state of the licenses of a second state when the latter state extends the same recognition to licenses of the first state. Licensing requirements in the two states usually must be equivalent before formal or informal reciprocal agreements are made. Reciprocity is often used interchangeably with the term *endorsement.* Theoretically, licensure by endorsement requires only that the qualifications of the licensee, or the standards required for licensure in the original licensing state, be deemed equivalent to the licensure requirements of the state in which licensure is being sought; it does mean not that the two states have a reciprocal arrangement.

recreational therapist: An individual who directs or coordinates recreational activities for the elderly or other special groups or is responsible for such activities in long-term-care facilities.

recurring clause: A provision in some health *insurance* policies that specifies a period of time during which the recurrence of a condition is considered a continuation of a prior period of *disability* or *hospital* confinement rather than a separate *spell of illness* or *episode of illness.*

referral: The practice of sending a *patient* to another practitioner or to another program for *services* or *consultation* that the referring source is not prepared or qualified to provide. In contrast to referral for consultation, referral for services involves a delegation of responsibility for patient care to another practitioner or program, and the referring source may or may not follow up to ensure that services are received.

Regional Medical Program (RMP): A program of federal support for regional organizations, called regional medical programs, that seek to improve care of patients with heart *disease,* cancer, strokes, and related diseases in their respective geographic regions. The legislative authority, created by P.L. 89-239, is found in Title IX of the *PHS Act.* The programs are heavily oriented toward initiating and improving *continuing education, nursing care,* and *intensive care units.* Some features of the RMP program were combined into the new *health planning* program authorized by P.L. 93-641 (see *health systems agency*).

registered nurse (RN): A *nurse* who has graduated from a formal program of nursing education (see *diploma school, associate degree*

R

program, and *baccalaureate program*) and has been *licensed* by appropriate state authority. Registered nurses are the most highly educated of nurses with the widest scope of responsibility for all aspects of *nursing care.* See also *licensed practical nurse, nurse practitioner,* and *nurse anesthetist.*

registered record administrator (RRA): An individual who administers *medical record* systems for health care facilities and implements policies and procedures for the collection, storage, classification, and release of data for medical, legal, and administrative purposes. See *medical record administrator.*

registration: The process by which qualified individuals are listed on an official roster maintained by a governmental or nongovernmental agency. Standards for registration may include successful completion of a written examination given by the *registry,* membership in the *professional* association maintaining the registry, and specified education and experience, such as graduation from an approved program or equivalent experience. Registration is a form of *credentialing,* similar to *certification.* Registration is also used to describe the recording of *notifiable* diseases, or the listing and follow-up of *patients* with such diseases.

registry: A list of individuals who have given explicit indication (for instance by contracting for *membership*) that they use or rely upon a given health *professional* or program for the *services* that the professional or program is able to provide. Panel is sometimes used in preference to registry with respect to individual practitioners. The nature of the actual financial and other relationships between a program and the people on its registry is quite variable. Registry also refers to an organization that conducts a *registration* program for *health manpower* or the list of individuals such an organization has registered. See also *catchment area, enroll,* and *roster.*

regressive tax: A tax that takes a decreasing proportion of total *income* as income rises, such as sales tax and the social security *payroll tax* (not applicable on earnings above the maximum level). A regressive tax is a constant percentage of income up to the maximum level (wage base) or a *proportional tax* up to that level. See also *progressive tax* and *marginal tax rate.*

regulation: The intervention of government in the health care or health *insurance* market to control entry into or change the behavior of participants in that marketplace through specification of rules for the participants. This intervention does not usually include programs that seek to change behavior through financing mechanisms or incentives. Private *accreditation* organizations may become involved in government regulation when their services are utilized in regulatory programs, such as the role of the *Joint Commission on Accreditation of Healthcare Organizations* under *Medicare. Regulatory programs* can be described in terms of their purpose (control of *charges*), who is regulated (*hospitals*), who regulates (state government), and method (prospective rate review). They include *certification; certain registration; licensure; certificate of need;* the *Economic Stabilization Program;* and *maximum allowable cost* and *peer review organization* programs. Regulation is also a synonym for a *rule* published by the executive branch of the federal government in implementing a law.

regulatory agency: Any agency of government that adopts and enforces *regulation* in a given area of responsibility.

rehabilitation: The combined and coordinated use of medical, social, educational, and vocational measures for training or retraining individuals *disabled* by *disease* or *injury* to the highest possible level of functional ability. Rehabilitation services are usually distinguished according to these types of measures (vocational, social, medical, and educational). Habilitation is the term for similar activities undertaken for individuals born with limited functional ability, compared with rehabilitation used for people who have lost abilities because of disease or injury (see *developmental disability*). A rehabilitation center is a health program or facility that specializes in rehabilitation.

R

reimbursement, cost control: In health care finance, *DRG* reimbursement methods used in determining *rates* of payment to health care institutions for *services*. Rates can be set either as price per case or by indexation. Under price per case, the patient population is distributed among the groups. Rates are then set prospectively for each DRG without regard to costs incurred or length of stay. Under indexation, per diem reimbursement is paid with reasonable costs being adjusted to reflect *case mix*.

reimbursement, retroactive: A payment by a *third party* to a health care *provider* not included in the original request or arrangement for reimbursement. See also *retrospective reimbursement*.

reinsurance: The practice of one insurance *underwriter* buying *insurance* from a second company for the purpose of protecting itself against part or all of the *losses* it might incur in the process of honoring the *claims* of its policyholders. The original company is called the ceding company; the second is the assuming company or reinsurer. Reinsurance may be sought by the ceding company to protect itself against losses beyond certain amounts in individual cases where competition requires it to offer policies providing coverage in excess of these amounts; to offer protection against catastrophic losses in a certain line of insurance, such as aviation accident or polio insurance; or to protect against mistakes in *rating* and *underwriting* when entering a new line of insurance, such as *major medical*.

relative value scale or schedule (RVS): A coded listing of *physicians* or other *professional services* that uses units indicating the relative value of the services they perform. Taken into account are the time, skill, and overhead cost required for each service, but not usually the relative cost-effectiveness of the service, the relative *need* or *demand* for it, or its importance to people's *health*. The units in this scale are based on median *charges* by physicians. Appropriate conversion factors are used to translate the abstract units in the scale to dollar fees for each service. Given individual and local variations

R

in *practice,* the relative value scale can be used voluntarily by physicians as a guide in establishing *fee-for-service* schedules. Insurance *carriers* and government agencies may also use the RVS in determining appropriate reimbursement (for example, by *Medicare* in areas where there is no *customary charge* or *prevailing charge* for a covered service). The California Medical Association, for instance, prepares and periodically revises a scale that includes independent scales for medicine, anesthesia, surgery, radiology, and pathology. Relative value scales may contain biases favoring certain specialties (such as surgery) or types of services (highly technical or specialized) over others. See also *fractionation.*

release form: A written acknowledgement whereby one person releases another from a past or prospective claim. It is also used to authorize release of confidential information or patient information.

reliability: In research, the reproducibility of an experimental result, that is, how closely a second study would yield the same answer whether or not it is correct. See also *validity.*

request for proposal (RFP):   A solicitation from a foundation or governmental agency notifying interested parties that funds are available for selected or specified projects, research, or other undertakings.

required services: *Services* that must be offered by a health program in order to meet some external *standard.* Under *Title XIX* of the Social Security Act, each state must offer certain *basic health services* before it can qualify as having a *Medicaid* program (and thus be eligible for federal matching funds). These services include *hospital* services; laboratory and x-ray services; *skilled nursing facility* services for individuals age 21 and older; *early and periodic screening, diagnosis, and treatment program* for individuals under age 21; *family planning* services; *physicians'* services; and *home health care* services for all persons eligible for skilled nursing facility services. It is important to note that within these require-

R

ments states may determine the scope and extent of *benefits* (for example, limiting hospital care to 30 days a year). States may offer additional services in their Medicaid program. These are called *optional services,* because they are offered at the option of the state.

res ipsa loquitur: Literally, "the facts speak for themselves": in *malpractice,* a legal doctrine that presumes the defendant is negligent when an *injury* occurs to a plaintiff through a situation under the sole and exclusive control of the defendant and where such injury would not normally occur if the one in control had used due care. The doctrine applies, for example, in the classic case of a surgeon who leaves a sponge in the patient's abdomen.

rescission: In the federal *budget,* enacted legislation canceling *budget authority* previously provided by the Congress. Rescissions proposed by the president must be transmitted in a special message to the Congress. Under Section 1012 of the Congressional Budget and Impoundment Control Act of 1974, the budget authority in question must be made available for *obligation* unless Congress approves a rescission bill within 45 days of continuous session. In *insurance,* rescission refers to policy cancellation with repayment of *premiums.*

research: Conscious and purposeful action to acquire deeper knowledge or new facts about scientific or technical subjects. Different types of research are distinguished by their concern (such as *biomedical research* and *health services research*) or method.

reserves: Balance sheet accounts set up to disclose the *liabilities* faced by an insurance company under outstanding *insurance policies.* Their purpose is to secure as true a picture as possible of the financial condition of the organization (by permitting conversion of disbursements from a paid to an accrual basis). The company sets the amount of reserves in accord with its own estimates, state laws, and recommendations of supervisory officials and national organizations. Regulatory agencies can accept the reserves or refuse them as

R

234

inadequate or excessive. For *Blue Cross plans,* for example, reserves are set aside to cover average monthly *claims* and operating expenses for some period of time. Reserves, although estimated, are obligated amounts and have four principal components: (1) reserves for known liabilities not yet paid; (2) reserves for losses incurred but unreported; (3) reserves for future benefits; and (4) other reserves for various special purposes, including *contingency reserves* for unforeseen circumstances.

residency: A prolonged period (usually one or more years) of on-the-job training that may be either part of a formal educational program or be undertaken separately after completion of a formal program, sometimes in fulfillment of a requirement for *credentialing.* In *medicine,* dentistry, podiatry and other health *professions,* residencies are the principal part of *graduate medical education* that begins either after graduation (increasingly) or *internship* (traditionally), lasts two to six years, and provides *specialty* training. Most *physicians* now take residencies in one of 23 specialties offered, although they are not necessarily required for *licensure.* Residencies are needed for *board eligibility.*

resident: A graduate of a medical or osteopathic school serving an advanced period of graduate training.

residential care: A house or other lodging with a program to meet the resident's nutritional, social, and spiritual needs.

resources: Sources of support available to an individual in addition to regular earned or unearned *income.* Generally, resources refer to an individual's wealth or property (including cash savings, stocks and bonds, a home, other real estate, the cash value of life insurance, an automobile, or jewelry) that can be converted to cash if necessary. Existing programs for the *poor* generally set a limit on the total amount of resources an individual or *family* may have to be eligible for the programs. Most existing resource tests exempt a home of reasonable value on the basis that it would not be reasonable to

R

require selling a home to qualify for *benefits*. The term is also used to mean the *providers*, institutions, *health manpower*, and *facilities* used for provision of health services in the total health care system.

respondeat superior: In *malpractice*, a form of vicarious *liability* whereby an employer is held liable for the wrongful acts of an employee even though the employer's conduct is without fault. Before liability predicated on "respondeat superior" may be imposed upon an employer, it is necessary that a master/servant (i.e., controlling) relationship exist between employer and employee and that the wrongful act of the employee occur within the scope of employment. The doctrine does not absolve the original wrongdoer, the employee, of liability for the wrongful act. Not only may the *injured* party sue the employee directly, but the employer may seek indemnification from the employee for any loss incurred by the employer.

restraint: The act of restraining a *patient* or holding a patient down by use of physical restraints or tranquilizing *drugs*.

retention: A period of time that records must be kept in permanent or copied form. See *risk charge*.

retrospective reimbursement: A payment to a *provider* by a *third-party payer* for *costs* or *charges* actually incurred by *subscribers* in a previous time period. This is the method of payment used under *Medicare* and *Medicaid*. See also *prospective reimbursement*.

retrospective study: An inquiry to observe events that have already occurred (a *case-control* study is usually retrospective); compare with a *prospective study* planned to observe events that will occur at a future time.

rider: A legal document that modifies or amends the protection of an *insurance policy*. A rider can expand or decrease *benefits* or add or *exclude* certain conditions from the policy's original coverage.

R

risk: Generally, any chance of *loss*. In *insurance*, it designates the individual or property *insured* by an *insurance policy* against loss from some *peril* or *hazard*. The term is also used to refer to the probability that the loss will occur. See also *insurable risk* and *at risk*.

risk charge: The fraction of a *premium* that is used to generate or replenish *surpluses* an insurance *carrier* must develop to protect against the possibility of excessive *losses* under its policies. *Profits,* if any, on the sale of insurance are also taken from the surpluses developed using risk charges. Risk charge may also refer to *retention* of records or retention rate.

risk management: The assessment and control of risk within a health care facility, including the analysis of possibilities of liability, methods to reduce risk of liability, and methods to transfer risk to others or through insurance coverage. Risk management is commonly used to mean a formal program of malpractice reduction.

risk manager: The administrator charged with the responsibility of overseeing the risk management program.

Rolfing: See *structural integration.*

room rate: basic *inpatient* charge per day (room, board, and basic medical services) for a stay in a health care *facility.*

roster: A list of *patients* served by a given health *professional* or program. The roster belongs to the professional or program and is usually prepared from a *registry* or list of *encounters.* An individual's name on a roster does not necessarily imply any ongoing relationship between the program and that individual. See also *catchment area.*

rounds: The process whereby *physicians* (or other health *providers*) visit the patient at bedside to review medical progress.

R

routine care: *Inpatient* servicess within a health care *facility* provided an individual with a disorder that is not sufficiently serious or unusual to require special care of the patient.

rule: In the executive branch of the federal government, an agency statement of general or particular applicability and future effect designed to implement, interpret, or prescribe law or *policy*, or to describe the organization, procedure, or practice requirements of an agency; also commonly called a regulation. Rules are published in the *Federal Register*. The process of writing a rule is called a rule making. A rule adopted in accordance with the procedures specified in the Administrative Procedure Act (Title V, U.S.C.) has the force of law.

rural health centers: A *facility* that offers basic *primary care* and emergency services staffed by allied health personnel.

R

Ss

SADR: Severity adjusted death rate.

safety: The probability that use of a particular *drug, device,* or medical *procedure* will not cause unintended or unanticipated hurt, *disease,* or *injury.* Safety in this context is a relative term that must be balanced against the *effectiveness* of the drug or procedure in question. Drugs or procedures known to cause hurt, disease, or injury are not usually considered unsafe if the benefits they offer exceed the damage. The federal Food, Drug, and Cosmetic Act requires a demonstration of safety for drugs marketed for human use. No similar requirement exists for most other medical procedures paid for or regulated under federal or state law.

safety committee: A hospital committee composed of departmental representatives who plan, implement, and monitor a facilitywide safety program under the direction of a *safety manager* or risk administrator.

safety manager: An administrative person responsible for safety and a safety program that includes fire and disaster protection and prevention activities within a health care facility.

sanatorium: A *facility* where *patients* with chronic physical or mental illnesses are treated (i.e., tuberculosis).

satellite clinic: A *primary care* facility located near a workplace or in a residential area, thus providing accessibility to essential *health* services for a specific patient population.

saturation: In marketing *insurance* or *HMOs,* the point at which further *penetration* is improbable or excessively costly.

scarcity area: An area lacking an adequate *supply* of one or more types of health *service* (such as *physicians*). The term is essentially synonymous with *medically underserved area*.

Schedule A: A list of occupations that the Department of Labor considers to be in short *supply* throughout the United States for purposes of *labor certification*. All occupations now listed on Schedule A are health occupations, but some health occupations (such as *dentists*) are not listed.

schedule of controlled substances: The classification of *drugs* under the Drug Abuse Prevention and Control Act of 1970. Drugs are placed in Schedules 1 through 5 in descending order of potential harm.

scheduled benefit provision: See *allocated benefit provision*.

Scientology: A religious movement or order begun in 1952 that teaches immortality and reincarnation. It claims to have a virtually certain psychotherapeutic method that will free the individual from personal problems, increase human abilities, and speed recovery from *sickness, injury,* and *mental disorder*.

scope of services: The number, type, and intensity or complexity of *services* provided by a *hospital* or *health* program. Scope of services is measured in different ways so that the capacity and nature of various programs may be compared. A program's scope of services should reflect, and be adequate to meet, the *needs* of its *patient mix*.

screening: The application of quick, simple, or preliminary *procedures* to identify and separate apparently well persons who have, or have a risk of contracting, a *disease* from those who probably do not have the disease or the risk. It is used to identify suspects for more definitive diagnostic studies. Multiple screening (or multiphasic screening) is the combination of a battery of screening tests for various diseases performed by technicians under medical direction and applied to large groups of apparently well persons. See also *sensitivity, specificity,* and *preventive medicine.* Screening also refers to initial, cursory *claims review* by insurance companies intended to identify claims obviously not covered or that may be deficient in some respect.

screening clinic: A *clinic* where an initial assessment of *patients* seeking care is performed to determine the *services* they *need* and priority requirements. *Treatment* of minor problems is also available at some screening clinics. See also *triage.*

screening panels: In *malpractice,* screening panels are used as fact-finding bodies during the early stages of a malpractice dispute. There are two basic types of screening panels in use. *Physicians'* defense panels seek to develop the best possible defense for the physician who faces a real or potential malpractice claim; joint physician and lawyer panels examine the facts of a case for both the physician and the plaintiff and decide whether the case has sufficient merit for trial.

scut work: A term used by *housestaff* and others in hospitals to describe work they dislike, usually trivial in nature; paperwork; or work that could be readily done by others.

secondary care: *Services* provided by medical *specialists* who generally do not have first contact with *patients* (e.g., cardiologists, urologists, and dermatologists). In the United States, however, there has been a trend toward self-referral by patients themselves for these services, rather than *referral* by *primary care* providers. It differs from the custom followed in England, for example, where all patients first seek care from primary care *providers* who refer them to secondary or tertiary providers as *needed.* See also *tertiary care.*

Section 222: A section of the Social Security Amendments of 1972, P.L. 92-603, authorizing the secretary of Health, Education, and Welfare (now called Health and Human Services) to undertake studies, experiments, or demonstration projects with respect to

Medicare concerning the following: (1) *prospective reimbursement* of *facilities,* ambulatory surgical centers (*surgicenters*), *intermediate care facilities,* and *homemaker services* (relating to the extended care *benefit* under Medicare); (2) elimination or reduction of the three-day prior hospitalization requirement for *admission* to a *skilled nursing facility*; (3) determination of the most appropriate methods of reimbursing the services of *physician assistants* and *nurse practitioners*; (4) provision of day care services to older persons eligible under Medicare and *Medicaid*; and (5) possible means of making the services of *clinical psychologists* more generally available under Medicare and Medicaid. The projects are now for progress in most of these areas of concern.

Section 223: A section of the Social Security Amendments of 1972, P.L. 92-603, requiring the secretary of Health, Education, and Welfare (now called Health and Human Services) to establish limits on overall *direct costs* or *indirect costs* that will be recognized as *reasonable costs* under *Medicare* for comparable *services* in comparable *facilities* in an area. The secretary is also permitted to establish maximum acceptable costs in such facilities with respect to items or groups of services (for example, food or standby costs). The *beneficiary* is liable (except in the case of *emergency care*) for any amounts determined as excessive (except that he or she may not be charged for excessive amounts in a facility in which the admitting *physician* has a direct or indirect ownership interest). Under *rules* issued for this section, reimbursement for hospital *inpatient* routine service costs is limited, effective July 1, 1975, to a figure derived from the 80th percentile (plus 10 percent of the median) for each class of hospitals. Classification of hospitals is based on whether or not the hospital is located in a Standard Metropolitan Statistical Area (SMSA), on per capita *income* in the area, and on hospital *bed* capacity. The total number of hospital classes is 32.

Section 224: A section of the Social Security Amendments of 1972, P.L. 92-603, that places a limit for purposes of *Medicare* and *Medicaid* reimbursement on *charges* recognized as *reasonable charges*. The law recognizes as reasonable those charges that fall within the 75th percentile of all charges for a similar *service* in a *locality*. Increases in *physicians'* fees allowable for Medicare purposes are *indexed* to a factor that takes into account increased costs of *practice* and the increase in general earnings levels in an area. Charges for physician services under *Medicaid* may not exceed this amount. Section 224 further provides that, with respect to reasonable charges for medical *supplies* and *equipment*, only the lowest charges at which supplies and equipment of similar *quality* are widely and consistently available in a locality may be recognized.

Section 314(d): A section of the *PHS Act* that authorizes *formula grants* by the federal government to the states for their unrestricted use in funding state and local health programs and activities. It is sometimes called a health revenue-sharing program.

Section 1122: A section of the Social Security Act added by P.L. 92-603. The section provides that payments will not be made under *Medicare* or *Medicaid* with respect to certain disapproved *capital* expenditures determined to be inconsistent with state or local health plans. P.L. 93-641, the National Health Planning and Resources Development Act of 1974, requires states participating in the Section 1122 program to have its *state health planning and development agency* serve as the Section 1122 agency for purposes of the required review. See also *capital expenditure review* and *certificate of need*.

self-care: Care that individuals can give themselves by learning to self-administer medical procedures and self-treat. Seventy percent of all illnesses do not require professional services.

self-insure: The practice of an individual, group of individuals, employer, or organization assuming complete responsibility for *losses,* such as *malpractice* losses or medical expenses and other losses due to *illness*. In the latter cases, medical expenses are usually financed by current *income*, personal savings, a fund specifically developed for the purpose, or a combination of personal assets. Self-insurance is contrasted to the practice of purchasing *insurance* from a *third party* (an insurance company or government agency) by the payment of a *premium*.

senior citizen policies: *Insurance policies* for persons age 65 or older that supplement *Medicare* and other senior citizen health care programs.

sensitivity: A measure of the ability of a *diagnostic study* or *screening test* or other predictor to identify correctly the positive (or sick) people, that is, the proportion of true positive cases (sick people) correctly identified as positive. Sensitivity equals true positives divided by (true positives plus *false negatives*). A test may be quite sensitive without being very specific (see *specificity*).

serology: The study of serums, their analyses, development, and therapeutic uses.

service: A unit of health care. It is interesting that there is no standard term for a single unit of health care, whatever that unit may be. Both service and procedure are often used to refer to units of health care, such as a health service or a medical procedure, but neither has any constant definition. Service is sometimes used synonymously with *encounter*, but they should be differentiated, since an encounter may include several services. It is also used synonymously with *department*, a quite different meaning.

service area: See *medical trade area* and *catchment area*.

service benefits: Those received as a result of *prepayment* or *insurance*, whereby payment is made directly to the *provider* of *services,* the hospital, or other medical care program (such as a *prepaid group practice)* for covered services provided to eligible persons. Service benefits may be full service benefits, meaning that the plan fully reimburses the hospital or program for all services provided during a period so that the patient has no out-of-pocket expenses. Partial service benefits cover only part of the expenses, the remainder to be paid by the beneficiary through some form of *cost sharing.* See also *indemnity benefits* and *vendor payment.*

service-connected (SC) disability: In the Veterans Administration health care program, a *disability* incurred or aggravated in the line of duty during active military service. In this context disability includes *disease*. These disabilities are the primary concern of the program. See also *nonservice-connected disability* and *adjunct disability*.

service patient: A *patient* whose care is the responsibility of a health program or institution (usually a *hospital*). Service patients are often cared for by an individual practitioner paid by the program (typically a member of a hospital's *housestaff*), but the program, not the practitioner, is paid for the care. The term sometimes refers to a public or ward patient. See also *private patient*.

shared services: The coordinated, or otherwise explicitly agreed-upon, sharing of responsibility for provision of medical or nonmedical *services* by two or more otherwise independent hospitals or other health practitioners or programs. The sharing of medical services may include, for example, an agreement that one hospital provides all pediatric care needed in a community but no obstetrical services, while another hospital provides obstetrical, but not pediatric, services. Shared nonmedical services may include joint laundry or dietary services for two or more nursing homes. Common laundry services purchased by two or more health programs from one independent retailer of laundry services are not usually thought of as shared services, unless the health programs own or otherwise control the retailer.

shorting: Dispensing a quantity of a *drug* that is less than the quantity *prescribed* for the purpose of increasing *profit* by charging for the prescribed amount. See also *kiting* and *fraud*.

short-term facility: A facility in which more than 50 percent of all inpatients stay less than 30 days.

short title: In the Congress, the shorter, less formal common title given an act of Congress by its authors. Health Maintenance Organization act of 1973 (P.L. 93-222) and National Health Planning and Resources Development Act of 1975 (P.L. 93-641) are short titles. Not all acts have short titles. The long title, also known as the purpose clause, is a more formal statement of an act's purposes, but it is rarely used.

sickness: Used synonymously with *disease* and *illness*; generally not clearly defined. The term is common in the *insurance* field.

skilled nursing facility (SNF): Under *Medicare* and *Medicaid*, an institution (or a distinct part of an institution) that has in effect a transfer agreement with one or more *participating hospitals*. Requirements for this type of facility include:

1. A primary function of providing skilled *nursing care* and related services for *patients* who require medical or nursing care or *rehabilitation* services for the rehabilitation of *injured, disabled,* or sick persons.

2. Formal policies developed with the advice of a group of *professional* personnel that includes one or more *physicians* and one or more *registered nurses* to govern the skilled nursing care and related medical or other services provided.

3. A physician, a registered professional nurse, or a medical staff responsible for the execution of the institution's policies.

4. Health care of each patient under the supervision of a physician and an available physician to furnish *necessary* medical care in emergencies.

5. *Medical records* maintained for all patients.

6. Nursing service on a 24-hour basis and at least one registered professional nurse employed full time. To the extent that this provision may be deemed to require that any skilled nursing facility engage the services of a registered professional nurse for more than 40 hours a week, the Social Security Amendments of 1972 (effective October 30, 1972) permit the secretary of Health, Education, and Welfare (now Health and Human Services) to waive the requirement if certain conditions are met.

7. Provision for *appropriate* methods and procedures to be used in dispensing and administering *drugs* and *biologicals.*

8. A *utilization review* plan in effect that meets the requirements of the law.

9. *Licensure* pursuant to the law of the state in which the institution is located, according to applicable state and local jurisdiction *licensing* requirements (or approval by the agency of the state or *locality* responsible for licensing such institutions as meeting the *standards* established for such licensing).

skimming: A practice used in health programs paid on a *prepayment* or *capitation* basis and in health insurance that seeks to *enroll* only the healthiest people as a way of controlling program *costs* (income is constant whether or not services are actually used). This practice is sometimes known as creaming. It can be contrasted with *adverse selection*. See also *skimping*.

skimping: A practice in health programs paid on a *prepayment* or *capitation* basis that denies or delays the provision of services needed or demanded (see *need and demand*) by enrolled *members* as a way of controlling costs (income is constant whether or not services are actually used). The classic example is the denial or delay of a cataract extraction. See also *skimming* and *adverse selection*.

sliding scale deductible: A *deductible* that is not set at a fixed amount but rather varies according to *income*. A family is usually required to spend all (a *spend-down*) or a set percentage of its income above some base amount (for example, all or 25 percent of any income over $5,000) as a deductible before a member can receive medical care benefits. There may be a maximum amount on the deductible. The sliding scale concept also can be applied to *coinsurance* and *copayments*.

slip law: In the Congress, the final version of an act of Congress and its first official publication. Each public law is printed in the form of a slip law that also lists, but does not include, the *legislative history* of the act. This pertains to any earlier act amended by the new law, how it is amended, and any explanation or interpretation of the law.

See also *Public Health Service Act*.

SOAP: A method of recording information in a patient's *medical record* based on a problem oriented medical approach. It stands for "subjective" (that which was told by the patient), "objective" (that which was observed), "assessment" (affirmative statement of the situation), and "plan of action," (based on the other three components).

social health maintenance organization (SHMO): An *HMO* that incorporates social services with medical services for a membership composed solely of senior citizens (persons age 65 or older). *Medicare* funding is used with the aim of prolonging wellness among the elderly and thus reducing the need for alternate health care.

social insurance: A device for the pooling of *risks* by their transfer to an organization, usually governmental, that is required by law to provide *indemnity* (cash) or *service benefits* to or on behalf of covered persons upon the occurrence of certain predesignated *losses*. Social insurance is usually characterized by all of the following conditions: (1) coverage is *compulsory* by law; (2) eligibility for benefits (except during a transition period following introduction) is derived, in fact or in effect, from contributions having been made to the program by, or on behalf of, the claimant or a person who is a *dependent* of the claimant; (3) there is no requirement that the individual demonstrate inadequate financial *resources*, although *qualification* may need to be established; (4) methods for determining benefits are prescribed by law; (5) benefits are not usually directly related to contributions made by, or on behalf of, an individual; rather *income* is usually redistributed to favor certain groups, such as those with low former wages or a large number of dependents; (6) there is a definite plan for financing benefits that is designed to be adequate in terms of long-range considerations; (7) the cost is borne primarily by contributions usually made by covered persons, their employers, or both; (8) the plan is administered or supervised by the government; and (9) the plan is not established by the government solely for its present or former employees. Examples of social insurance in this country include social security, railroad retirement, *workers' compensation programs*, and *unemployment insurance.* In other countries, health insurance is often a government-sponsored social insurance program.

Social and Rehabilitation Service (SRS): The federal *administrative agency* under which social service and related programs are managed. For example, *Medicaid* is the responsibility of the *Medical Services Administration* under SRS.

Social Security Administration (SSA): The federal *administrative agency* that manages the social security program. *Medicare,* for example, is the responsibility of the *Bureau of Health Insurance* under SSA.

social services designee: A person in an *extended care facility,* or *long-term care facility* who provides social services to *patients* under the direction of a *social worker* consultant. A designee should have at least two years of college education and, preferably, a degree. State *licensure* is not required by any state because the function of social service designee is not itself an occupation, but a role specified in *Medicare* regulations that is assigned to an otherwise employed member of the facility's staff.

social worker: A trained *professional* who provides social services as a member of a health team or a social service section of a *health facility* or on a consultant basis. Social services are provided to enable a *patient, family* members, or others to deal with problems of social functioning affecting the *health* or well-being of the patient. Most trained social workers now hold a master's degree in social work (MSW). It is estimated that there are 140,000 trained social workers in the current social service labor force of about 300,000. Approximately 30,000 social workers are employed in health-related settings. Social workers increasingly are engaging in private and independent *practice*, on both a full-time and part-time basis.

The National Association of Social Workers (NASW) requires that social workers engaging in independent practice have at least an MSW degree and two years of professionally supervised training in methods employed in independent practice.

socialized medicine: A medical care system where the organization and provision of medical care *services* are under direct government control, and *providers* are employed by or contract for the provision of services directly with the government; also a term used more generally, without recognized or constant definition, referring to any existing or proposed medical care system believed to be subject to excessive governmental control.

Society of Prospective Medicine (SPM): An organization that provides an opportunity for individuals to stay abreast of the rapid advances in health care. Identifying actual and prospective health *risks* of an individual, coupled with a plan of risk reduction, is considered a sound approach to wellness planning. Many organizations utilize the SPM concept as the foundation of their wellness programs.

solo practice: Lawful *practice* of a health occupation by a self-employed individual. Thus, solo practice is by definition *private practice*, but it is not necessarily *general practice* or *fee-for-service* practice (solo practitioners may be paid by *capitation*, although fee for service is far more common). Solo practice is common among *physicians, dentists, podiatrists, optometrists,* and *pharmacists.*

special hospital: A health *facility* for mentally ill *patients* who are a danger to themselves and must be kept in secure facilities.

specialist: A *physician, dentist,* or other health *professional* who voluntarily limits *practice* to a certain branch of medicine or dentistry related to (1) specific *services* or procedures (e.g., *surgery,* radiology, pathology); (2) certain age categories of *patients* (e.g., pediatrics, geriatrics); (3) certain body systems (e.g., dermatology, orthopedics, cardiology); or (4) certain types of *diseases* (e.g., allergy, psychiatry, periodontics). Specialists usually have special education and training related to their respective practices and may or may not be *certified* as specialists by the related *specialty board*. See also *board eligible, general practice, secondary care,* and *relative value scale.*

specialty boards: Organizations that certify (see *certification*) *physicians* and *dentists* as *specialists* or subspecialists in various fields of medical and dental *practice*. The standards for certification relate to length and type of training and experience; they include written and oral examination of applicants for specialty certification. The boards are not educational institutions, and the certificate of a board is not considered a degree. Specialties and their boards are recognized and approved by the American Board of Medical Specialties in conjunction with the Council on Medical Education of the *American Medical Association*. See also *board certified* and *board eligible.*

specialty care: A specialized area of medicine or narrowly focused approach to health care.

specificity: A measure of the ability of a *diagnostic study* or *screening* test or other predictor to identify correctly the negative (or healthy) people, that is, the proportion of true negative cases (healthy people) correctly identified as negative. Specificity equals true negative divided by (true negatives plus *false positives*). A test may be quite specific without being very sensitive.

specified disease insurance: *Insurance* providing *benefits,* usually in large amounts or with high maximums, toward the expense of the *treatment* of the specific *disease* or diseases named in the policy. These policies are now rare. They were more common in the past for such diseases as poliomyelitis and spinal meningitis, but coverage of end-stage renal disease under *Medicare* can be considered an example.

speech pathologist: A specially trained individual who evaluates, habilitates, and performs research related to speech and language problems.   A speech pathologist plans, directs, and conducts remedial programs designed to restore or improve the communication efficiency of children and adults with language and speech impairments arising from physiological and neurological disturbances, defective articulation, and foreign dialect. Approximately 35,000 persons are employed as speech pathologists and *audiologists*. *Licensure* usually requires a master's degree. The *American Speech and Hearing Association (ASHA)* awards a *certificate* of clinical competence that requires academic training at the master's degree level, one year of experience in the field, and passing a national examination. Nearly half of ASHA members are employed in elementary or secondary schools. A large majority are engaged in either diagnostic or therapeutic clinical work. Some speech pathologists are also trained as audiologists.

speech therapy: The study, examination, and *treatment* of defects and *diseases* of the voice, of speech, and of spoken and written language, as well as the use of appropriate substitutional *devices* and treatment. See also *speech pathologist.*

spell of illness: In *Medicare*, the *benefit period* or *episode of care* during which Part A hospital insurance benefits are available. A benefit period begins the first time an *insured* person enters a *hospital* after the hospital insurance begins. It ends after the insured has not been an *inpatient* in a hospital or *skilled nursing facility* for 60 consecutive days. During each benefit period the insured individual is entitled to up to 90 days of hospital care, 100 days in a skilled nursing facility, and 100 home health visits. An additional *lifetime reserve* of 60 hospital days may be drawn upon when more than 90 days of hospital care are needed in a benefit period. There is no limit to the number of benefit periods an insured person may have. The spell-of-illness concept means that the program may pay for more than 90 days in a hospital in a given year, because with a new spell of illness the benefit becomes available again. When a spell of illness continues for a long period of time, such as several years, the program pays less than 90 days of care per year, because it does not pay in the second or third year if there has not been a break in the spell of illness. Additionally, under Medicare, the *deductible* is tied to each spell of illness. Thus, an individual who is hospitalized three times in a year, each in a separate spell of illness, has to pay the deductible of the cost of an inpatient hospital stay three times.

spend down: A method by which an individual establishes eligibility for a medical care program by reducing gross *income* through incurring medical expenses until net income (after medical expenses) becomes low enough to make the individual eligible for the program. In effect, the individual spends income down to a specified eligibility standard by paying for medical care until the bills become high enough in relation to income to allow the person to qualify under the program's *standard* of *need*, at which point the program *benefits* begin. The spend-down is the same as a *sliding scale deductible* related to the overall income level of the individual. For example, if a person is eligible for program benefits if income is $200 per month or less, a person with income of $300 per month would be covered after spending $100 out-of-pocket on medical care; a person with an income of $350 would not be eligible until incurred medical expenses reached $150. The term spend down originated in the *Medicaid* program. An individual whose income makes him or her ineligible for assistance although it is insufficient to pay for medical care can become Medicaid-eligible as a *medically needy* individual by spending some income on medical care.

sponsored malpractice insurance: A *malpractice insurance* plan involving an agreement by a *professional* society (such as a state medical society) to sponsor a particular *insurer's* medical *malpractice* insurance coverage and to cooperate with the insurer in the *administration* of the coverage. The cooperation may include participation in marketing, claims review, and review of rate making. This was the predominant approach to malpractice coverage until 1975 when a number of *carriers* with such arrangements announced they were withdrawing from them. They have been replaced by professional society-operated plans, *joint underwriting associations*, state insurance funds, and other arrangements.

staff privilege: The privilege, granted by a *hospital* or other *inpatient* health program to a *physician* or other independent practitioner, to join the hospital's *medical staff* and to hospitalize *private patients* in the hospital. A practitioner is usually granted privileges after meeting certain *standards*, being accepted by the medical staff and board of trustees of the hospital, and agreeing to carry out certain duties for the hospital, such as teaching without pay or providing emergency or *clinic* services. Most community and other private hospitals in this country are staffed by physicians in *private practice* who obtain access to hospital facilities in this manner. It is common for a physician to have staff privileges at more than one hospital. On the other hand, since hospitals accept a limited number of physicians, some practitioners are excluded from staff privileges and have no access to hospital facilities. The standards used to determine staff privileges sometimes include evaluation by the county medical society, which may give preference to or require membership in that society and, in turn, membership in the *American Medical Association (AMA)*. This practice is formally opposed by the AMA. Some hospitals limit privileges for certain services to *board-eligible* or *certified* physicians. Full-time or *hospital-based physicians* and physicians working in a system such as a *prepaid group practice* with its own hospital are not usually considered to have staff privileges. These physicians have privileges that may be called admitting, hospital, practice, or clinical privileges. Many hospitals have several different types or grades of staff privileges with names like active, associate, courtesy, or limited; however, these names have irregular and unsystemized meanings.

staffing patterns: Under Medicare, the rule that *facilities* must provide the state survey agency information disclosing the average number and type of personnel on each tour of duty for one week per quarter as randomly selected by the survey agency.

standards: Generally, measures set by competent authority as rules to determine quantity or *quality.* Conformity with standards is usually a condition of *licensure, accreditation,* or payment for *services.* Standards may be defined in relation to the actual or predicted effects of care; the performance or credentials of *professional* personnel; and the physical plant, governance, and *administration* of *facilities* and programs. In the *PRO* program, standards are professionally developed expressions of the range of acceptable variation from a *norm* or *criterion.* Thus, the criteria for care of a urinary tract infection might be a urinalysis and urine culture; the standard might require a urinalysis in 100 percent of cases and a urine culture only in previously untreated cases.

state comprehensive health planning agency (state CHP or 314(a) agency): A *health planning* agency assisted under Section 314(a) of the *PHS Act* in accordance with P.L. 89-749, the Comprehensive Health Planning and Public Health Service Amendments of 1966. Each state agency develops *comprehensive health planning* programs with the assistance of a health planning council that is broadly representative of public and private health organizations in the state and that includes a majority of *consumers* among its members. P.L. 89-749 has been superseded by P.L. 93-641, the National Health Planning and Resources Development Act of 1974, which authorizes assistance for *state health planning and development agencies* to replace 314(a) agencies. These agencies prepare an annual state health plan and a medical facilities plan (*Hill-Burton*). Each state agency also serves as a designated *Section 1122* review agency and *administers* a *certificate-of-need* program.

state cost commissions: State agencies assigned *regulation* of various health service *costs* and *charges* or review of hospital responsibilities in these areas. The duties of a commission may include assuring that (1) total hospital costs are reasonably related to total services offered, (2) aggregate rates bear a reasonable relationship to aggregate costs, and (3) rates are applied equitably to preclude any possibility of discriminatory pricing among various services and patients of a hospital.

state health manpower plan: A plan developed by a *state health planning and development agency* that is concerned with health manpower within the state.

state health plan (SHP): A comprehensive plan that recommends a state's proposed strategic actions and expected health resource changes over the next five years.

state health planning and development agency (SHPDA): Section 1521 of the *PHS Act*, added by P.L. 93-641, requires the establishment of a state health planning and development agency in each state. As a replacement for the existing *state comprehensive health planning agency*, a SHPDA prepares an annual preliminary state health plan and the state medical facilities plan (*Hill-Burton*). The agency also serves as the designated review agency for purposes of *Section 1122* of the Social Security Act and administers a *certificate-of-need* program.

statement of managers: See *conference*.

statewide health coordinating council (SHCC): A state council of *providers* and *consumers* required by Section 1524 of the *PHS Act*, added by P.L. 93-641. Each SHCC generally supervises the work of the *state health planning and development agency* and reviews and coordinates plans and *budgets* of the state's *health systems agencies* (HSA). It also prepares annually a state health plan from HSA plans and the preliminary plans of the state agency. The SHCC also reviews applications for HSA planning and resource development assistance.

statutes of limitations: A time period within a legal action must be commenced and beyond which it is barred.

step-rate plan: Health insurance coverage in which premiums automatically increase with the age of the enrolled member.

stillbirth: The delivery of a fetus that dies before or during delivery. The term is used to refer to either the delivery or the fetus. Some definitions are limited to fetuses of an age or weight that are potentially or usually viable (e.g., 1,000 grams). A fetal *death* is sometimes synonymous, but the term may be limited to deaths that occur before delivery. See also *perinatal mortality*.

stock insurance company: A company owned and controlled by stockholders and operated for the purpose of making a *profit*. It is contrasted with a *mutual insurance company*. In the former the profits go to the owners; in the latter they go to the *insureds*.

stop order: A standing medical order to discontinue drug therapy automatically after a set period of time.

strict liability: To be legally responsible for harm or injury to another even if not at fault.

structural integration: A deep-massage technique that is designed to help a person realign the body by altering the length and tone of myofascial tissues. Practitioners of Rolfing, as the technique is commonly known, believe that misalignment resulting from inaccurate learning about posture, as well as emotional and physical trauma, may have a detrimental effect on an individual's *health,* energy, self-image, perceptions, and muscular efficiency.

structural measure: See *input measure*.

subrogation: A provision of an *insurance policy* that requires an *insured* individual to assign any rights he or she may have to recover damage from another party to the *insurer,* to the extent the insured has been reimbursed by the insurer. Some experts have argued that private health insurance (including *Blue Cross plans* or *group insurance*) should have subrogation rights similar to those in most property insurance policies (e.g., automobile, fire). Having paid the *hospital* bill of a policyholder, the health insurance company could assume the insured's right to sue the party whose negligence may have caused the hospitalization and be reimbursed for its outlay to the policyholder. Subrogation rights could help insure prompt payment of medical expenses without *duplication of benefits*. (Refer to Michigan Hospital Service *v.* Sharpe, 339 Mich. 357, 63 N.W. 2d., 638, 1954, for ruling on subrogation by the Michigan Supreme Court.) Others respond that subrogation is time-consuming and expensive and may not offer companies adequate protection against loss. Few insurers use it voluntarily, and some state *insurance commissioners* forbid its use.

subscriber: Often used synonymously with either *member* or *beneficiary,* but in a strict sense it means only the individual (*family* head or employee) who has elected to contract for, participate in, or subscribe to an *insurance* or *HMO* plan for himself or herself and eligible *dependents.*

substance abuse plan: A state plan that addresses the provision of services to those individuals who are abusers of *drugs* or intoxicants.

substitution: The filling of a *prescription* by a *pharmacist* with a *drug* product that is a *therapeutical equivalent* and *chemical equivalent* of the specific brand prescribed, but not the brand itself. Many states have *antisubstitution laws* that prohibit the pharmacist from filling a prescription with any product other than the specific product of the manufacturer whose *brand name* is used on the prescription. See also *maximum allowable cost* and *generic name.*

succession of care: The continuity of *patient* care from one health care *facility* to another.

supervisory care facility: A facility that provides limited nursing or medical care to the elderly or infirm. The facility may or may not be licensed, depending upon state law, and is usually administered by a *registered nurse* or a *licensed practical nurse.*

supplemental health insurance: Health *insurance* that covers medical expenses not covered by separate health insurance already held by the *insured* (i.e., supplements another insurance policy). For example, many insurance companies sell insurance to people covered under *Medicare* that covers either the costs of *cost sharing* required by Medicare, services not covered by Medicare, or both. Where *cost sharing* is intended to control *utilization*, the availability of supplemental health insurance for this purpose limits the *effectiveness* of cost sharing as a control measure.

supplemental health services: The *optional services* that *HMOs* may provide in addition to *basic health services* and still qualify for federal assistance. Supplemental services are defined in section 1302(2) of the *PHS Act.*

supplemental security income (SSI): A program of *income* support for low-income aged, blind, and disabled persons established by Title XVI of the Social Security Act. SSI replaced state assistance programs for the aged, blind, and disabled on January 1, 1972, with a federally administered program. States may supplement this basic benefit amount. Receipt of a federal SSI benefit or a state supplement under the program is often used to establish *Medicaid* eligibility.

Supplementary Medical Insurance Program (Part B, SMI): The voluntary portion of *Medicare* in which all persons entitled to the *Hospital Insurance Program* (Part A) may *enroll.* The program is financed on a current basis from monthly *premiums* paid by persons insured under the program and a matching amount from federal *general revenues.* About 95 percent of eligible people are enrolled. During any calendar year, the program will pay (with certain exceptions) 80 percent of the *reasonable charge* (as determined by the program) for all covered *services* after the *insured* pays a *deductible* on the costs of such services. Covered services include *physician* services; *home health care* (up to 100 visits); medical and other health services; *outpatient* hospital services; laboratory, pathology, and radiologic services; and prescription drugs. Any individual age 65 or older may elect to enroll in Part B. However, individuals not eligible for Part A who elect to buy into Part A must also buy into Part B. State welfare agencies may buy Part B coverage for elderly and disabled public assistance recipients and pay the premiums on their behalf. The program contracts with *carriers* to process *claims* under the program. The carriers determine amounts to be paid for claims based on reasonable charges. The name, Part B, refers to part B of Title XVIII of the Social Security Act, the legislative authority for the program.

supplementation: Partial payment for a portion of the cost of *nursing home* care by the *patient* or the patient's *family*. Under a system of supplementation, a state pays a rate that the nursing home does not agree to accept as full payment; the individual or family must supplement the state rate. The amount a nursing home collects in supplemental payments is not controlled by the state. Supplementation generally has been used where the state rate was admittedly not sufficient to pay for the cost of the care.

supplier: Generally, any institution, individual, or agency that furnishes a medical item or *service*. In *Medicare*, suppliers are distinguished from *providers* (such as *hospitals* and *skilled nursing facilities*). Institutions classified as providers are reimbursed by *intermediaries* on a *reasonable cost* basis; suppliers, including *physicians*, nonhospital laboratories, and ambulance companies, are paid by *carriers* on the basis of *reasonable charges*.

supplies: Inexpensive medical items, usually of a disposable nature, such as bandages, tongue depressors, and rubbing alcohol. Supplies should be distinguished from permanent and durable *capital* goods (those whose use lasts over a year).

supply: In health economics, the quantity of *services* supplied as the price of the services vary, if *income* and other factors are held constant. For most services increases in price induce increases in supply; for all services price increases ration the existing supply. Increases in *demand* (but not necessarily in *need*) normally induce an increase in price.

surgery: Any operative, invasive, or manual procedure undertaken for the *diagnosis* or *treatment* of a *disease* or other disorder; the branch of *medicine* concerned with diseases that require or are responsive to such treatment; or the work done by a surgeon (one who practices surgery). See also *operation, psychosurgery, major surgery, minor surgery, elective surgery,* and *cosmetic surgery.*

surgicenter: An ambulatory health care *facility* offering surgical services beyond what can be safely performed in a *physician's* office but not sufficiently serious to warrant hospitalization.

surplus: In *insurance,* the excess of a company's assets (including any *capital*) over *liabilities.* Surpluses may be used for future dividends, expansion of business, or to meet possible unfavorable future developments. They may be developed and increased intentionally by including an amount (known as a *risk charge)* in the *premium* in excess of the pure premium needed to meet anticipated liabilities. Surpluses are sometimes earmarked in part as *contingency reserves* and in part as unassigned surplus.

suspension list: A hospital policy requiring *physicians* to complete and sign all *medical records* or face suspension of rights to *staff privileges.*

swap maternity: A provision in *group* health *insurance* plans providing immediate *maternity benefits* to a newly covered woman but terminating coverage on pregnancies in progress upon termination of a woman's coverage. See also *switch maternity* and *flat maternity.*

switch maternity: A provision in group health insurance plans providing *maternity benefits* to female employees only when their husbands are covered in the plan as their *dependents*. It has the effect of denying maternity benefits to single women. See also *flat maternity* and *swap maternity*.

Tt

target group: A geographic area or population selected to receive special medical care based on a perceived need or demand for additional services.

tax: To assess or determine judicially the amount of levy for the support of certain government functions for public purposes; a charge or burden, usually pecuniary, laid upon persons or property for public purposes; a forced contribution of wealth to meet the public needs of a government. See also *tax credit, tax deduction, regressive tax, proportional tax,* and *progressive tax.*

tax credit: A reduction of *tax* liability for federal *income* tax purposes. Several *national health insurance* proposals allow businesses and individuals to reduce their taxes dollar for dollar for certain defined medical expenses. The effect of using a tax credit approach rather than a *tax deduction* is to give persons and businesses an equal benefit for each dollar expended on health care. A tax credit favors lower- over higher-income people, while a tax deduction is worth more to the business or person with a higher the *marginal tax rate.* See also *Medicredit.*

tax deduction: A reduction in the *income* base upon which federal income *tax* is calculated. Health insurance expenditures are deductible by businesses as a business expense. Because the *marginal tax rate* is related to income and is higher for higher-income persons and businesses, the value of a tax deduction for income spent on medical care increases as income increases. Thus, the subsidy is effectively greater for the higher-income person or more profitable corporation. See also *tax credit.*

tax expenditure budget: In the federal *budget,* an enumeration of revenue losses resulting from *tax expenditures*. Section 301 of the Congressional Budget and Impoundment Control Act of 1974 requires that estimated levels of tax expenditures be presented by major *functions* in the *congressional budget* and the *president's budget*.

tax expenditures: Revenues lost to government because of any form of legal *tax* reduction or tax forgiveness, including *tax credits* and *deductions*. The term emphasizes that such revenues foregone for specific purposes (such as subsidizing private purchase of health insurance through the federal income tax deduction for health insurance) are budgetarily equivalent to actual federal expenditures. See also *tax expenditure budget*.

teaching hospital: A *hospital* that provides *undergraduate medical education* or *graduate medical education*, usually with one or more medical, dental, or osteopathic *internship* and *residency* programs (approved by AMA, ADA, or AOA, respectively) and *affiliation* with a medical school. Hospitals that educate *nurses* and other health personnel without training physicians are not generally considered teaching hospitals, nor are those that offer only programs of *continuing education* for practicing *professionals*. See also *housestaff* and *affiliated hospital*.

teaching physician: A *physician* who has responsibilities for the training and supervision of medical students, *interns,* and *residents.* Teaching physicians are often, but not necessarily, salaried by the institution in which they teach. A common arrangement is that a physician in *private practice* must donate a certain amount of time for teaching and supervision in return for *staff privileges*.

team nursing: A system whereby a head *nurse* assigns nursing care to each nurse on the team who carries out the same activities for the duration of the shift; an opposite approach to *primary care* nursing.

tertiary care: *Services* provided by highly specialized *providers* (e.g., neurologists, neurosurgeons, thoracic surgeons, and *intensive care units*). Such services frequently require highly sophisticated technological and support facilities. The development of these services has been largely a function of diagnostic and therapeutic advances attained through basic and clinical *biomedical research*. See also *primary care* and *secondary care*.

therapeutic agent: Any substance that promotes healing in a maladaptive person.

therapeutic equivalents: *Drug* products with essentially identical effects in *treatment* of some *disease* or condition. Such products are sometimes, but not necessarily, *chemically equivalent* or *bioequivalent*.

therapy: The *treatment* of *disease*.

third-party advances: Monies paid in advance of *services* by insurance *underwriters* to *providers* of care.

third-party payer: Any organization, public or private, that pays or *insures* health or medical expenses on behalf of *beneficiaries* or recipients (e.g., *Blue Cross* and *Blue Shield*, commercial insurance companies, *Medicare*, and *Medicaid*). The individual generally pays a *premium* for such coverage in all private and some public programs. The organization makes payments on the insured's behalf. Such payments are called third-party payments and are distinguished by the separation among the individual receiving the *service* (the first party), the individual or institution providing it (the second party), and the organization paying for it (the third party). See also *service benefits* and *indemnity benefits*.

tissue committee: A committee usually functioning in a *hospital* setting that reviews and evaluates all *surgery* performed in the hospital on the basis of the extent of agreement among the preoperative, postoperative, and pathological *diagnoses* and on the relevance and acceptability of the procedures undertaken for the diagnoses. The name derives from the use of pathologic findings from tissue removed at surgery as a key element in the review. See also *tissue review*.

tissue review: A review and evaluation of *surgery* performed in a *hospital* on the basis of agreement or disagreement among the preoperative, postoperative, and pathological *diagnoses*. In particular, the pathological or tissue diagnosis is used to determine if the procedure was necessary. Studies have shown that hospitals with *tissue committees* have lower rates of unnecessary surgery than those without these committees.

Title V: A U.S. government public law that created a health program for maternal and child health and crippled children's services.

Title XVIII: The title of the Social Security Act that contains the principal legislative authority for the *Medicare* program. It is commonly used as the name for the program.

Title XIX: The title of the Social Security Act that contains the principal legislative authority for the *Medicaid* program. The program is commonly referred to by this name.

titled patient: One who is covered for health services under Titles V, XVIII, or XIX of the Social Security Act.

tort: A wrongful act done to another (excepting breach of contract). See *negligence* or *malpractice*.

total inpatient service days: The sum total of all days of *service* provided to a person as an *inpatient* of a health care *facility*.

total length of stay: The total of all days of stay by all *inpatients* as determined by the number of inpatients discharged during a specified time period.

tracers: Selected conditions or *diseases* chosen for appraisal in programs that seek to assess the *quality* of medical care because it is believed that the quality of care given for the tracers is typical or representative of the quality of care given generally or to all diseases.

trade name: See *brand name*.

transfer agreement: As used in *Joint Commission long-term care* facilities accreditation, a written arrangement that provides for the reciprocal transfer of *patients* between health care facilities.

trauma center: An *emergency care* unit specially staffed and equipped to handle emergency care or trauma cases.

trauma registry: A hospital *emergency care* database that discloses the type of *injury* and the resulting *treatment* in the emergency department.

treatment: The *management* and care of a *patient* for the purpose of combating *disease* or disorder.

triage: Commonly used to describe the process of sorting out or screening *patients* seeking care to determine the *service* initially required and with what priority. A *patient* coming to a *facility* for care may be seen in a triage, screening, or walk-in *clinic* where it will be determined, possibly by a triage *nurse*, whether, for example, the patient has a medical or surgical problem or requires some nonphysician service, such as consultation with a *social worker*. Such rapid assessment units may merely refer patients to the most appropriate treatment service, or they may also give treatment for minor problems. They word was originally used to describe the sorting of battle casualties into groups of those who could wait for care, who needed immediate care, and who were beyond care.

trim points: In *DRGs*, a high or low *length of stay*, typically five percent of the total *Medicare* inpatient population that falls beyond anticipated extremes in required hospitalization.

trolley car policy: A facetious name for an *insurance policy* on which it is difficult to collect *benefits*. The policy is referred to as providing benefits only for *injuries* resulting from being hit by a trolley car. The term is typically used for *mail-order insurance*.

trust funds: Funds collected and used by the federal government for carrying out specific purposes and programs according to terms of a trust agreement or statute, such as the social security and unemployment trust funds. Trust funds are administered by the government in a *fiduciary* capacity for the beneficiaries. They are not available for the general purposes of the government. Trust fund receipts whose use is not anticipated in the immediate future are generally invested in interest-bearing government securities and earn interest for the trust fund. The *Medicare* program is financed through two trust funds. The Federal Hospital Insurance Fund finances Part A; the Federal Supplementary Medical Insurance Trust Fund finances Part B. See also *social insurance, funded, congressional budget,* and *President's budget*.

Uu

unallocated benefits: A provision in an *insurance policy* providing reimbursement up to a maximum amount for the costs of all extra *hospital* costs without specifying the amount to be paid for each service.

unbundling: Payment for nonphysician services provided to *inpatients* within a health care *facility*. The practice of billing *Medicare* for physician services under Part B for outside services has been referred to by lawmakers as "unbundling."

uncompensated care: Free care by health care *providers* for which no compensation is expected.

undergraduate medical education: Medical education given before a doctor of medicine or equivalent degree is granted. It is usually the four years of study in medical, osteopathic, dental, or podiatric school leading to a degree. This use of the term undergraduate contrasts with that in general where undergraduate education refers to college education leading to the bachelor degree.

underwriting: In *insurance*, the process of selecting, classifying, evaluating, and assuming *risks* according to their *insurability*. Its fundamental purpose is to verify that the group insured has the same probability of *loss* and probable amount of loss, within reasonable limits, as the universe on which *premium* rates are based. Since premium rates are based on an expectation of loss, the underwriting process must classify risks into classes with similar expectations of loss.

underwriting profit: That portion of the earnings of an *insurance* company that comes from the function of *underwriting*. It excludes earnings from investments (other than interest earnings required by law or regulation that are assumed to have been earned for purposes of determining the *reserves* held) either in the form of income from securities or sale of securities at a *profit*. The remainder is found by deducting incurred *losses* and *expenses* from earned *premium*.

unemployment insurance: A form of *social insurance* that operates by means of a *payroll tax* paid by employers. The revenues from the tax are used to pay calculated *benefits* for defined periods to people who qualify (usually by virtue of accumulated amounts of covered employment) as being unemployed, as defined in the law. Individuals receiving unemployment insurance benefits do not usually continue to receive *group* health *insurance* coverage obtained through their most recent place of employment.

Uniform Anatomical Gift Act: A law existing in most states that specifies procedures for donating organs and the use of cadavers for organ transplant or teaching purposes.

uniform cost accounting: The use of a common or standard set of accounting definitions, procedures, terms, and methods for the accumulation and communication of quantitative data relating to the financial activities of similar enterprises. The *American Hospital Association*, for example, encourages the use of its Chart of Accounts as an accounting system by *hospitals* in the United States.

Uniform Hospital Discharge Data Set (UHDDS): A defined set of data which gives a minimum description of a *hospital* episode or *admission*. Collection of a UHDDS is required upon discharge for all hospital stays reimbursed under *Medicare* and *Medicaid*. The UHDDS was defined in a policy statement of the secretary of Health, Education, and Welfare (HEW), HEW publication number HSM 73-1451, Series 4, no. 14, as extended by a policy statement approved June 24, 1974, and included data on the age, sex, race, and residence of the *patient; length of stay; diagnosis;* responsible *physicians; procedures* performed; disposition of the patient; and sources of payment. The *PSRO* program (now the peer review organization

(PRO) program) used a slightly larger data set called the PSRO Hospital Discharge Data Set (PHDDS). The Uniform Hospital Discharge Abstract (UDHA) used to collect the UHDDS is one example of a *discharge abstract*.

Uniform Individual Policy Provisions: A set of provisions regarding the nature and content of individual health *insurance* policies that was developed in a recommended model law by the *National Association of Insurance Commissioners (NAIC)*. It is permitted in all jurisdictions and has been adopted (with minor variations) by almost all of them.

unit dosage system: A *drug* dispensing system of individually packaging each dosage unit by which *patients* pay for the actual doses administered.

United States Adopted Names Council (USAN): A private group of representatives of the American Medical Association, the American Pharmaceutical Association, the United States Pharmacopeial Convention, and the Federal Food and Drug Administration, plus one public member.

United States Pharmacopeia (USP): A legally recognized *compendium* of *standards* for *drugs*, published by the United States Pharmacopeial Convention, Inc., and revised periodically. It includes also assays and tests for the determination of strength, *quality* and purity. See also *National Formulary*.

U.S. Public Health Service (USPHS): A branch of the federal government responsible for oversight of various public health programs.

UR: See *utilization review*.

USC: United States Code.

USCA: United States Code Annotated.

usual charge: See *customary charge*.

usual, customary, and reasonable plans (UCR): Health *insurance* plans that pay a *physician's* full *charge* if it does not exceed his usual charge, it does not exceed the amount customarily charged for the service by other physicians in the area (often defined as the 90 or 95 percentile of all charges in the community), or it is otherwise *reasonable*. In this context, usual and customary charges are similar, but not identical, to *customary charges* and *prevailing charges*, respectively, under *Medicare*. Most private health insurance plans, except for a few *Blue Shield plans*, use the UCR approach.

utilization: Use. Utilization is commonly examined in terms of patterns or rates of use of a single *service* or type of service (e.g., *hospital* care, *physician* visits, or *prescription drugs*). Measurement of utilization of all combined medical services is usually done in terms of dollar expenditures. Use is expressed in rates per unit of population at *risk* for a given period; for example, number of *admissions* to hospitals per 1,000 persons age 65 or older per year, or number of visits to physicians per person per year for *family planning* services.

utilization review (UR): Evaluation of the *necessity*, *appropriateness*, and *efficiency* of the use of medical *services*, procedures, and *facilities*. In a hospital this includes review, both on a concurrent basis and retrospective basis, of the appropriateness of *admissions*, services ordered and provided, *length of stay*, and discharge practices. Utilization review is performed by a *utilization review committee*, *PRO*, *peer review* group, or public agency. See also *medical review*.

utilization review committee: A staff committee of an institution or a group outside the institution responsible for conducting *utilization review* activities for that institution. *Medicare* and *Medicaid* require, as a *condition of participation*, that *hospitals* have a utilization review committee in operation.

Vv

valid criteria: As used in *utilization review*, health care *standards* stated in objective rather than descriptive terms in order to provide accurate evaluation.

validity: The degree to which data or results of a *study* are correct or true; the extent to which a situation as observed reflects the true situation. See also *reliability*.

vendor: A *provider*; an institution, agency, organization, or individual practitioner who provides health or medical *services*. *Vendor payments* go directly to these providers from a *third-party* program, such as *Medicaid*.

vendor payment: Used in public assistance programs to distinguish payments made directly to *vendors* of service from cash income payments made directly to assistance recipients. The vendors, or *providers* of health services, are reimbursed directly by the program for services they provide to eligible recipients. Vendor payments are essentially the same as *service benefits* provided under health *insurance* and *prepayment* plans.

Veterans Administration Hospital: A long-term health care facility rendering care to veterans with service-related disabilities.

veterinarian (D.V.M.): An individual trained and licensed to provide medical and health care to all types of animals and other nonhuman species; a doctor of veterinary medicine.

visit: An *encounter* between a *patient* and a health *professional* that requires either the patient to travel from his or her home to the professional's usual place of practice (an office *visit*) or the professional to travel to the patient (a *house call* or home visit).

visiting nurse association (VNA) or visiting nurse service: A *voluntary health agency* that provides *nursing* services in the home, including health supervision, education, and counseling; bedside care; and the carrying out of *physician's* orders by *nurses* and other personnel, such as home health aides who are trained for specific tasks of personal bedside care. These agencies had their origin in the visiting or district nursing provided to sick poor in their homes by voluntary organizations, such as the New York City Mission in the 1870s. The first visiting nurse associations were established in Buffalo, Boston, and Philadelphia in 1886-87. See also *home health agency.*

vital signs: Signs produced by normal body function, such as temperature, pulse, respiration, and blood pressure.

vital statistics: Statistics relating to births (natality), *deaths (mortality)*, marriages, *health,* and *disease (morbidity).* Vital statistics for the United States are published annually by the National Center for Health Statistics of the Health Resources Administration in the *Department of Health and Human Services.*

vivarium: A shelter for animals used in medical and health research.

voluntary health agency: Any nonprofit, nongovernmental agency, governed by lay or *professional* individuals and organized on a national, state, or local basis, whose primary purpose is health-related. The term usually designates agencies, supported primarily by voluntary contributions from the public at large, engaged in a program of service, education, and research related to a particular *disease, disability,* or group of diseases and disabilities; for example, the American Heart Association, American Cancer Society, National Tuberculosis Association, and their state and local affiliates. The term can also be applied to such agencies as nonprofit *hospitals,* *visiting nurse associations,* and other local service organizations that have both lay and professional governing boards and are supported by voluntary contributions in addition to charges and fees for services provided.

voluntary hospital: A nonprofit health care organization that is self-supported and nongovernmental in nature.

volunteer: A person who works in a health care facility without expectation of compensation.

Volunteers of America (VOA): A national organization that establishes volunteer services for health care facilities throughout the United States.

Ww

Wagner-Murray-Dingell Bill: One of the original *national health insurance* proposals, first introduced by Congressmen Wagner, Murray, and Dingell in the 1940s.

waiting list: Individuals waiting admission to a *hospital* or *nursing home*; implies acceptance on a sequential basis.

waiting period: A period of time an individual must wait either to become eligible for *insurance* coverage or to become eligible for a given *benefit* after overall coverage has commenced (see *exclusions*). This does not generally refer to the amount of time it takes to process an application for insurance, but rather it is a defined period before benefits become payable. Some policies will not pay *maternity benefits,* for example, until nine months after the policy has been in force. Another common waiting period occurs in *group insurance* offered through a place of employment where coverage may not start until an employee has been with a firm more than 30 days. For disabled persons to be covered under *Medicare,* there is a waiting period of two years; a person must be entitled to social security *disability* benefits for two years before medical benefits start.

waiver of premium: A provision included in some policies that exempts the *insured* from paying *premiums* while *disabled* (during the life of the contract).

ward clerk: A clerical person who undertakes ministerial-type work within a *hospital* (e.g., directing visitors and answering telephones).

ward patients: *Medically indigent* patients who are treated in a city or other governmental hospital.

ward rounds: See *rounds.*

warranty: In *malpractice,* actions against *physicians* are normally based on negligence, but in certain circumstances the plaintiff can bring his action on the basis of a warranty. A warranty arises if the physician promises or seems to promise that the medical procedure to be used is *safe* or will be *effective.* One of the advantages to bringing an action on warranty grounds, rather than for negligence, is that the statute of limitations is usually longer. A warranty action may be brought and maintained if there is an express warranty offered by the physician to the *patient.*

wholistic health: See *holism.*

workers' compensation programs: State *social insurance* programs that provide cash *benefits* to workers who are *injured,* disabled, or deceased in the course, and as a result, of employment or to their dependents. The employee is also entitled to benefits for some or all of the medical services necessary for treatment and restoration to a useful life and possibly a productive job. These programs are mandatory under state laws in all states.

working capital: The sum of an institution's investment in short-term or current assets, including cash, marketable (short-term) securities, accounts receivable, and inventories. Net working *capital* is defined as the excess of total current assets over total current liabilities.

W

Xx

x-ray technician: An individual trained in the use of x-ray equipment for the *diagnosis* or *treatment* of *disease*.

X

Yy

yellow-dog contract: An illegal contract with a (health care) worker that forces the worker to agree not to join a union.

Zz

zoonoses: Diseases that are naturally transmitted between animals and humans.

APPENDIX A

Commonly Used
Abbreviations and Acronyms

A	allergy
AA	Alcoholics Anonymous
AAAHC	Accreditation Association for Ambulatory Health Care
AACHP	American Association for Comprehensive Health Planning
AAHCF	American Association of Health Care Facilities
AAHE	Association for the Advancement of Health Education
AAMC	Association of American Medical Clinics, Association of American Medical Colleges
AAPS	American Association of Physicians and Surgeons
AB	Aid to the Blind
ACFMR	Accreditation Council for Facilities for the Mentally Retarded
ACHA	American College of Hospital Administrators (*See* American College of Healthcare Executives)
ACHE	American College of Healthcare Education; *also* American College of Healthcare Executives
ACNHA	American College of Nursing Home Administrators
ADA	American Dental Association; a*lso* American Dietetic Association
ADAMHA	Alcohol, Drug Abuse, and Mental Health Administration
ADC	average daily census

ADL	adolescent medicine
ADS	alternate delivery system
ADT	admission/discharge/transfer
AFDC	Aid to Families with Dependent Children
AGPA	American Group Practice Association
A&H	accident and health insurance
AHA	American Hospital Association
AHCA	American Health Care Association
AHEC	area health education center
AHIP	Assisted Health Insurance Plan
AHPA	American Health Planning Association
AHR	Association for Health Records
AHSR	Association for Health Service Research
AI	allergy and immunization
AIP	annual implementation plan
ALOS	average length of stay
AM	aerospace medicine
AMA	American Medical Association; also against medical advice
AMPAC	American Medical Political Action Committee
AMRA	American Medical Record Association
AN	anesthesia
ANA	American Nurses' Association
AOA	American Optometric Association; also American Osteopathic Association
APA	Administrative Procedures Act; also American Psychiatric Association
APhA	American Pharmaceutical Association
APHA	American Public Health Association; also American Protestant Hospital Association
APTD	Aid to the Permanently and Totally Disabled
ART	accredited record technician
ASCP	American Society of Consultant Pharmacists
ASHA	American Speech and Hearing Association
ASLM	American Society of Law and Medicine

ASTHO	Association of State and Territorial Health Officials
AUPHA	Association of University Programs in Health Administration
BA	budget authority
BCA	Blue Cross Association
BCHS	Bureau of Community Health Services
BHI	Bureau of Health Insurance
BHM	Bureau of Health Manpower
BHPRD	Bureau of Health Planning and Resources Development
BLB	bloodbanking
Blue Sheet	Drug Research Reports
BNDD	Bureau of Narcotics and Dangerous Drugs
BQA	Bureau of Quality Assurance
BS	Blue Shield
CARE	Computerized Audit and Record Evaluation System
CAP	community action program
CAPER	Computer Assisted Pathology Encoding and Reporting System
CBO	Congressional Budget Office
CCME	Coordinating Council for Medical Education
CCU	coronary care unit; see also cardiac care unit
CD	cardiovascular disease
CDC	Centers for Disease Control (formerly Communicable Disease Center)
CER	capital expenditure review
CHAMPUS	Civilian Health and Medical Program of the Uniformed Services
CHAMPVA	Civilian Health and Medical Program of the Veterans Administration
CHC	community health center
CHIP	Comprehensive Health Insurance Plan

CHN	community health network
CHP	comprehensive health planning
CHSS	Cooperative Health Statistics System
CL	current liabilities
CMHC	community mental health center
CMS	Council of Medical Staffs
Co	coinsurance
COB	coordination of benefits
COTH	Council of Teaching Hospitals
COTRANS	Coordinated Transfer Application System
CPA	certified public accountant
CPHA	Commission on Professional and Hospital Activities
CPI	Consumer Price Index
CPT	Current Procedural Terminology
CRVS	California relative values studies
CT	computerized tomography
C&Y	children and youth project under the Maternal and Child Health Program
D	dermatology
DD	developmental disability
DDS	doctor of dental surgery
DEA	Drug Enforcement Administration
DES	diethylstilbestrol
DESI	Drug Efficacy Study Implementation
DI	double indemnity
DIA	diabetes
DO	doctor of osteopathy
DOA	dead on arrival
DRG	diagnosis related groups
DSM	Diagnostic and Statistical Manual of Mental Disorders
DVM	doctor of veterinary medicine
ECF	extended care facility

ECFMG	Educational Commission for Foreign Medical Graduates
EHIP	Employee Health Insurance Plan
EHSDS	experimental health service delivery system
EM	emergency services
EMCRO	experimental medical care review organization
EMSS	emergency medical service system
EMT	emergency medical technician
END	endocrinology
EPSDT	Early and Periodic Screening, Diagnosis, and Treatment Program
ER	emergency room
ERIC	Education Resources Information Center
ESP	Economic Stabilization Program
FDA	Food and Drug Administration
FEHBP	Federal Employees Health Benefits Program
FFP	federal financial participation
FHIP	Family Health Insurance Plan; also Federal Health Insurance Plan
FICA	Federal Insurance Contributions Act
FLEX	Federation Licensing Examination
FMC	foundation for medical care
FMG	foreign medical graduate
FNP	family nurse practitioner
FP	family practice
FRSH	Fellow in the Royal Society of Health
FY	fiscal year
GAO	General Accounting Office
GER	geriatrics
GHA	Group Health Association of Washington, D.C.
GHAA	Group Health Association of America

GP	general practitioner
GPM	general preventative medicine
GRAE	generally recognized as effective
GRAS	generally recognized as safe
GYN	gynecology
HAC	Health Advisory Council
HANES	Health and Nutrition Examination Survey
HASP	Hospital Admission and Surveillance Program
HB	House Bill
HCC	health care corporation
HCFA	Health Care Financing Administration
HEM	hematology
HEW	Department of Health, Education, and Welfare; see Department of Health and Human Services
HFMA	Health Care Financial Management Association
HHS	Department of Health and Human Services
HI	Hospital Insurance Program of Medicare (Part A)
HIAA	Health Insurance Association of America
HIBAC	Health Insurance Benefits Advisory Council
HIC	Health Insurance Claim Number
H-ICDA	Hospital International Classification of Diseases Adapted for Use in the United States
HIMA	Health Industry Manufacturers Association
HIP	Health Insurance Plan of Greater New York, Inc.
HMEIA	health manpower education initiative award
HMO	health maintenance organization
HR 1	Social Security Amendments of 1972, P.L. 92-603; also see health care corporation for American Hospital Association's

	proposal in the 94th Congress
HRA	Health Resources Administration
HSA	health service area; *see also* Health Services Administration; *see also* health systems agency
HSI	Health Service, Inc.
HSMHA	Health Services and Mental Health Administration
HSP	health systems plan
HUP	Hospital Utilization Project of Pennsylvania
HYP	hypnosis
IBNR	incurred but not reported
ICDA	International Classification of Diseases, adopted for use in the United States
ICF	intermediate care facility
ICF/MR	intermediate care facility for the mentally retarded (see intermediate care facility)
ICU	intensive care unit
ID	infectious diseases
IG	immunology
IL	intermediary letter
IM	internal medicine
IMR	institution for the mentally retarded
IND	investigational new drug
IOM	Institute of Medicine of the National Academy of Sciences
IPA	individual practice association
IPR	independent professional review
IRP	individual responsibility program
Joint Commission	Joint Commission on Accreditation of Healthcare Organizations
JUA	joint underwriting association
LAR	laryngology

LCGME	Liaison Committee on Graduate Medical Education
LCME	Liaison Committee on Medical Education
LM	legal medicine
LOS	length of stay
LPN	licensed practical nurse
LVN	licensed vocational nurse
MAA	Medical Assistance for the Aged
MAC	maximum allowable cost
MAP	Medical Audit Program
MAST	Military Assitance to Safety and Traffic
MCAT	Medical College Admission Test
MCE	medical care evaluation study
MCH	maternal and child health services
MCHR	Medical Committee for Human Rights
MCPI	Medical Consumer Price Index
MDC	major diagnostic categories
MEDIHC	Military Experience Directed into Health Careers
MEDIPHOR	Monitoring and Evaluation of Drug Interactions in a Pharmacy-Oriented Reporting System
MEDLARS	Medical Literature and Analysis Retrieval System
MFS	maxillofacial surgery
MGMA	Medical Group Management Association
M&I	maternal and infant care project under the Maternal and Child Health Program
MIA	Medical Indemnity of America, Inc.
MIB	Medical Impairment Bureau
MIC	mobile intensive care
MMIS	Medicaid management information system
MR	mentally retarded
MSA	Medical Services Administration
MUMPS	Massachusetts General Hospital's Multi-Programming System

N	neurology
NA	neuropathology
NABSP	National Association of Blue Shield Plans
NACo	National Association of Counties
NADSP	National Association of Dental Service Plans
NAEMT	National Association of Emergency Medical Technicians
NAIA	National Association of Insurance Agents
NAIC	National Association of Insurance Commissioners
NAMH	National Association for Mental Health
NARC	National Association of Retarded Citizens
NARD	National Association of Retail Druggists
NBME	National Board of Medical Examiners
NCHCT	National Center for Health Care Technology
NCHS	National Center for Health Statistics
NCHSR	National Center for Health Services Research
ND	neoplastic diseases
NDA	new drug application
NEP	nephrology
NF	National Formulary
NFLPN	National Federation of Licensed Practical Nurses
NHI	national health insurance
NHSC	National Health Service Corps
NIH	National Institutes of Health
NIMH	National Institute of Mental Health
NIRMP	National Interns and Residents Matching Program
NLN	National League for Nursing
NM	nuclear medicine
NMA	National Medical Association
NP	nurse practitioner
NPM	neonatal-perinatal medicine
NPRM	notice of proposed rule making

NREMT	National Registry of Emergency Medical Technicians
OAA	old age assistance
OASDHI	Old-Age, Survivors, Disability and Health Insurance Program
OB	obstetrics
OB-GYN	obstetrics and gynecology
OC	oral contraceptive
O/E	order/entry system
OEO	Office of Economic Opportunity
OHMO	Office of Health Maintenance Organizations
OM	occupational medicine
OMB	Office of Management and Budget
ON	oncology
OPD	outpatient department
OPH	ophthalmology
OPSR	Office of Professional Standards Review
OR	operating room
OSHA	Occupational Safety and Health Administration
OT	occupational therapist; see also occupational therapy; see also otology
OTA	Office of Technology Assessment
OTC (drug)	over-the-counter drug
OTO	otorhinolaryngology
P	psychiatry
PA	physician assistant; see *also* Proprietary Association
PAHO	Pan American Health Organization
Part A	Hospital Insurance Program of Medicare
Part B	Supplementary Medical Insurance Program of Medicare
PAS	Professional Activity Study
PCMR	President's Committee on Mental Retardation

PD	pediatrics
PDR	Physicians' Desk Reference
PF	Physicians' Forum
PH	public health
PHP	prepaid health plan
PHS	see U.S. Public Health Service
PHS Act	Public Health Service Act
PM	physical medicine
PMA	Pharmaceutical Manufacturers Association
PNHA	Physicians' National Housestaff Association
POMR	problem-oriented medical record
PPO	preferred provider organization
PRO	peer review organization
PSRO	formerly, Professional Standards Review Organization; see also peer review organization
PT	physical therapist; *see also* physical therapy
PUD	pulmonary diseases
PYA	psychoanalysis
PYM	psychosomat
QAP	Quality Assurance Program for Medical Care in the Hospital
R	radiology
RCC	ratio of costs to charges
RCT	random controlled trial
RFP	request for proposal
RHU	rheumatology
RMP	Regional Medical Program
RN	registered nurse
RRA	registered record administrator
RVS	relative value scale or schedule
SAC	Subarea Advisory Council; see Health Advisory Council
SADR	severity adjusted death rate

SC	service-connected (disability)
SHCC	statewide health coordinating council
SHMO	social health maintenance organization
SHP	state health plan
SHPDA	state health planning and development agency
SMI	Supplementary Medical Insurance Program of Medicare
SMSA	standard metropolitan statistical area
SNF	skilled nursing facility
SPM	Society of Prospective Medicine
SRS	Social and Rehabilitation Service
SSA	Social Security Administration
SSI	supplemental security income
Title XVIII	Medicare
Title XIX	Medicaid
UCR	usual, customary, and reasonable plans
UHDDS	Uniform Hospital Discharge Data Set
UR	utilization review
USAN	United States Adopted Names Council
USC	United States Code
USCA	United States Code Annotated
USP	United States Pharmacopeia
USPHS	U. S. Public Health Service
VNA	visiting nurse association
VOA	Volunteers of America
WBGH	Washington Business Group on Health
WHO	World Health Organization
WRMH	Washington Report on Medicine and Health
314(a) agency	state comprehensive health planning (CHP) agency

314(b) agency   areawide comprehensive health planning (CHP) agency

ABOUT THE AUTHOR

Arnold S. Goldstein has been actively involved in health care administration and education for more than 25 years. Dr. Goldstein is a professor of health care administration and law at Northeastern University and has taught health care law and policy at several graduate schools of health care administration. He has also served as legal counsel to several health care organizations, including the National Pharmacy Insurance Council, American Society of Consultant Pharmacists, and National Drug Cooperatives Associated. An active writer in the field, he has been a columnist and editor for several health care journals and is the author of many books on the subject, including *The Nurses' Legal Advisor* and *EMS and the Law*. Dr. Goldstein is a doctoral candidate in health policy at Northeastern University. In addition, he holds a bachelor's degree in pharmacy, a master's in business administration, and a doctorate in jurisprudence and master of laws.